MW00849808

The Horoscope in Manifestation

The Horoscope
in Manifestation

Psychology and Prediction

Liz Greene

The Wessex Astrologer

Published in 2023 by
The Wessex Astrologer Ltd
PO Box 9307
Swanage
BH19 9BF
England

For a full list of our titles go to www.wessexastrologer.com

First published 1997 by the CPA Press, BCM Box 1815,
London WC1N 3XX, England
www.cpalondon.com

First paperback edition published 2001 ISBN 1900869292

Copyright © 1997 by Liz Greene.
Liz Greene asserts the moral right to be identified as the
author of this work.

ISBN 9781910531983

A catalogue record for this book is available at The British Library

No part of this book may be reproduced or used in any form or by any
means without the written permission of the publisher.
A reviewer may quote brief passages.

Table of Contents

Part One: Complexes and Projection

Part Two: A Psychological Approach to Transits and Progressions

Part One: Complexes and Projection

This seminar was given on 25 May, 1996 at Regents College, London, as part of the Summer Term of the seminar programme of the Centre for Psychological Astrology.

The psychological model

The subject of complexes is, if you will excuse the expression, highly complex. But it is immensely valuable as a psychological model, because it can give us remarkable insight into the dynamics of a horoscope. Of all the many available psychological perspectives, that of complexes is one of the most useful to the astrologer, and one of the most profound. We can view complexes reductively to understand personal conflicts and family dynamics more clearly. Or we can view complexes from an archetypal or mythic perspective, and get a glimpse of the deeper meaning behind a person's experiences and development pattern. Both views are valid. What we are really looking at is a psychological model of fate.

Complexes and Greek myth

Although the term "complex" is relatively modern, awareness of its dynamics is very ancient. Greek myth, with its vivid portrayals of the "family curse" and the compulsions visited upon humans by gods, gives us our earliest models of how a complex operates. The Greeks understood that "something" – some compulsive inner pattern which created dramatic repercussions in outer life – had an irrevocable way of passing from father to son, from mother to daughter, and this "something" was usually linked with one or another of the gods. Not only family curses, but also family gifts could be inherited in this way. What is most psychologically relevant about these mythic portrayals is the compulsive nature of this "something" which drives human beings into beliefs, actions and feelings over which they have no conscious control and which are often in violent opposition to their ethics and values.

By presenting these compulsive patterns as the signature of a dynamic relationship between human and god, myth highlights the numinous nature of complexes. To the Greeks, the enactment of an inherited pattern was fate in the most profound sense. When Orestes killed his mother to avenge his father's death, he was compulsively acting out yet another of a long line of offences against deity which began with his ancestor Tantalos and ended only when his efforts to find an alternative solution created a new relationship between the gods themselves. The Greeks also seem to have understood that, although complexes are fate, human intervention can alter their expression, if not their essential "divine" core. In modern dynamic psychiatry, complexes were initially explored almost solely in terms of pathology. But the mythic portrayal of their workings gives us an entirely different perspective. Complexes are not only fate – they are the primary factor in both human and divine evolution.

Early research: Charcot, Janet and Freud

We can trace the history of the complex in modern psychology back to Charcot at the end of the 19th century. In his work with hysterical patients at the Salpêtrière in Paris, he came to the conclusion that behind particular kinds of mental disease lay pockets of associated ideas at work in the unconscious. These were in some way disconnected from consciousness and had a life of their own. Rather than trying to paraphrase him, I will read you a quote from Charcot, given in a lecture on hysterical paralysis in May 1885, which puts this first formulation of the complex quite clearly:

> "...an idea, a coherent group of associated ideas settle themselves in the mind in the fashion of parasites, remaining isolated from the rest of the mind and expressing themselves outwardly through

corresponding motor phenomena...The group of suggested ideas finds itself isolated and cut off from the control of that large collection of personal ideas accumulated and organised from a long time, which constitutes consciousness proper, that is the Ego."[1]

Charcot believed that split-off fragments of the personality can follow an invisible development of their own, accrue enormous power, and eventually express themselves through clinical disturbances which thwart the ego's wishes and goals. Although it may seem a long way away from the Greek gods, "possession" by a deity and the repercussions of the "family curse" are different ways of describing the same phenomenon. Something other than conscious volition is master in the psyche's house.

Pierre Janet took Charcot's idea and developed it further. He coined the term *idée fixe subconsciente* to describe these split-off personality fragments which seemed to wield such power. A quote from Janet is also in order here, to give you a flavour of how these early psychological pioneers perceived the workings of the psyche.

"...The idea, like a virus, develops in a corner of the personality inaccessible to the subject, works subconsciously, and brings about all disorders of hysteria and of mental disease."[2]

Janet had enormous influence on modern psychology and psychiatry, and as we shall see in a moment, what Jung called the complex was originally simply the equivalent of Janet's "subconscious fixed idea". In these early days, the complex was viewed solely as a facet of pathology, and the split-off fragments were understood to be repressed conflicts – primarily sexual – which the ego could not face or deal with. During the course of the day we will see that this view of the complex is still relevant in specific individual situations, since personal conflicts flesh out the bones of

---

[1]J. M. Charcot, *Leçons sur les maladies du système nerveux*, in *Oeuvres Complètes*, III, 335-337, quoted in Henri F. Ellenberger, *The Discovery of the Unconscious*, Basic Books, Inc., New York, 1970, p. 146.
[2]Pierre Janet, *L'Automatisme psychologique*, Alcan, Paris, 1889, p. 436, quoted in Ellenberger, *ibid.*

the complex and may need to be dealt with as a source of pathology. But the core of the complex is not pathological.

The next important researcher into complexes was Freud. Although he rarely named the sources for his ideas, he did acknowledge Janet's priority, both in the discovery of "subconscious fixed ideas" and in the cure of the patient through catharsis and conscious awareness of the troublesome *idée fixe*. The essential techniques of psychoanalysis – dream interpretation and free association – are ultimately geared toward raising the complex into consciousness. Freud, like Charcot and Janet, initially viewed the complex as essentially comprised of repressed personal memories and conflicts. Only later did he begin to acknowledge complexes as universal factors which provided the motivating force in every individual's development.

Jung, while still Freud's disciple, introduced the term "complex" into psychoanalytic thought. The Oedipus complex might otherwise have been called the Oedipal fixed idea – the inevitable and universal incestuous triangle of childhood, with all its attendant desire, fear, guilt, aggression and shame. Likewise, Alfred Adler took up Jung's term and utilised it in his concept of the inferiority complex – the fixed idea of inferiority at work beneath the threshold of awareness, which leads to a compulsive power-drive that can both achieve greatness and destroy the individual.

The complex in Jung's analytical psychology

At the turn of the century, while working at the Burghölzli Clinic, Jung developed the famous "word association test" to demonstrate the existence and nature of unconscious complexes. The test had been around for a while in crude form, but Jung restructured and refined it. At this time Jung was still a Freudian, if that is the right way of putting it. For any of you who might be unfamiliar with this test, it consists of reading a succession of carefully chosen words to the subject, who has to respond with the first word that occurs to him or her. The reaction time is measured precisely, and anomalies, such as a delayed response, no response, a stutter or mispronunciation, or the repetition of one word over and over again, are carefully noted. Then the connections between the responses are examined.

I have taken this test as well as giving it to others during my clinical training, and although you may all think it very amusing and a bit of a waste of time, it is in fact a very strange and powerful experience. We believe we are in control of what we think and how we respond verbally, but if one takes this test in an open and spontaneous fashion, it is extraordinary how much is revealed by it. The subject is almost invariably unaware of the connection between his or her answers and the complex underlying the responses, even though it may be screamingly obvious to the person administering the test.

Jung's main objective in developing this test was the detection of complexes. Initially he distinguished between normal, accidental, and permanent complexes. The existence of a "normal" complex had not really been considered prior to this, since most of the early research was done with severely disturbed patients in psychiatric clinics. To Charcot and Janet, and also to Freud, complexes were invariably linked to pathology. What Jung initially meant by "normal" complexes involved fundamental areas of human experience, such as sexual feelings, family relationships, and money. For example, a powerful drive toward success might be viewed as a "normal" complex – it is compulsive and consuming, but it may lead to great productivity and creative fulfillment, and does not necessarily distort the individual's relationship to reality.

In other words, a complex, although unconscious, may not be pathological. It may be an unconscious web of feelings and associations, "normal" in itself, which exerts a compulsive but positive influence over conscious life. "Accidental" complexes, in contrast, relate to specific events which have happened in a person's life, often traumatic in nature, which have left powerful unconscious emotions and associations in their wake. These are not universal, as are the "normal" complexes, because they are related to particular experiences. For example, a childhood rape may form the nucleus for an "accidental" complex which has powerful destructive effects on the individual's ability to relate to others. "Permanent" complexes are, in the main, pathological and inclined to overwhelm the ego. They are resistant to integration, and are particularly relevant to progressive conditions such as schizophrenia. Although Jung did not use the term, I would be inclined to call these "hereditary" complexes, reflecting unresolved conflicts which extend back into the fabric of the family psyche.

Gradually Jung extended the narrow early concept of the complex, and postulated many different stages – conscious, partly conscious, fully unconscious, and strongly or less strongly emotionally charged. This latter issue preoccupied him, because it was directly linked with the compulsiveness of the complex. He began to think in terms of psychic energy, and evaluated the complex as strong or weak according to the amount of psychic energy charging it. Ultimately he extended his scope beyond the personal unconscious and formulated his theory of the archetypes. In doing this he brought the idea of the complex full circle, and returned to the Greek myths as representations of the archetypal core of the complex. It is at this juncture that we, as astrologers, can come in and view the whole spectrum, from the mythic to the personal, and recognise in planetary configurations a precise picture of this archetypal core.

The application of the model

The psychological model of the complex is quite sophisticated on its own, but it is utterly transformed when viewed through an astrological lens. It is a great pity that psychology has not, in the main, availed itself of astrological imagery, because, as I said earlier, complexes are really what we mean by fate. I also find it very interesting to play about with the model of the complex in the context of esoteric thought. For example, if one is sympathetic to the idea of reincarnation, one will probably view the various issues that one grapples with in one's present life as the continuing unfoldment of the efforts, failures, successes, and conflicts carried over from other lifetimes. Complexes are not mutually exclusive with the idea of "karma" as substance accrued from past lives.

Thus the complex may be seen as an encoded energetic container of past life patterns, in the same way that DNA is an encoded container of heredity. We can also see complexes as part of our genetic inheritance, and it may be that our complexes as well as our physical traits are, in part, a product of the line from which we come. Complexes are a quintessential model of how the psyche works. This model not only gives the whole theory of conscious-unconscious dichotomy a demonstrable basis, but also gives the astrological chart a firm basis in psychological dynamics. When we look at aspect configurations, singletons, angular planets – anything in the chart we deem to be energetic – we are looking at complexes. When we look at transits and progressions, we are looking at the timing of the emergence of a complex, or part of a complex, from the unconscious into conscious life.

 I shall now put a sequence of very crude maps on the overhead projector, just to orientate those of you who may be unfamiliar with the material I have been outlining. Please bear in mind that all maps are very limited. They are meant to sketch in the territory, not to provide a vicarious experience of it. The map, as Ian Gordon-Brown always used to say about Assagioli's "egg diagram", is not the country. This diagram is one of many valid, albeit simplistic maps to help us navigate a deeply mysterious realm. It is not meant to state categorically, "That's how it is." Please take it in the Mercurial spirit in which I am offering it.

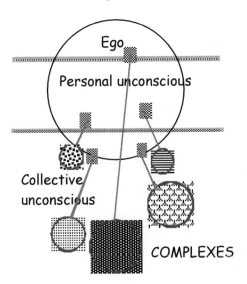

This diagram is, of course, a lie; there is constant movement in the psyche. Life is not static like a two-dimensional black-and-white drawing, and neither are we. We don't go around with a conscious ego like a perspex bubble containing fixed perceptions and ideas, and a personal unconscious full of seething unmentionables, and a bottomless collective unconscious with little globules that have lines ending in arrows. There is constant interchange between the different dimensions of the human psyche, and the boundaries are fluid and always shifting. Things that one is aware of at any given time may slide back into the unconscious, which, although I have drawn it as "below" in the diagram, may actually be above, or within, or all around. Unconscious qualities that are not yet developed, or have been suppressed for various reasons, may enter conscious awareness at different times in life. They may be triggered by events or the natural process of aging. Or they may simply be ripe.

As the American poet Walt Whitman once wrote, we contain multitudes. The psyche has many facets, and some of them are in the dark – not necessarily negative, but beyond the threshold of consciousness. Our awareness of ourselves and of the world is necessarily limited, not only by our limited personal experience, but also by our limited psychological "spectacles". We see only what we are best suited to see, which tends to leave out a lot. That is why the word association test fascinated Jung – it provides a vivid demonstration of what we have left out. We are also usually unconscious of the larger psyche to which we all belong, and therefore don't really register what human beings as a collective are going through at any given time, although we may act it out blindly.

This unconsciousness about the complexes which drive us as a mass makes us very vulnerable to collective movements of a compulsive kind. That is one of the reasons why the outer planets, which are symbols of collective drives, can wreak such havoc if there is an insufficiently solid individual ego to mediate them. We tend to think that what we see is all there is to see of reality, both inner and outer, and if we encounter people who see things differently, they are at best misguided or mistaken, and at worst mad. We may also believe that our experiences are unique, unlike anyone else's, and that no one has ever experienced, or ever will experience, love, hate, pain or longing as we do.

On one level, that is true – we process our experiences through a unique personality which isn't quite like anyone else's, even if we find a perfect "astrological twin". The mysterious chemical combination of individual experience and the inherent temperament reflected by the individual horoscope creates a particular perception of life which is uniquely our own. But complexes, at their core, are not unique. They are archetypal patterns, neither pathological nor individual, and they motivate all human beings – perhaps even all life, according to the level of awareness.

Here is the same diagram, altered slightly, to give you an idea of what I mean. Once again I will remind you that the map is not the country.

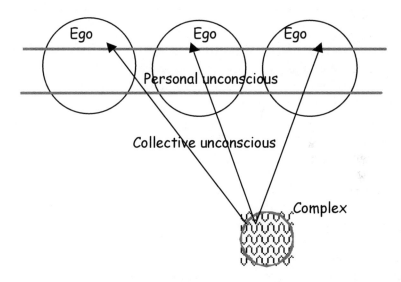

Each of these three individuals will experience the impact of the same complex in highly individual ways, according to their early environment, subsequent experiences, and inherent temperaments. And they will react accordingly. But the core of the complex is the same, because it is a pattern within the collective psyche, forming part of and motivating each individual psyche.

Because the same complex is at work, the issues which emerge at the personal level will draw these three people into certain kinds of relationship patterns based on the complex. We will look at this more carefully later, in an astrological context.

The archetypal level of complexes

Now we need to go back to the Greeks, who invariably thought of everything first. In assigning compulsive behaviour to a deity, they recognised that, beyond the personal level of experience, there are areas of life in which we all share the same unconscious needs, drives and patterns. The same deity can interfere with the lives of a multitude. The Trojan War, for example, does not begin with one individual leader deciding to invade another leader's territory. We think mainly in political and sociological terms these days. The Trojan War begins with a beauty contest between the gods. Human beings are the helpless counters in a divine game in which enmities between the Olympians are unavoidably visited on hapless mortals.

Have any of you ever seen a wonderful early animatronics film called *Clash of the Titans?* There is a superb scene on Olympus, where the gods are sorting out their conflicts on a chessboard. Zeus, played with great style by Laurence Olivier, makes a particularly clever move, and down below, poor Perseus is unknowingly saddled with his fate. Anything the gods can't work out between themselves winds up getting tossed into the court of the innocent humans who happen to be favoured by them and are both their pawns and their vessels of embodiment. Although we tend now to see this "pawns on the chessboard of the gods" view of life as cynical and depressing, it may be truer than we think. We are certainly pawns on the chessboard of our complexes, and the more we believe we are always in conscious control of ourselves and life, the more compulsively we seem to behave.

For "gods", read "planets". That is, after all, what we are dealing with in astrological symbolism. Because we all share the same planets, we are not isolated individuals. We are like every other human being who ever has lived and who ever will live, because the same archetypal patterns, symbolised by the planets, are alive within us. In this sense all the planets are collective, because they reflect universal human qualities. The basic drives which we share with every human being may make an individual pattern in the birth horoscope, but the planets themselves are universal, like the core of a complex.

For example, we have all had parents. They may be good, bad or indifferent. One or both may be absent. And it is even possible, through *in vitro* fertilisation, for a child to have a father who died ten years earlier and had his sperm frozen, or a mother whose fertilised egg has been implanted into someone else. But however bizarre the nature of the parental experience, we have not yet found the secret of immaculate conception, and still depend on a sperm and an egg to keep things going. The experience of parenting is not just my personal experience. Everyone has been parented – badly, lovingly, violently, absently, smotheringly, or whatever. In our very different ways we all experience the process of coming from two parents, male and female, whether they are present or absent, and however they treated us. The experience of mother and father is part of the collective level of experience, which is why in myth we have a king and queen of the gods or, even in the oldest and most primal of myths, a maternal deity who has a male self-fertilising capacity.

Mythic images are images of basic psychological drives, fundamental and irrevocable patternings in life and in the psyche. They don't have to be mystified. One doesn't have to believe in gods in the supernatural sense. One can be a supremely rational scientist who has observed that crystal formation always follows certain fixed patterns, and snowflakes always have six sides, and frogs always start off with gills and end up with lungs.

To understand these archetypal patterns, astrologers use the shorthand of planets, or a combination of planets and mythic images. But the arrangement of the patterns is different in each person. We get different emphases and different challenges. Out of the huge range of archetypal images of father, for example, a particular individual may live out a very specific facet, depending on what the significators of the father-principle look like in the individual chart, and what kind of experiences shape the way the complex develops.

Sun-Saturn, for example, is very special kind of father-image. It is reflected in a compulsion to express the father-complex – the energetic web of feelings, ideas and associations pertaining to father – in a certain way. Sun-Neptune will describe another, entirely different experience and expression of the father-complex. Sun-Mars will describe yet another.

The Sun-Neptune person may experience the archetypal father as an invisible spiritual source, or a poet, or a wounded victim, and the energy of this special kind of father-complex will generate certain kinds of perceptions, feelings, and actions. The Sun-Saturn person may experience father as a law-giver, or a tyrant, or a strong and stable protector. The Sun-Mars person may experience him as a fighter, a bully, a leader, or a violent aggressor. All these aspects are concerned with the father-principle and colour the father-complex, but they are different. We all have a father-complex, but we don't all have the same way of enacting and experiencing it.

Sun-Saturn as a father complex

When we try to understand what a complex looks like in astrological terms, we need to look at individual planets as well as aspects between planets. Saturn, as we know, symbolises the archetypal principles of law, authority, structure and limitation. This is its nature as portrayed in myth, and this is what it represents as an archetypal pattern within human beings. It is one dimension of the father-principle, or, in human terms, the father-complex – a web of associated ideas, feelings and experiences which reflects all we humans know of father, both personal and transpersonal.

Saturn is, of course, not the only planet connected with the father-principle. The Sun symbolises a different facet – the radiant creator-god who makes the universe and then sustains it with love and light. In Greek art, Saturn is always an old man, but Apollo the Sun-god is always young, beautiful, and perfectly proportioned.

When we meet a person in whose chart there is a Sun-Saturn contact, the father-complex in that individual will be coloured by this combination of planets, so that the creator and source of life is also the stern and implacable enforcer of law and limitation. However joyful and inspired the creative urge, it will always run up against irrevocable laws which define its limits.

This combination may be manageable with a trine or sextile – a complex with a fairly low energy charge. Or it may be disturbingly compulsive with a conjunction, square or opposition – a complex with a high energy charge, because two facets of the father-archetype are in conflict. When this conflict comes through into the personal unconscious, it forms a kind of energy field, gathering personal feelings and associations around it like a big magnet. It is both a pattern of development and a specific mode of perception. From infancy onward, all experiences pertaining to father will be perceived through its lens. When it begins to influence consciousness, the individual with the Sun in hard aspect to Saturn will experience his or her father as either Saturnian or solar, and feel compelled to do battle on the side of one against the other.

Let's create a hypothetical example – a man called George. We meet George at a friend's house, and in the course of a personal conversation the subject of parents comes up. He mentions that he will be spending the weekend with his father. Something in his tone rings oddly. Being psychologically inclined, we become curious, and ask him, "How did you get on with your father when you were young?" He replies politely, "Well, he was a very responsible person. He worked terribly hard. I didn't see much of him because he was away at work all the time. But I have a lot of respect for him. He always insisted that we play by the rules."

Because we are astrologers, we ask him for his birth data – although ethically we have no business doing so, because George has not asked for advice. But being ignorant of what a chart can reveal, he complies. We go home and calculate his chart, and are not surprised to find that the Sun is opposition Saturn. We then know what he edited out, but might have said if he had had the courage and the consciousness: "The bastard ignored me. I felt rejected all the time. Nothing I did was ever good enough. He made me feel

stifled, because he was so authoritarian. And the last thing in the
world I want to do is spend the weekend with him. I always leave
feeling upset, undermined, and resentful."

The archetypal father-complex is universal, and it is
neither positive nor negative. It simply *is*, and contains all human
experience of the life-principle which we call father. We associate
law, order, authority and discipline with Father Saturn, and the
creative power in the cosmos with Father Sun. We associate the
cosmic or heavenly design with Father Uranus, as in "Our Father
Who art in Heaven". We associate strength, aggression and
leadership with Father Mars. We all have these planets in the
birth chart, and all of them tell us something about the qualities
and patterns connected with the father archetype and the father-
complex.

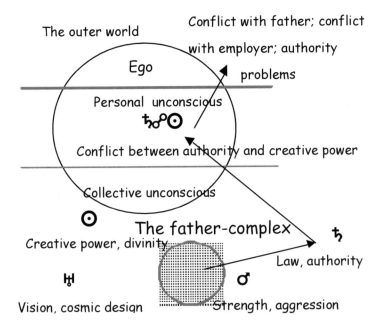

I have neglected to include Jupiter in the diagram, although
he may also be a father-image. He is the Giver of Gifts, the father
who bestows good fortune and turns our eyes to the future. I also
haven't included Mercury, god of the roads, who is father as teacher

and educator. And the planets we consider "feminine" in astrology may also be associated with father, especially if we find them in the 4th house. Father Moon is the nurturing or unreliable father, Father Venus is the beautiful beloved, Father Neptune is the divine source with which we seek to merge, and Father Pluto visits divine retribution on those who transgress natural law. We all have a father-complex of some kind. Unless one of you has been immaculately conceived, you will have a father, present or absent, alive or dead. If you *were* immaculately conceived you will still have one, albeit divine. And it seems that we all have a solar component to our father-complex, because we are created, not self-engendered.

George, our hypothetical example, has the Sun opposition Saturn in his birth chart, so he will experience a particular dimension of the father-archetype in a particular way. This is how we each partake of specific facets of a universal human pattern. We don't get to work on the whole picture in one incarnation – and maybe not even in several. We each have a highly individual destiny, or fate, or any other word we might care to use to describe our necessity.

Because these two planets were in conflict at the moment of George's birth, the archetypal father-principle was in conflict with itself. There was a special kind of disharmony within the cosmos when George was born. The father-complex on the collective level had a bug in it, and such bugs are cyclical, because all planets form cyclical aspects to each other. The gods were fighting one of their recurrent fights (because the Sun opposes Saturn once every year). Kronos-Saturn the Titan was battling it out with Apollo the Lord of Light. As the alchemists used to say, creation itself is still imperfect, and so too is God; and God depends upon human consciousness to achieve that perfection which is potential but not yet manifest.

So George's particular father-complex, symbolised by his Sun-Saturn opposition, has coloured his perception of his actual father right from the beginning of life. Whatever his father says or does, George experiences him through the lens of his Sun-Saturn opposition. In the early years of life, this perception will be unconscious, which is why I have put the Sun-Saturn opposition in the area of the diagram labeled "personal unconscious".

As George grows up and his personal ego begins to form, he will unconsciously make a choice as to which end of this opposition he experiences as his, and which end he will project on his father. This isn't pathological. It tends to happen with any difficult aspect in a birth chart, because the human ego doesn't seem to handle inherent conflict very well and will usually try to suppress one end in favour of the other. Also, our family background can virtually coerce us into taking sides between quarrelling gods. Successive hard aspects from transiting Saturn to this natal opposition, as well as other important transits and progressions, may reflect experiences which make George feel cornered and impelled to "split" the opposition in order to avoid anxiety and stress. And the actual behaviour of George's father may tip the scales strongly one way or the other. If his father really is a tyrannical bastard, then George won't be especially enthusiastic about owning Saturnian qualities in himself.

We can never be certain, from looking at a hard aspect, which end the ego will "claim" and which end will remain unconscious. But we can get some clues. If George is a Capricorn with Taurus rising and the Moon in Virgo trine the Sun and sextile Saturn, and nothing except Pluto in fire, then we can make an educated guess that he will favour Saturn over the Sun, and project the solar side of the opposition onto his father. The father might then appear artistic or charismatic, but possibly also weak or childish, or inaccessible like the Sun in the heavens. If George is a Leo with Sagittarius rising, the Sun conjunct Jupiter, and Venus and Mercury in Leo trine Mars in Aries, we can make an educated guess that he will favour the Sun, and project Saturn. This latter possibility is the line I will take as I develop our story about the Madness of George.

As fiery George begins to interact with the outer world and encounters any thing or person that is connected with the archetype of father – school authorities, police, his weekly allowance, even his own body – his complex will push against his conscious perceptions and subtly colour them, distorting his relationship with reality. Saturnian people and institutions will invariably seem authoritarian and restrictive, the outer world will seem to be blocking him at every turn, and George will go about thinking to himself, "It's tough out there. The world is a rotten place. Everybody heaps shit on me." This is how he perceives his father. At this point he is unlikely to recognise that the hard, tough, authoritarian figure who keeps him down isn't really his father, or, for that matter, the world. His father is a hook upon which he is projecting some of the energy of his father-complex – the half he cannot yet digest and make his own.

In infancy George is already predisposed through his innate psychic structure – which is what complexes are – to perceive his father and all father-surrogates in this way. But it is direct experience that will flesh out the bare archetypal bones of the complex. For the moment, let's leave George's mother out of the picture, although we all know she will play a very important part in influencing how this Sun-Saturn opposition is experienced. Let's say, then, that his father really isn't too bad a chap. He too has a Sun-Saturn aspect, a square. But unlike George, the father's Sun is in an earth sign, and there isn't any fire in his chart except for the Moon in Leo, so he identifies with Saturn's earthbound voice, and rejects the individualistic solar principle. He is secretly a dreamer, a frustrated artist. He adores his son – his Moon is, after all, conjunct George's Sun-Venus-Jupiter – and wishes the boy could have all the creative opportunities he himself never got. But he feels he must support his family, so he puts on a Saturnian face and tries terribly hard to be responsible.

But George is predisposed to seeing him as nothing but negative Saturn. So his father is going to start feeling rejected. George gets sullen around him, and resents any attempts at discipline, and doesn't like the wooden horse his father has spent hours carving for him for his birthday. After a while, the father says to himself, "This boy is impossible. I just can't talk to him. Whatever I try to do, I can't get it right. I'm not going to bother with him any more. His mother can deal with him."

The father withdraws and becomes distant, and increasingly feels a failure as a father. After all, he has a Sun-Saturn square, and his experience of his own father, George's grandfather, wasn't exactly a piece of cake. He doesn't really know much about fathering. George meanwhile secretly feels a failure as a son, because he thinks his father doesn't love him – even though, on the conscious level, he blames his father for their mutual alienation. This very personal experience of father-and-son conflict starts fleshing out the bones of George's complex. Our childhood experiences, which we remember and interpret selectively, contribute personal associations, personal memories, and personal feelings to something that is essentially impersonal or transpersonal. And thus the complex grows, with an archetypal pattern at its core and a highly personal layering of experiential flesh around that core. On first viewing, a pathological expression of George's complex has begun to form. It is accumulating a high energy charge of a negative kind. But its ultimate meaning and purpose have not yet revealed themselves.

As he reaches adulthood and moves toward his Saturn return, George's disappointment, hurt and resentment toward his father will generate feelings of anger and failure in all relationships and situations which involve the father-archetype. He may not be conscious of some of this, or even any of it. But at the same time that he is carrying around a negative perception of father, the secret respect and admiration he feels for his father's self-control and self-discipline is not negative. Although he is unlikely to admit it, he may envy his father, because this man had the toughness and commitment to sacrifice his own aspirations for the family, and George knows this, deep down. He may also know, since he is fiery, that he is rather narcissistic and childish in assuming that the world "ought" to recognise his specialness and grant him exemptions. By the time he reaches his Saturn return, the complex contains a complicated mass of highly ambivalent personal associations and feelings.

At twenty-nine, George is doing very well working for British Telecom. He is aiming for a good managerial position, perhaps as a regional manager. He wants to move up in the company, and he believes, on the conscious level, that he deserves to reach the top. But fate plays a very nasty trick on him – or so it would appear. George doesn't know he has a father-complex which predisposes him to problems with authority, because he hasn't yet encountered the full impact of the complex. He has had glimpses – at around fifteen, when Saturn opposed Saturn and conjuncted the

Sun and he had his first really big fight with his father about his punk friends and his poor performance at school, and at twenty-two, when Saturn squared the Sun-Saturn and he got thrown out of his job at Sainsbury's because he wore jeans and an earring to work.

But now he is having his Saturn return. He is a grownup, and he thinks he has left his adolescent rebellion behind. Yet the very nature of the work he has chosen will inevitably constellate the complex. The moment one goes to work as an employee of a company, one will encounter an authority to whom one must answer. One goes along and applies for the job. Somebody is already there who says, "I will look at your application, and I will decide whether you are good enough." From the outset the father-complex is constellated, because there is an authority to whom one must go in order to get the job in the first place. Before George even gets through the door at BT, his father-complex is already starting to pulsate, because he might get rejected. Somebody there might say, "We don't want you." He is already primed, even though he doesn't realise it.

For a time, all seems to go well. But then his boss moves up, just in time for George's Saturn return, and he acquires a new boss who has the Sun opposition Saturn. Wherever in the world he goes, George will always meet this Saturnian figure when the moment is ripe. This is what I mean by fate. There is no rational explanation of how this happens. On one level, we can see the cause-and-effect principle in operation. George is a company man because his Sun-Saturn compels him to seek security and structure. Within companies it is likely that those at the top will also have Sun-Saturn natures, and the odds are he will wind up working for one of them. But such causal reasoning cannot explain the mysterious ways in which we encounter our complexes in the outer world.

Sometimes the chain of causes and consequences is so obscure that we cannot find the beginning of it, because it may lie in the family background before our birth. Sometimes our choices are made when we are so young that we cannot in any sense be deemed responsible. Sometimes we are forced to make certain choices because the world is what it is. Sometimes the collective has set things in motion which lead to consequences which affect us personally. In this area personal "blame" may be irrelevant and inappropriate.

All we know is that, if we look at enough life histories, including our own, we can see this strange synchronicity occurring constantly. We always meet our secret selves in the outer world, even if we have to go around the world to do it. We always find those people whose birth charts fit our birth charts and whose complexes match our own, so that we can act out our drama with those individuals and thereby, hopefully, discover ourselves. It is generally through the dynamic of relationship that we start becoming aware of our complexes. That is how they usually manifest in life – not just in romantic relationships, but in all relationships in which we are deeply involved.

So George will unerringly be assigned to the particular executive at BT who also has a father-complex of the Saturnian kind, and then, guess what happens?

Audience: There is a power-battle.

Liz: Yes, eventually, although initially there is more likely to be antipathy based on mutual projections. Our problems with other people usually begin with small, unnoticed gestures, words, and actions generated by our complexes, before they flower as full-blown power-battles.

Something difficult starts going on between George and his employer, and at first it is quite unconscious. The employer may be a bit tight-lipped and officious, but he is basically a nice chap. But his Sun-Saturn makes it hard for him to delegate authority or show warmth to his employees, and George feels unappreciated and put down all the time. His boss doesn't know what the problem is. All he knows is that there is friction between them. The relationship is not working. George's unconscious complex is making him cast his boss in the same role in which he cast his father. He feels criticised. He is not being acknowledged as special. He gives off a sullen atmosphere. His boss, in turn, feels that whatever he does, George is going to sabotage it. He senses George's tacit insubordination, and worries that he might turn out irresponsible, or even dishonest.

Audience: I wonder if George's employer may have a tendency to feel threatened by the talents or strengths of any employee, so he *is* going to put him down.

Liz: Yes, that could be part of it. It is not just George whose father-complex is on the rampage, but also his employer. We don't know the exact nature of George's employer's father-complex. But he may feel envy of George because George seems so fiery and outgoing, and this man, like George's father, may have stifled all his playful *puer* instincts to achieve success.

Audience: Or George's boss may be scared of him.

Liz: That, too. Saturn in myth was frightened of his children, because he was certain one of them would overthrow him. Or the man may feel in some way inferior to George, or he may feel that he is trying to be a good father and here is a son who is rejecting him. All of these feelings may be involved. You are quite right – the situation may constellate envy in the employer. It may also constellate envy in George. All we know initially is that these two are going to find each other, and once they start getting into their psychic punch-up – once that joint father-complex takes over without any conscious awareness – a concrete punch-up is inevitable.

George gets fired, and then turns up on an astrologer's doorstep wanting a chart consultation. To help *him* understand the real nature of this tangle, *we* must understand it. At core, it has nothing to do with employers or jobs. That is only one possible concrete manifestation of the complex. Even if George goes into psychoanalysis for ten years, no amount of conscious effort will make the complex go away. After ten years of analysis George might discover that his father is not really Saturn-Kronos, but he will still be left with his complex, peeled of its purely personal associations. The complex is a living, dynamic centre of energy, and it contains the pattern of George's development as a man. Ultimately he has to find a way to be this combination of Sun and Saturn himself, and express it in as creative and constructive way as he can.

He can only get to that level of consciousness by going through many different experiences, both pleasant and unpleasant, gradually gaining insight into his father-complex through the Saturnian people and situations he encounters. He may accumulate such experiences for many years, each time his natal Sun-Saturn is triggered by a transit or progressed aspect, until the time arrives when the complex has gathered sufficient energy to emerge into consciousness and be at least partly integrated. Complexes may sleep for a long time, and only make themselves known when the time is right. That is what predictive astrology is all about, although the more concrete-minded astrologer may miss the meaning and slow emergence of the complex, and focus only on the material event which is its by-product – George losing his job. On the inner level, transits and progressions tell us when complexes are ripe.

We can work on an intellectual level to understand what our complexes are all about. We can use our charts to "spot the complex". This is great fun, and also very useful because it can prepare us and help us to deal more sensibly with what is coming up. But it will not alter the timing of the development and emergence of the complex. When complexes begin to intrude on life, the actual experience is rather different from an intellectual recognition. Then it is wise to turn inward to meet them, in order to understand what they are and where they are leading us.

The possibility of change

Audience: Are you saying that complexes never change, even if we recognise them? That they just stay fixed and never alter?

Liz: No, I'm not saying that. When we try to understand complexes, we need to think in paradoxes. Complexes change constantly according to our experiences and the consciousness we bring to them, and the way we handle them at any given time may alter the way they are expressed in the future. If George had understood even a little of the ambivalent feelings he held toward his father, the outcome of his confrontation with his employer might have been different. But we cannot stand in front of the mirror and shout, "Come out, you bastard!" if the complex is not yet ripe for integration. And the archetypal core will remain the same, no matter how successful we are in integrating the personal material attached to the complex.

The core of a complex is archetypal, and is reflected astrologically by the configurations in the birth chart. We cannot send in and order a new birth chart because we feel something should be changed. I don't think working constructively with our complexes is a question of transforming something into something else. It is a question of consciousness, which can help us to stop projecting our complexes and engaging in compulsive relationship patterns with other people. It can also help us to be freer of the inner compulsions which drive us against our values and ethics, and it can help us to find new creative avenues for expressing the energy of the complex. Whether such consciousness can help us to alter the future is a question to which I have no answer. It is possible. It is also possible that certain experiences are necessary and unavoidable.

Complexes are very mysterious, and take us into very deep philosophical and spiritual waters. If we do not limit ourselves to the psychoanalytic framework, and come at the subject from a more esoteric perspective, we are facing the dilemma the medieval alchemists struggled so hard to resolve – the cosmos isn't finished yet. God has not yet finished the work of creation, or, to put it even more heretically, God himself, herself or itself is not yet finished. It isn't fully cooked yet. In this world-view, complexes are bits of God, if you want to be very mystical about it. What we call the collective unconscious is the *unus mundus*, the living cosmic whole of which human beings are a part.

When a person works to integrate a complex by making a relationship with the unconscious, the complex is given new avenues of expression which, on a purely instinctual level, it would never have. Complexes without any consciousness to mediate them have limited levels of expression, as they do in the animal kingdom. Most life forms are bound by the archetypal patterns which dictate their evolution in accordance with survival needs, and this was understood by the Greeks as the "Law of Nature" – the most rudimentary form of fate or *moira*. There are not many things your cat can do with its complexes, except enact them within the limits of its species. If it is feeling aggressive, it can bite its owner or another cat, or it can tear apart the furniture, or run madly around the house. But it does not, as far as we know, possess the capability of reflecting on the source of the aggressive feelings, which might shift them onto another level.

Deservedly or not, a human has a conscious ego which can make considered choices. This does not imply inherent superiority over other life-forms, nor do we always use our capacity for choice wisely. And many people prefer to lie back and let the complex take over, because it is so much easier. It could even be argued that, because we have so many choices, we have found far more destructive outlets for our complexes than other living things would ever pursue. But for whatever reason, if there is indeed a reason and it isn't just a cosmic accident, we have been given the gift of reflection, and can look forward and back, inward and outward. Therefore we can establish a different relationship with these energy centres within us, and encourage a dialogue between the complex with its compulsions and the ego with its capacity for choice.

By making the complex conscious, and taking responsibility for containing its inherent conflicts, the individual gives something back to the collective psyche. Like the alchemists, we have worked on nature, and transformed its expression, if not its essential archetypal core. It may be that, if enough individuals work in this way, the compulsive and destructive manner in which some collective complexes habitually enact themselves – the aggressive compulsions which leads to war, for example – would be transformed. I have no answer to the question of whether this is possible. I personally believe it is, but I doubt that it will happen by next week. Some complexes seem not to have changed their expression at all in several thousand years. Others clearly have. But even with the latter, the archetypal core of the complex doesn't seem to change.

In Jung's *Answer to Job*,[3] he suggests that, after many millennia of human life, the tyrannical Old Testament Yahveh is transformed by Job's dignified acceptance of suffering, and learns compassion. This is a hopeful perspective on the potential for change in complexes, but it certainly took a bloody long time. And even with such a vast collective shift, the archetypal core of our complexes remains the same, because complexes are the structure of our psychic reality. So yes, I think there is a possibility of change – but also there isn't. How is that for a Mercurial answer?

Audience: Let me make sure I have got what you are saying. The archetypal core of the complex is there, and it is what it is, but the way that it seats itself in an individual's unconscious is the thing which can change. George will always have a Sun-Saturn opposition, so that's his father-complex, but he doesn't have to pick a fight with his boss and get fired. And he doesn't have to blame his father. He could become more Saturnian and live both sides.

Liz: Yes. The way in which consciousness contains the complex and works with it can radically change its "seating", as you put it.

Complexes in manifestation

There are a lot of different ways in which complexes express themselves, and I wanted to spend some time on this because it is another way of describing the different ways in which astrological configurations express themselves. Complexes are usually expressed through projection. We may suddenly start reacting very powerfully to something or someone in the environment.

When parts of a complex are projected, the energy charge is out of proportion to what the situation merits, and if we have the wit to recognise this, we may discover that there is something

---

[3]C. G. Jung, "Answer to Job", in *Psychology and Religion, Collected Works, Vol. 11*, Routledge & Kegan Paul, London, 1973, pp. 355-474.

within us that has got its own life, its own ideas about reality, and its own emotional responses. And it is not doing what we want. We say to ourselves, "I shouldn't be reacting this way," or, "I'm not going to allow this to happen again," and then we encounter the same person or situation and we find ourselves in the grip of our compulsion all over again.

Projection is a "normal" way in which complexes may gradually emerge into conscious awareness. Projection is not an indication of pathology. It is a natural psychological mechanism through which unconscious components seek consciousness. How we handle our compulsive responses can make an enormous difference to our lives, on many levels. We can begin to question ourselves, or we can blindly act out our compulsions. We can blame ourselves or others, or we can try to contain and understand our emotions.

In some people, the boundary between conscious awareness and the unconscious is very fluid. This may make it easier to work with complexes, although too much fluidity may also mean we identify with the complex and do not develop enough ego strength. But some people nail all the windows shut and put padlocks on the doors. The ego becomes rigid and defended, and when that happens and a complex is moving toward consciousness, it can't get through in a "natural" way. So it may take an uncomfortable way instead.

The somatising of the complex

Audience: I can identify with what you are talking about. I have a Saturn-Pluto square in my chart, and I dread that square when anything transits it. I have got Saturn in the 8th. I'm not projecting it, honestly! But I am often ill.

Liz: Let's look at what kind of complex this configuration might reflect. Any ideas?

Audience: It's control versus passion. I can't think of a good name for it, like the Oedipus complex, but I'm sure there are examples of this in myth.

Liz: Yes, there are many examples. One good one is the relationship between King Pentheus and Dionysus in Euripides' *The Bacchae*. Pentheus is big on control. He tries to lock the god in prison and forbids his worship. Dionysus eventually drives him mad and leads him to his death.

A more contemporary example is Thomas Mann's novel, *Death in Venice*, which many of you will know from Visconti's film. The composer, von Aschenbach, is a worshipper of rationality, and repudiates the instincts. He believes that art should be a product solely of the intellect and spirit, rather than being corrupted by emotion and sensuality. Von Aschenbach has a bad heart, on the emotional as well as the physical level. The beautiful boy, Tadzio, with whom he falls in love, is an image of Eros, who is a god of death as well as love. The boy's mother is a thinly disguised Aphrodite, who in myth becomes extremely ill-tempered whenever anyone rejects her delights. Mann has taken the ancient myth and given it contemporary relevance. Literal death is not usually the outcome of a struggle between Saturn and Pluto, but the death of control, on some level, will usually be required. Von Aschenbach is overwhelmed by an unwelcome passion. This is often the death required by Saturn-Pluto, which could ultimately transform the ego. Maybe we should call Saturn-Pluto the Death in Venice complex.

If Saturn in your chart is blocking Pluto, and is placed in Pluto's natural house, then the Plutonian end of the complex may project itself in an extremely powerful way, and you may find yourself in painful power battles with other people. What house is Pluto in?

Audience: The 5th.

Liz: Then I would guess that you have had this kind of power struggle in intimate relationships, and sexual issues may be the apparent cause.

Audience: Yes, I know that one.

Liz: The complex may also somatise, and manifest through the body. You seem to have made a connection between being ill and the conflict Saturn-Pluto represents. I personally believe that all illnesses involve a complex. They may also have physical or physiological causes, but this is not necessarily mutually exclusive with an archetypal core – especially when there is a repetitive pattern of illness, or a certain kind of illness that recurs. An archetypal pattern is both physical and psychological, and our bodies are prone to particular types of illnesses which mirror our psychological qualities and conflicts. Every homeopath knows this, although the knowledge appears, so far, to have eluded most orthodox medical practitioners.

Audience: When a complex gets projected outward onto another person or a situation, it doesn't need to somatise. I think that the somatising happens when the complex is being projected inside the person, like a conflict between two subpersonalities, to use the Psychosynthesis terminology. We can have conscious or unconscious ideas about the ego, the body, the higher self, and so on. So we can project a Sun-Saturn aspect onto our own higher self, or a Saturn-Pluto onto our body. Do you follow what I mean?

Liz: I follow what you mean, and I agree that this can happen. Your example of "projecting" Sun-Saturn onto the higher self is a good one – our images and interpretations of God are usually heavily coloured by our complexes, and if we perceive God as a punishing Saturnian tyrant, we will be attracted to religions which are heavily Saturnian. We will unconsciously arrange our own punishment when we think we have sinned, and then blame it on God.

But I don't think this is the only reason why a complex somatises, and I am more inclined to associate what you are describing with situations where the person compulsively maltreats the body – anorexia, bulimia, self-inflicted injury, and so on. Certainly, in the case of this lady's Saturn-Pluto, we could hypothesise that Pluto is being projected onto the body, which is perceived as the carrier of all her dark, uncontrollable instincts, and which has to be ruthlessly controlled. So Pluto hits back through the body. That is a valid way of looking at it, although perhaps not the only one. Pluto is an outer planet, and what it symbolises is collective, not personal. So the collective nature of the body, which is, after all, made just like all other bodies of the same sex, may exacerbate the conflict.

But I am a little worried about the term "subpersonality" to describe something archetypal. I have no difficulty in working with this terminology, and in terms of individual personality qualities, attributes and drives, "subpersonality" is as good a word as any to describe the different facets of the psyche. But behind the "subpersonality" on an individual level lies something much larger. The body's darkness and "evil" provide the main theme of many myths, especially the Gnostic and Christian ones, and this is very much bigger than one individual's negative projection on an errant subpersonality. I think you are right, and one might fruitfully begin with this perspective – but on the personal, not the archetypal level.

In terms of quality, there seems to be no difference between a person who projects a complex and a person who enacts a complex internally in a compulsive way. The person who acts a complex out through an illness is also engaged in splitting, because the body is carrying one side of the aspect and the ego is carrying the other. I don't think that one expression of the complex indicates a greater degree of consciousness or evolution than the other.

People express their complexes differently. This may be connected with the overall chart balance. For example, people who are weak in the element of earth may show a propensity to somatise their complexes because the physical side of life is more sensitive, more vulnerable, and more unconscious. This may be a reflection of the body's extreme receptivity. People with planets in the 6th house may somatise their conflicts as well, even if the individual is very earthy. And people with a powerful angular Moon may somatise a complex, because the Moon reflects an instinctual level of response which is physical as well as emotional. If the Moon is unhappy or blocked, the body may act out the misery because it is like a sensitive photographic plate.

There doesn't seem to be an easy way of determining from a chart whether a complex is going to come out through projection or through illness. Often it is both. We might see a stellium of planets in the 7th house in one chart and the same stellium in the 6th in another, and we can at least get a hint that, with the former, complexes may be expressed through relationships, and with the latter, through the body. But the 6th house may also indicate a propensity to enact complexes through work and one's relationship with employers and employees, so we still can't be sure. As a complex comes into consciousness, it generally splits. There is usually a conflict, which we initially try to avoid by farming out one half. This unwelcome half may be projected on the body, or it may be experienced through the body, which is rather different. Or it may attach itself to another person, or a type of person, or a group of people, or an abstract thing like an ideology, or a concrete thing like a particular place or environment. The onset of an illness, and compulsive relationship patterns due to projection, are two characteristic manifestations of the emergence of a complex into consciousness. They are not necessarily due to pathological blocking. The high energy charge around a complex can create enormous anxiety when we get a whiff of its power. We know that something is going on inside which we don't understand. It frightens us, and we try to back off from the conflict and the challenge of increased consciousness by splitting.

That is a human, not a pathological thing to do. If we use astrological language, we may come to the same conclusion, because when a major transit or progression is approaching and it has got within orb, we know something is happening, and we may become frightened. We may not know on the rational level (unless we are astrologers), but we know it intuitively, and we start reacting. Often anxiety is the first response. Change is imminent, and one starts putting metaphorical tank traps in the drive. Do any of you know Byron's poem about the Kraken? A huge primordial creature from the depths of the sea begins its slow ascent to the surface, and the first harbingers are the tidal waves and the boiling of the waters.

Complexes and psychosis

Audience: And then what happens? Mental breakdown?

Liz: Sometimes, yes, if the ego is badly dissociated from the rest of the psyche, or is too lopsided or poorly formed. What I said about illness also applies to psychotic breakdowns. There is invariably a complex at work, a complex with a very high energy charge, and the ego may be shattered – temporarily or permanently – by its emergence. The complex has no other way to enter life, so it smashes down the ego's walls, and the ego is overwhelmed. This may happen if the ego cannot stretch enough to take the complex on board. In extreme cases of psychosis, such as schizophrenia, the archetypal nature of the complex is very much in evidence, because the person's fantasies are often mythic in nature. This mythic quality may also be present when a breakdown is a one-off and eventually leads to a breakthrough and a major and positive change in awareness.

If the ego can provide an appropriate vehicle, then creative work is one of the ways in which the enormous energy of the complex can express itself. When we look at some of the great creations of literature, such as *Faust*, we can see the expression of the author's complex through the characters and plot. But it isn't just a personal Oprah Winfrey-type confession thinly disguised as fiction. The relationship between Faust and Mephistopheles is a magnificent vehicle for Goethe's Sun-Pluto square. When the author chooses an archetypal theme and then makes it his or her own through individualising it, the complex really has a chance to unfurl its wings rather than pouring out its sludge. Perhaps that is the difference between the artist and the amateur. Wagner wrote *Tristan und Isolde* when he was caught in a fairly prosaic love triangle (as he usually was), but the poignant yearning of the music and the mythic inevitability of the plot have transcended the personal level of his complex and put the listener – as well as the composer – in touch with the archetypal level.

We have been looking at Sun-Saturn as a father-image, and as a symbol of a particular kind of father-complex. Just for contrast, let's look at another aspect. What kind of father-image might be suggested by Sun-Uranus?

Audience: Full of light. Changeable.

Liz: Yes, that might be the kind of feeling a child has about his or her father. But we need to start with the archetypal core, and then we will understand the different images associated with the father, some of which may seem mutually exclusive. Uranus is concerned with revelation. It is the fire of illumination, the sudden Promethean vision of the orderly workings of the cosmos. Uranus is inspirational, because it reveals the system behind material manifestation. It is God as the lightning bolt, the flash of inspiration. If the energy of such a complex breaks through into ego-consciousness, we may experience an enormous burst of creative energy, or an important spiritual revelation. Equally, we may have a shattering psychotic breakdown. Or the complex could be projected, and we could have a very disturbing and compulsive encounter with a Uranian person in the outer world.

But what has this to do with father? A great deal, actually. If father is experienced as a sudden, illuminating force, a shattering revelation of power and cosmic intelligence, we are likely to be afraid of him in childhood. He seems so impersonal, so full of power, so far away. A great deal depends on how inimical or positive we experience his energy to be, and how willing we are to be the recipients of it. This may be linked to the kind of aspects Uranus makes in the natal chart, as well as the overall element balance. It may also be linked to the behaviour of the actual father. If we can relate to father as a person, then he may be able to mediate the archetype sufficiently so that we are not so terrified – even if Sun and Uranus are in hard aspect. Then, when we ourselves experience Uranian revelations later in life, we feel safe enough to acknowledge and be transformed by them, because we have a positive expectation of their creative power.

But if father is a tyrant, a negative example of Uranian suppression of the instincts, we may experience a deep split between the mind and the body. We may identify with him and reject the body, or we may identify with the physical world, and reject Uranus. And if father is absent, as he often is when Uranus is a father-significator, then the sudden illuminating power of the archetypal father has no human mediator, and is all bound up with his sudden disappearance and its shattering consequences. Then we may try to block the advent of any Uranian experience, because we are afraid it will herald a painful separation and the same shattering consequences we encountered early in life. Or we may try to identify with Uranus in the hope of getting close to a father we never had. And then we may have a lot of trouble later.

Freeing the energy of the complex

Audience: I have noticed that when a parent dies, these kinds of issues often seem to explode in the person's life. Is this because the complex can't be projected any more?

Liz: Yes, it means the energy of the complex can no longer be contained by projecting it on another person. So it bounces back, although this may take quite some time to register on consciousness. Of course there are situations where projections remain intact on a dead parent, child, guru, or lover. Then we may see a person fighting tooth and nail, sometimes for years, to maintain a particular view of that dead person, despite the increasing intrusion of reality.

Let's go back to George. He has managed to farm Saturn out by plastering it firmly on his father, thereby avoiding the conflict inherent in the complex. This is perfectly "normal", in the sense that we need to do this with our complexes until we are able to deal with them ourselves. Perhaps we always need to have some bits farmed out, since this is the "glue" which binds us in relationship with others. But George has been doing it a little too much, for a little too long. He has found the perfect solution for a problematic Sun-Saturn: don't talk to the old man.

One day, George's father dies, and all the energy from this complex which has been invested in his father begins to boomerang back to its owner. This will probably take place under an important transit or progression which triggers the Sun-Saturn. A huge quantity of psychic energy caroms back into George, and of course this will create a major disturbance in his psychic equilibrium. He may not understand what is happening, and may not link his depression or physical symptoms or sexual lassitude or sudden increase in aggression with his father's death. The process of reclaiming the complex may result in a creative opening up, or a great deal of suffering, or both. But whenever we project our complexes in long-term relationships – with parents, children, partners, and institutions or groups with which we have been involved for a long time – we have made a secret pact with these people and situations in the outer world. They will carry this bit of our complex and we will carry that bit of theirs. Families do this all the time, with each member carrying a particular bit of the family complex. The moment there is a change in the relationship, especially a dramatic change such as a death, energy is freed.

Sometimes this freeing of energy is experienced as a wonderful release by one person and a terrible threat by the other. There is no clause in the contract guaranteeing that both parties will gracefully accept the breaking down of the *participation mystique* created by a shared complex. Some people will do anything, however ruthless and vicious, in order to prevent it. Of course this is fruitless, and cannot prevent the process from happening. In families we can see this kind of thing happening all the time. One child – usually the "black sheep" or scapegoat, the "identified patient" as he or she is called in family therapy, elects to leave the enmeshed family unit, and suddenly everyone starts acting all sorts of stuff out, because the "black sheep" bit of the family complex, which that child has been carrying for many years, has boomeranged back into the bosom of the family, where it always secretly belonged. Then other family members may unconsciously work to immobilise or even destroy the person who has unleashed so much transformative energy, in the hope that all the pieces can be put back in their places again – which is impossible.

I have heard a good many people talk about this experience after they have been in therapy for some time, and have begun to understand and respond differently to the complexes at work in the family. This kind of genuine expansion of consciousness generally releases energy, and changes start happening in the family, some of them sometimes very positive. And strangely, often there is the synchronicity of a parent dying, which is the outer expression of a deep and mysterious transformation taking place within. Just at the moment when the child who has been carrying a complex for the parent has begun to break free, the parent makes an exit – as though the parent too has been released to move on, on another level.

Hooks for the projection of complexes

Audience: What happens when you don't actually find a hook? I have been thinking about the case of a person I know who has the Sun in Leo in the 9th house, opposition Jupiter and trine Neptune. His father is an absolute Uranian – full of very democratic ideas, but everyone has to do what he wants them to do. This Leo person is very far away from being spiritual or philosophical, which you would think he ought to be with those aspects. He lives with a sense of constant restlessness – he loves to wander. Those Sun-Jupiter and Sun-Neptune aspects don't really show. I cannot see any hook in his father for those aspects. What I mean is, can a complex feel lost because it hasn't found a hook or a mediator?

Liz: When you say your friend – I assume he is a friend? – loves to wander, I would have thought you were describing one of the obvious expressions of both Sun-Jupiter and Sun-Neptune. The philosophising side of Jupiter and the mystical side of Neptune are apparently absent, but maybe that isn't the only expression for these aspects, or maybe the time hasn't come yet. But you have described the father's overt behaviour. He may be harbouring a secret mystic in him, a lost wanderer buried underneath the Uranian dogmatism, and your friend picks this up but can't link it up with anything he sees in outer life.

He may also secretly feel that his father is a failure, a *puer aeternus*, and because he can't find a strong masculine model, he himself can't put down roots or build anything solid. That may be why he can only find one expression for the solar aspects – not because the father isn't a hook, but because the hook is an atmosphere or undercurrent rather than a demonstrable personality type, so there is no behavioural model. I think you should have a look at this father's chart, before you decide whether he is or isn't a hook. Not all father-complexes will fix themselves on the personal father in as obvious a way as they have with George, our hypothetical example. In other words, not all complexes involving "masculine" planets will project themselves as personality qualities which the person associates with his or father. It may be that your friend's Jupiter-Neptune side is not going to form part of his conscious perception of his father, because his father is suppressing his own Jupiter-Neptune side. I would be very surprised if the father had nothing in his chart to serve as a hook for these planets, but I wouldn't be surprised if they were suppressed.

This mystical, philosophical, other-worldly, idealised father-image may be projected on a brother, or even on your friend's mother, if she displays a strongly religious or philosophical "animus" side to her nature. Jupiter-Neptune is in many ways the image of the priest-teacher, and your friend may have perceived it – for good or ill – in his local vicar or his headmaster at school. It may be projected on the country where he was born. It may be projected on his definition of God. It may appear as a characteristic of a particular social or racial group. It may not actually hook onto his father as he recognises him, although at core it is concerned with the father-principle. When a complex is deeply unconscious, it forms part of the fabric of our perception of reality in a way that doesn't necessarily register as a specific image of one of the parents.

How many of you have ever idealised a place – for example, the place of your birth, or a particularly beautiful piece of countryside that you visited as a child, or another country such as India? During the 1970's many people believed that India is a place where, as soon as you get off the plane at Delhi airport, you achieve instant spiritual enlightenment. You are more likely to have your handbag slit open and your wallet stolen than you are to achieve enlightenment, but complexes do not take account of such things. A place, real or fantasised, can provide a hook for the projection of a father- or mother-complex involving planetary significators such as Jupiter or Neptune, because the place is both the Eden that one lost long ago and the Eden that one hopes to find one day. I think this might be the case with your friend. His wandering spirit is fuelled by a deep longing to "go home" – he sounds a bit like ET. Home is father, but not his actual flesh-and-blood father as he perceives him. It is the Isles of the Blessed, the Garden of the Hesperides, where one finds immortality. If he could just locate it and get there, everything would be fine. A place can be the symbol of the Neptunian return to the source.

When we project our complexes onto places in this way, it doesn't necessarily cause harm. Projection is the natural mechanism by which a complex first makes itself known, and perceiving a place through the lens of a complex is not likely to be as destructive as insisting that somebody close to us carries the complex for us. This kind of projection may not make us unhappy. There isn't anything disturbing the surface of consciousness enough to make us think, "What is going on here?" We don't realise how much of our energy is actually invested in this way, until something happens which causes the ego conflict. Sometimes this coincides with actually visiting the idealised place, and discovering that the thing we are seeking isn't really there. In your friend's case, at least until now, he just moves on to another place.

Audience: The way I finally interpreted the Jupiter-Neptune was that it's the father my friend never had. I just couldn't see the correlation between him and the traditional method of seeing the aspects to the Sun as descriptive of the father.

Liz: Aspects involving the Sun are concerned with the father-principle, but they may not form part of a person's conscious evaluation of his or her father, if the father's overt conscious behaviour cannot provide a hook. And with respect, you have told us about your impression of your friend's father as a Uranian, but do you know what your friend really feels about his father deep down? You might not like this father much, but your friend may love and idealise him, even if he feels rejected or stifled. The Jupiter-Neptune may truly be the father your friend had, but a father whom your friend couldn't ever get close to because the Uranian side got in the way. Also, the complex may be too highly charged to be satisfied with just one hook, and will be projected on any father-surrogate. And father-surrogates may not always be people.

Audience: The Church, for example.

Liz: Yes, the Church may be a father-surrogate, and so might one's priest or vicar. Any of you who are involved in counselling will already have worked out that George's therapist may also provide the perfect hook for the projection of his complex. The terms "transference" and "countertransference" are clinical definitions of what is essentially the mutual enactment of a complex within therapy. For that matter, George's astrologer may also provide a perfect hook.

Audience: Let's say that George is an astrologer.

Liz: Very well, George is an astrologer. In that case he might project his complex onto the planets, and view astrology, or other astrologers, in a particularly rigid, compulsive, or doom-laden way. It is always worth considering our own complexes in terms of what we view as the certainties of astrological interpretation and philosophy. We may also project a great deal on our astrological colleagues, and conceal this under the guise of "professional disagreement". The giveaway is always the high charge attached to the projection. And George will probably also have an astrological teacher, won't he? George goes to CPA seminars, and there is somebody up at the front of the room teaching, who gets to be you-know-what.

Audience: And then he sets up a practice and has a client...

Liz: Exactly. He sets up a practice, and has a client who comes to him with this very same complex. Inevitably, a good many of his clients will have this complex, as most of you who are practising astrologers will know. We always get the clients we deserve. You can all see, I am sure, that every dimension of life that in any way partakes of this archetypal pattern is going to get coloured by the complex.

Complexes and traumas

Audience: The classic attitude is that a complex is the result of a trauma, that it's in some way pathological. Do childhood events cause complexes?

Liz: In the early days of psychoanalysis the answer would have been, "Yes, complexes are created by traumas." But Freud himself moved beyond that, and postulated the Oedipus complex as a universal psychological pattern. He believed that traumas distorted or "fixed" the complex, and caused blockages and destructive expressions of it. In other words, a trauma can contribute negative personal associations to the archetypal core of the complex. In the ordinary Freudian run of things, there is a resolution to the Oedipal conflict, ending in healthy compromise and the "latency" period before puberty. But a severe Oedipal "defeat" – for example, a boy's experience of deliberate crushing and humiliation at the hands of the rival father, or an inability to make any emotional bond whatsoever with the mother – may twist the complex into pathological forms.

Astrology goes further than that. We know that the blockages and destructive expressions of a complex may not be "caused" by trauma, but may be reflected by difficult chart configurations which represent a tendency to experience certain events as traumatic in a highly subjective way. In other words, complexes are not caused by traumas, but we register a particular experience as traumatic because of our complexes.

I have met enough people who have been through virtually identical "traumatic" experiences when young – psychological or physical abuse in childhood, a near-fatal accident, rape or assault – to recognise that we respond to such events in radically different ways. One person might feel his or her entire life has been ruined by the experience, and uses this as a justification to inflict abuse or violence on others. A second person might suffer serious psychological disturbances, such as manic depression or hysteria. A third person may repeatedly put himself or herself in the position of the victim, unconsciously courting a replay of the original injury. A fourth person might be angry and mistrustful in certain situations, but remains relatively whole inside, still able to love and behave decently. Once again we are entering very deep waters. Remember Novalis' profound observation – "Fate and soul are two names for the same principle."

Astrologically, we can sometimes trace the presence of difficult "events" or periods in childhood which may have contributed to the more problematic expressions of a complex. Let's consider George's Sun-Saturn opposition once again. Let's say it is an applying opposition – the Sun is in 8° Leo and Saturn is in 14° Aquarius. When he was six years old, the progressed Sun moved into exact opposition to Saturn. That marks a time when this complex might have crystallised through some external event which was experienced as a "trauma". For example, George's father might have savagely beaten him, or he overheard his parents discussing divorce and believed his father was leaving because of him.

But equally, if we assume the existence of a specific, easily recognised event, we may find ourselves in trouble, because there might not have been such an event. There might have been a powerfully repressive and cold atmosphere, to which George himself unconsciously contributed. This moment of the exact Sun-Saturn opposition really describes the way that George perceived the events going on around him, not the events themselves.

Nothing at all may have "happened" to George, except that he may have been recovering from a bout of flu and was therefore unusually sensitive, and felt that everybody around him was rejecting him. If you say to him, "What happened when you were six?" he may look at you blankly and say, "Nothing." Or his father may have come home from work in a bad mood, and George went running up and shouted, "Daddy, daddy, can you show me how to make this electric train work?" and his father replied, "Oh, shut up and leave me alone, you little sod." Thirty years later, on the analyst's couch, George says, "And then he said this *terrible thing* to me." All over the world, millions of parents slap and snap at their children, but George's progressed Sun exactly opposite Saturn made that little outburst into a trauma. His own response to the environment crystallised his *a priori* perception of authority as a bad deal.

There will probably always be something in the early environment that crystallises the complex for good or ill. This is usually reflected by transits and progressed aspects. But when we begin to look more objectively at this "something", we realise that these events mean a great deal to the person because they mean a great deal to the complex. Sometimes they are events we can recognise as traumatic, and then we can say, "Oh, that's when George's father died in the war, and his mother had a breakdown."

A big thing happened, and we can understand why he would feel a terrible sense of loss, rejection and abandonment.

But not everyone whose father died in the war has Sun opposition Saturn, and not everyone interprets such an event as a personal abandonment. And in another chart with exactly the same configuration, we may not find any traumatic event. Somehow, during that sixth year, the complex has crystallised through a whole chain of little events that only mean something important to the person whose complex makes him or her register them as part of an important design. It is useful to explore the possibility of a traumatic event. But we mustn't be too upset if we don't find one.

Audience: If George's father dies, it can also go the other way, can't it? George might have been carrying projections from his father, and then suddenly they aren't there any more.

Liz: Yes, that can also apply. In fact it usually does, since parent-child interaction generally involves projections both ways. George may be carrying projections from his father, who might have perceived his son as a wastrel, an undisciplined *puer aeternus*. The father may also project certain dimensions of Saturn, while identifying with others. We not only split configurations in this way; we also split individual planets. Saturn, like all the planets, has many faces. It is an image of the authoritarian Kronos, but it is also the ass, an animal traditionally ruled by Saturn. The fool is a Saturnian figure, as demonstrated by the Roman Saturnalia. That is why, during the medieval period, the King always had a fool by his side at court. The fool is the chaotic, ass-like, asinine side of Saturn the stern ruler.

So George may have been playing the fool for his father – the dumb-head, the thicko. His father might have gone around saying to George, "Can't you *ever* get anything right?" The moment the father dies, George begins to realise he is not a fool. He is not an ass. When the cord which binds two people through a shared complex is cut, through death or permanent separation, we may discover things about ourselves that have previously been farmed out onto the other person. Equally, we may break free of the projections that we have been carrying for the other person, which are also in some way bound up with the shared complex.

Other manifestations of the complex

I would like to look briefly at other ways in which complexes make themselves known. We have touched on relationship dynamics and we have touched on illness. We have also looked at artistic expression, and have considered the state of psychological breakdown. In very severe situations, the complex may gather so much energy and autonomy that it forms a split-off personality dissociated from the ego. There have been some extraordinary cases of multiple personality in recent psychiatric history. Do any of you remember a film called *The Three Faces of Eve?* In such cases we can see the complex virtually saying to the ego, "Sod off, I'm going to go and have my own life. Don't mess with me." And the complex seems to take on an actual identity – sometimes even a name – and speaks through the person's mouth in a distinctive way, and gathers around it associations and feelings and attitudes that the rest of the psyche has rejected. The complex thus becomes an alternative ego, virtually fully formed.

More commonly, a complex may possess the ego on a temporary basis while consciousness is still present. This is often one of the expressions of a powerful transit across a relatively unconscious point in the birth chart, such as an unaspected planet or a singleton by element. When this happens on a small scale for a brief period of time, we usually don't realise it. It is only if somebody happens to record us at the time, and plays the tape back to us, that we suddenly think, "Who is this person saying all these things? Can I really have behaved like that?" When we are in the grip of extreme emotions, extreme polemics, or an extreme mood, the complex may simply have taken over consciousness for a while. We think that we are actually in control, but in fact the complex is running the show. It has moved into the house, and the ego has to camp out in the garage.

The complex has slipped in between the person and his or her relationship with external reality, and the conscious ego is rendered mute, unable to make its wishes, ethics, and values known. One of the hallmarks of this kind of temporary and all-too-common possession is the compulsiveness with which we begin to speak and act. In such a state we may be quite prepared to manipulate the truth, distort facts, willfully ignore what others are saying and intending, and coerce the external world to fit the perception of reality reflected by the complex.

Complexes tend to have one track only, and the person in the grip of the complex will remind everyone of that one track at every possible opportunity. We can all experience this on a temporary basis, when we feel very angry or very hurt and a highly charged complex has been triggered. We start saying and doing things which just seem to come out of nowhere. We say afterward, "That wasn't really me." But if not, then who is it? We also hear this kind of possession by a complex at political party conventions and mass meetings. The complex has a certain monotony of voice and vocabulary. It has one idea, one emotion, one unalterable world-view, and we can really see what Janet meant by *idée fixe*.

Complexes do not possess a sense of humour – that seems to be a mysterious property of ego consciousness. Freud discovered that the complex can communicate through unconscious puns and word slips, but this is not due to humour – it arises out of the sudden intrusion of the complex into consciousness. We may laugh ourselves silly at someone else's word slip, but no joke was intended by the speaker, consciously or unconsciously. I came across a recording once called *Pardon My Blooper*, which was a collection of word slips from radio and television programmes. There was one by an unfortunate Canadian news commentator, who unwittingly announced to his listening audience in a sonorous voice, "This is the Canadian Broadcorping Castration." I doubt that this poor man thought it was funny at all, although thousands of listeners all over Canada must have been rolling about on the floor creasing themselves. Nothing can budge the inflexible focus of the complex. What it perceives is absolutely true. There is no possible question about its authenticity and authority. This absolute authority is what comes out of the person's mouth, when in the grip of the complex.

Audience: You can actually hear it in the person's voice.

Liz: There is no discussion whatsoever, nor any tolerance. We may encounter the rigidity of the complex in religious as well as political spheres, and sometimes it is quite over the top – everyone must be converted, and against their will if necessary. On a collective level this kind of complex inflames a whole population, and then one is faced with witch-hunts and inquisitions. You should all read or, better still, go to see, Arthur Miller's play, *The Crucible,* in which "mass hysteria" – which is really another term for a complex erupting on a collective level – is unleashed in a persecutory way.

When we consider the terrorist mentality – whether it is terrorism for political or religious reasons, terrorism based on anti-abortion, or terrorism in the name of animal rights – there is no longer any contact with reality or with the possibility of dialogue, compromise, or different but equally valid perspectives. The mental and emotional attitude is utterly rigid and very frightening, because there is nobody home. The lift doesn't go to the top floor any more. We cannot deal with a person fixated in this way because there is no individual residing in the ego's house – only the complex. We cannot dialogue with a complex in the ordinary human way. The complex is mythic. It has come straight from the primordial levels of the psyche. It is not going to sit down and have a cup of tea with us.

Audience: How do you cope when someone says, "I'm right, and I will bludgeon you into accepting it!"?

Liz: If at all possible, I get out of the way quickly. It is not worth bothering to waste time and energy in arguing. All astrologers have met this kind of virulence in the so-called "skeptic", who is not really a skeptic at all in the true sense of the word. My *Chambers Twentieth Century Dictionary* defines a skeptic as "an inquirer who has not arrived at a conviction". The word comes from the Greek school of philosophy founded by Pyrrho, who asserted nothing positively and doubted the possibility of absolute knowledge. This is not the "skeptic" who feels compulsively driven to ridicule astrology. Such people are in the grip of a complex, and see any challenge to their personal control of the universe as extremely dangerous. Many of you have no doubt encountered such people, who are not remotely interested in a genuine discussion. They simply wish to humiliate the person who makes them feel threatened. There is a difference between this kind of thing and someone who is genuinely agnostic or doubtful, but who is willing to listen, discuss, and form his or her own conclusions.

Naturally there are enough astrologers suffering from the same complex to satisfy the appetite of the more virulent "skeptic", and the two will inevitably attract each other. I have met colleagues in the astrological field who seem to suffer an unusual degree of this kind of persecution, and they invariably hang about trying to argue their case with the people who are least likely to ever listen to it. They will even agree to television interviews in which they know they are going to be ridiculed by an utterly unscrupulous presenter, or edited into incomprehensibility before the programme is ever aired, but they still go ahead and ask to have their hands and feet nailed to the cross. They will even do the nailing themselves, by agreeing to "tests" or "contests" which they could not possibly win. These situations are very sad, because both people are polarising on opposite sides of a powerful and highly charged complex, and cannot hear each other. The astrologer *must* prove astrology is valid, and the sceptic *must* prove it isn't. Have any of you ever watched a hamster going round and round on a wheel, moving nowhere?

The therapist or counsellor will often hear the complex speaking through the seriously disturbed client, and so may the astrologer. We must tread very carefully when this happens, because somewhere inside there is a suffering person who is being imprisoned by a complex that has taken over. Direct attempts to break down the rigidity of the complex do not usually work. A much slower and more careful process is required, slower than a two-hour chart reading can allow, in order to make contact with the person. This process almost always involves the gradual, patient building of an emotional relationship with the client, which can eventually grow strong enough to balance the power of the complex. In therapeutic terms, this is called a "working alliance".

Complexes and perception

Audience: I believe that some forms of schizophrenia can be treated this way.

Liz: Yes, there has been a good deal of remarkable work done in this area. Schizophrenia is not necessarily "incurable" if we adopt this approach rather than the approach of conventional psychiatry. In an ideal world, this is the way in which any psychotic state might be approached. But the trouble is that there aren't very many people who want to devote themselves to working that hard with psychotic patients. An enormous commitment is required, not to mention prolonged psychotherapy for the psychotherapist to ensure that one is not "infected" by the patient's complexes. And there are no guarantees of success. In principle it is possible. The moment we apply the theory of complexes to the more mysterious manifestations of the human psyche, we begin to realise that many of the extremes of human suffering reflect a relationship between ego and unconscious which has gone dreadfully wrong because of the disproportionate power of the complex. Complexes as archetypal life-patterns are not pathological in themselves. But if the ego cannot contain the energy of the complex and mediate it, then we may experience what is known as madness.

In some forms of madness, such as schizophrenia, one can hear the archetypal core of the complex speaking. With other forms of psychosis, the mythic element may be more difficult to perceive. In common or garden variety forms of temporary possession by the complex, such as can occur in any marital quarrel, the mythic element is usually very well hidden. But we shouldn't therefore assume that, because we have the privilege to be up and walking and relatively sane, we have nothing in common with the chronically mad. Every time we lose ourselves in a state where "something" takes us over, we are in the grip of the complex. Perhaps this state lasts for only ten minutes, but for those ten minutes we occupy the same mysterious psychic zone as the schizophrenic, who lives there on a fairly permanent basis. However, we have an ego to return to afterwards. The schizophrenic doesn't enjoy this luxury.

Audience: At least when I get into these states, my language is understandable.

Liz: Are you sure? Your partner might not always think so.

Audience: But a schizophrenic's words are incomprehensible.

Liz: Not always, if faculties other than the rational intellect are called into play. I don't want to spend too much time on this issue, because it deserves to be discussed in depth, and we could spend the rest of the day talking about it. But the language of schizophrenia is basically the language of myth. It is the native language of the complex, without a rational ego-filter. The ego "sorts" thoughts, feelings and associations and strings them together on a logical, A-leads-to-B basis. Any of you who work with computers will know that if you take a string of topics, and tell the machine to "sort", it will instantly arrange the topics in alphabetical order. The ego does the same kind of thing with the material of the complex. The language of schizophrenia is incomprehensible to many psychiatrists, because words and images are linked by unconscious association rather than by logic. The "sort" command isn't working. It does sound like gibberish most of the time, but if you tune your ear differently, you may hear little fragments of the myth being told.

Audience: There is another dimension to schizophrenia, when one is actually starting to have affected perception and starts seeing hands coming out of walls, and stuff like that.

Liz: You are touching on an extremely important issue connected with complexes. Our perception of the outer world is a complicated business. What we perceive, and how we define what we perceive, are deeply subjective things. Each of us here today assumes that what we perceive is actually what is out there. We have to live by this assumption, because otherwise anxiety would paralyse us, as it does the schizophrenic. But our perceptions, even if relatively well-grounded, are still subjectively coloured.

I remember somebody once waxing eloquent to me about my green eyes. This did not have the intended effect. I said, "I'm sorry to tell you this, but I don't have green eyes. They may be a little bloodshot today, but they aren't green. They're brown." This person persisted in stating categorically that my eyes were green. He wasn't colour-blind; he just perceived them that way. In the end, we have to assume that, if there is any doubt about our perceptions, a consensus of opinion will set us right. How many people here think my eyes are green? Nobody? Very good. How many think they are brown? All of you? *Ergo,* they must be brown, which presumably proves that I am not mad. But even a consensus may be suspect, in the grip of a collective complex.

Our physical perceptions are variable, according to our moods and projections and the power of our complexes. We may become obsessed with physical characteristics, in others or ourselves, which no one else notices or considers important. We look in the mirror and say, "Oh my God, a spot!" Nothing else exists on one's face except that spot, although it might be so small that no one except a dermatologist would notice it. Or we think to ourselves, "If only my nose wasn't so big, or my cheeks weren't so fat, I would be lovable."

This is what happens in anorexia. The perception of the body is totally distorted by the complex, and divorced from reality. The anorexic looks at his or her body and says, "I am disgustingly fat," and the horror is that the person may be thin to the point of life-threatening emaciation. The real issue is not the fat, of course, but lies in deeper emotional and sexual conflicts which focus on absolute control of the body and the power to overcome instinctual needs. The bodily perception of the anorexic is completely dominated by the complex. Even in so-called "normal" situations, our perceptions on every level are very fragile. They may be subtly or grossly distorted by our complexes.

When a complex is highly charged and is on the move in the psyche, all our perceptions may begin to be affected by it. Probably all of you will have had the experience of being very angry with someone you love, and seeing them as ugly, old, or just plain and uninteresting, when an hour before, the person seemed attractive or even beautiful. In an extreme state, our perceptions may become so badly infected by the energy of the complex that we are subject to hallucinatory phenomena, or experience "altered states" that seem totally out of touch with what would be defined by common consensus as objective reality. There is an ongoing and apparently irreconcilable argument, especially between the psychoanalyst and the mystic, about whether these "altered states" reveal the true nature of reality, or the true nature of one's personal pathology. But even in moments of so-called sanity, we often don't realise how subjective our perceptions are. The way we add things together and arrive at a conclusion about a person or an experience depends greatly on our complexes.

Let's say we meet George at the age of fifty. He has had his Saturn return, he has had his Uranus opposition, and he has had his second Saturn opposition. We say to him, "What's life about, George?" and he replies, "Life is tough. Life is hard work, and you get what you pay for." And there speaks his complex, because he has looked at his experiences, which may not be all that different from anyone else's, added them up, interpreted them, and come to a conclusion about the nature of the human condition. His conclusion may be workable and creative – for him. But it is a Sun-Saturn conclusion, and not everyone has this aspect in the birth chart.

Let's say that you have a Sun-Neptune-Jupiter conjunction in Sagittarius in the 9th. There is no point in saying to George, "But that's a really cynical and negative way to look at things. All you need is love. Life is meaningful. The soul reincarnates. Get your chart done. Try some meditation, and chill out." George is going to look at you and say, "Go back to California and stop wasting my time." His complex has obviously shaped his experiences. It has also made him perceive his experiences in a certain way, interpret them, and come up with a value system and a world-view which are imbued with the feeling-tone of the complex.

That may be "normal" for him. It may not be "pathological". It would only be problematic if George were being made miserable by his values and world-view, or if his complex were crushing all the life out of him, or making him crush all the life out of everyone around him. Then he might need help, although help could only be effective and valid if it is provided within the context of who he is, not who his astrologer or therapist wants him to be. But if his view of reality works for him, then he is entitled to respect, because he has given his complex a constructive channel in life. His world-view may not be your world-view, and if he is your client and you haven't got a Sun-Saturn, you may need to understand the nature of his complex and encourage him to live his world-view as creatively and decently as possible, rather than trying to convince him that his world-view is wrong.

Transits, progressions, and timing

Audience: Is there any technique which would help us bring complexes into the light of consciousness?

Liz: There are "techniques", if that is the right word, which can help us to focus on the emotional charge of the complex and gain a better understanding of its nature. This is what we try to do in psychotherapy. There are also many times when a complex is quasi-active, when we can get closer to its feeling-tone and content, and this might be reflected by transits. But I don't think we can arbitrarily decide that we are going to make something conscious because we see it in the chart. Am I right in assuming that is what you mean?

Audience: Yes, I suppose so. I am thinking of how we can see a certain complex in the chart, and I am wondering whether there are particular transits or particular psychological techniques which might help us to work through the complex before some heavy aspect hits and it gets really difficult.

Liz: We can certainly look at the chart and say, "Here is something that looks like a complex. This Moon square Venus and opposition Pluto is a very tense configuration, and it has something to do with the mess my relationships are in. I keep getting stuck in triangles and I feel overwhelmed with jealousy. I am sure it is connected with mother." We can think deeply about the kinds of unconscious issues which might be involved in such a configuration. We can look at our behaviour and see where there might be a compulsive split being acted out, and we can understand, by exploring certain childhood experiences, why a particular adult relationship didn't work. We can try to explore some of the emotional issues in counselling or therapy, and we may be able to release some of the anxiety and rage through the therapeutic relationship. We can also realise that, in a few years' time, transiting Uranus, Saturn or Pluto will move over this configuration and we will see a little action.

When this time arrives, our insights, and all the preliminary work we have done, may turn out to be extremely useful. These things might change the way in which we express the complex when things start hotting up. But the timing of a complex, and the way in which it gathers strength and demands expression in life at special moments, are things over which I believe the ego has no real control. We cannot stand in front of the mirror and shout, "Get conscious, you bugger!" any more than we can stand over a plant in the garden and shout, "Grow, you bastard!"

There are many therapists who assume that the moments of breakthrough in therapeutic work occur because of the therapeutic work. I don't actually believe they do. I believe these moments of breakthrough reflect certain transits and progressions which describe the release of the energy of the complex, and the therapeutic work provides a constructive outlet for the energy. Something important happens, and some healing takes place. But the therapist cannot will the client to change or transform a complex unless change is already on the way. Something new and creative may happen because of the therapeutic relationship, but it is the product of both therapist and client working with, not controlling the timing.

Complexes are the determinants of our development pattern. They set their own timing. Or perhaps, more accurately, the psyche as a totality sets the timing. The ego's role is to work as consciously as possible with what is ripe, so that something new can emerge, a creative product of the relationship between ego and unconscious, rather than a blind acting out of unconscious compulsions. I don't think we can hurry these things, or manipulate our astrological knowledge to avoid or accelerate a life process. We can acquire as much understanding as we can, and look at those times in the past when particular transits and progressions triggered an obvious "hot" place in the chart. We can review what happened during that time so that, when another transit or progression is moving toward the same point, we have some idea of the area that it is going to unlock. We can try to give the complex as many creative vehicles as we can. But I don't think there is a way of altering the timing – only the consciousness which we bring to the timing.

It is helpful to remember that the timing of transits and progressions is already given from the moment of birth. If you have the Sun conjunct Saturn in the natal chart, transiting Saturn will conjunct the Sun as well as itself when you are twenty-nine and a half. You can't send in a request form that says, "Could I please have transiting Saturn over the Sun when I'm twenty-three?" It takes transiting Saturn twenty-nine and a half years to make one revolution around the zodiac, and there is nothing you can do about it. You might say, "I will make every effort to understand this Sun-Saturn conjunction, and I will constantly try to own what I am projecting on others. And I will try to ensure that I face myself as honestly as possible when Saturn arrives on my Sun." But the complex will begin to emerge at its appointed time whether you interfere or not. It won't come out at your beck and call if it is unripe.

Audience: What you are saying rules out free will.

Liz: It rules out free will in terms of timing. We can all try standing outside and shouting to Saturn, "Speed up!". If we are offended because nothing happens, then we can go and complain to the Demiurge about not having any free will. This is not a very helpful thing to do. The inherent timing of complexes, which is the same as the inherent timing of the chart, does nothing to curtail free will in the sense of how we deal with our lives – whether we work creatively with our complexes, or get taken over by our compulsions, or rush about blaming somebody else for whatever happens to us. Our free will lies in the relationship we make with what we discover inside ourselves. This can have a profound effect on what happens to us in external life. But the timing has already been given from the moment of birth. Trying to alter it is like saying to your body, "I don't want to do puberty at twelve. Can I please have it at thirty-five?"

As astrologers, we can wind up in a lot of trouble if we think we can impose our wishes on the rate at which things grow. You are wanting to hear me say, "Yes, you are free. You can sort out your complexes whenever you like, regardless of the chart." Indeed, you *are* free, to work with your development pattern in any way you choose, including transforming things that are dark or stuck. But as far as getting the psyche to deliver its fruit when it is not yet ripe, any gardener can tell you that such tactics don't work.

Audience: All right, Saturn comes to conjunct the Sun when you're twenty-nine. But you have all that time between the year you are born and when you are twenty-nine. I know you are simplifying it to make it clear, and naturally the interim Saturn aspects are important, but it's still a long time between those aspects. So what happens during the in-between bits? Does the complex just sleep?

Liz: Complexes are light sleepers. They get woken up by smaller transits, although they might not get out of bed or get dressed to go out. That means there are many, many opportunities to get glimpses into what is at work underneath, and many chances to integrate bits which rise to the surface. The transiting Moon, which moves about half a degree an hour, will be making a major hard aspect to the natal Sun-Saturn every week or so. Transiting Mercury will wake the complex up, and so will transiting Sun, Venus, and Mars. A full Moon or an eclipse landing within a couple of degrees of the Sun-Saturn might release quite a lot of the energy of the complex. All the fast-moving personal planets will activate the complex on a regular basis.

I have only focused on one of the most powerful triggers, because, as you say, I am simplifying things for the sake of clarity. I also haven't mentioned progressions, for the same reason. But I believe the heavy planets in transit, together with major progressed aspects, reveal the overall shape of the inner pattern. The personal planets only reveal pieces of the pattern, a bit at a time. A complex is never "finished" because its core is archetypal. The big, important transits, especially those of the outer planets, give us the opportunity to experience the meaning and energy of the complex in great depth, and many things can shift at such times because the doors are wide open between ego-consciousness and the deeper levels of the psyche. These planets may reveal the mythic as well as the personal levels of the complex, because they themselves are impersonal or transpersonal. But every day of our lives, the inner structure of the psyche is being touched off by something, big or little. There is constant movement. I am sorry if I have given the impression that one sits about doing nothing until Saturn comes along. I am using it as an example of an important transit, and the really big ones are not that frequent. We get them at particular intervals during life, and that is when we have greatest access to the inner world. What we experience as "events" at these times are the tip of an iceberg. But when you start thinking about it, you will see that we are constantly in motion psychologically, because there will always be something happening in the chart, however small.

If we contemplate the endless interwoven movements of the planets, we might begin to glimpse a wonderful dance, constantly in motion, constantly changing, and constantly cyclical. It is a vision of the ongoing dance of what Jung called the "objective" psyche. When this dance intersects with our own birth charts through transits to natal placements, then our little part of the big pattern – our particular personal share of the archetypal domain of collective complexes – is activated. This is why I warned you all at the beginning that all psychological maps are crude. They are two-dimensional and simplistic, and they cannot communicate the sense of a constant dance. Our complexes are living, breathing, moving and changing all the time.

Audience: There is something more about transits. You can go through a critical point, say a square, of a transit cycle like Saturn. This may involve either particularly strong events or important internal decisions. After the square, you are between the square and the trine, and you are still reacting to those events or carrying out the consequences of those decisions and actions. There is continuing change, even after the aspect is passed.

Liz: Yes, you are right. The complex doesn't just fall back to sleep instantly when the aspect has passed. Things are still happening inside and outside, while the repercussions of decisions and actions percolate. All the transits that touch a certain configuration in the chart are part of a cycle, and natal planets have a kind of "memory". Our experiences keep adding layers to the way we express the various configurations in the chart. One stage of the cycle doesn't happen independently of the previous stages. There is a continuity.

Whenever any point in the chart is triggered, either by the same transiting planet's cycle or by another transit, the themes that are bound up with the complex will emerge. Depending on how we dealt with the last trigger, the next one will partake of whatever consciousness or blindness we exhibited when we previously encountered the same themes. The actors may be wearing different costumes, but they are playing the same roles. So there is a constant building up of associations around a complex. These personal associations start accruing from the time that we are infants. Things happen throughout our lives, some voluntarily chosen and some involuntarily experienced, which add layer after layer.

Once we start getting a sense of how this works, we can start doing the opposite. Every time something triggers the complex, we are in a position to peel away another layer of personal associations and let go of some unconscious projection or identification. So we peel away a particular negative father issue by discovering father as a living person with human flaws similar to our own. Then we peel off another layer and then another, and eventually we come close to the core, which is the archetypal level.

That is when we get a strange sense of the inner continuity of our experiences. We say to ourselves, "This means something. This event is not just an external happening. It is part of a pattern, and the pattern is purposeful." It is hard to describe that feeling, but I think many of you will recognise it. It is the sense of a deep and intelligent design at work, and one feels connected with a greater whole. Whatever we are going through, we can find a way of coping if we can perceive a meaning in what happens. Experiences then become part of one's journey, not merely random happenings. It doesn't matter if the meaning exists only within ourselves rather than "objectively" in the cosmos. The effect is the same. Our inner pattern is our fate, but this only becomes apparent if we can see beyond the personal associations.

Complexes and karma

Audience: Could that free you from taking the complex into the next life?

Liz: I don't know. If you think in these terms, then the answer would probably be, "To some extent." The personal conflicts layered around the complex might be partially if not wholly resolved, and would therefore not form the kind of "karmic" baggage which we carry from one life to the next. But the archetypal core may reflect the nature of the soul itself, or the ongoing theme and purpose of a series of incarnations. I cannot give you an answer. I am very wary of looking at reincarnation issues in a simplistic way. I always have the feeling that they are vastly more complex, if you will excuse the expression, than we think.

Audience: Could a complex be a memory of a past life?

Liz: I mentioned this possibility earlier. It is an interesting idea. I am not a "believer" in reincarnation in the usual sense, because people always seem to talk about "my" former incarnation, and this is very much an ego-perspective. If anything reincarnates, I do not think it is the ego, and memory of the linear kind – the kind we associate with "remembering" past events, whether in this life or another – is a property of ego-consciousness.

But I am open to the possibility that there is a continuity of some kind, and I am very interested in where certain deep-rooted patterns and perspectives come from. Clearly some of them lie beyond the family inheritance. Where do innate talents and knowledge come from? Where did Mozart get his musical talent, which made its appearance when he was virtually an infant? Admittedly his father was a musician, so we can argue that his gift was inherited, but what does that really mean? And inheritance does not explain the quality of Mozart's genius. Why does one person find the courage to utilise an inherent talent while another wastes it? Why is one person born under a Sun-Saturn, and another under a Sun-Uranus or Sun-Neptune? Or even more problematic, why does one person become a Hitler and another a Buddha?

These are fascinating questions, and I don't have any answers. Maybe there isn't an answer, and it's all merely accidental. Our birth charts *may* reflect certain themes of our "karmic" inheritance, but I am wary of interpreting configurations too literally in this light. After all, many chickens, goats and dragonflies were born at the same moment I was. Do they all have the same karma I do? Is there a chipmunk somewhere who shares my birth data and is teaching a seminar on complexes to other chipmunks out in the woods? Perhaps the archetypal core of the complex represents what Bailey writes about – the "ray" to which the soul is attached, the basic energy by which the soul operates life after life, because that is the soul's function as part of the whole. That's another interesting idea, which actually predates Bailey by a couple of thousand years. Plato believed that each human soul sprang from the "choir" of a particular god, and retained that allegiance life after life. I am afraid I have no idea where the truth lies in all this.

Audience: I feel what is important is whether seeing these things from a reincarnation perspective can help us to understand ourselves better, or whether it's just a way of avoiding something.

Audience: Surely a complex can form round any single planet which hasn't been integrated into the chart – for example, Neptune.

Liz: Yes, any planet in the horoscope can be viewed as a complex, because every planet reflects psychic energy of a certain kind. A planet can be understood as an image of an energy centre, with its own story, associations, and archetypal core. Some complexes, like some planets, are flammable. Others are quite well integrated. This may depend on how connected we are to the energy which the planet represents. Outer planets like Neptune and Pluto have a way of reflecting highly charged complexes in themselves, simply by virtue of what they are – collective rather than personal. Also, the society in which we presently live does not help us to understand or contain the energies outer planets represent, so there is often a high charge attached to them.

Complexes and unaspected planets

An unaspected planet is likely to reflect a complex that is very far away from consciousness – at least initially. That is because it does not have any easy, natural routes for integration into consciousness, which is what aspects to the personal planets provide. When such deeply unconscious points appear in the chart, they tend to have a very archaic and mythic quality when they are finally triggered. One of the most famous examples of this, although an extremely negative one, is the unaspected Neptune-Pluto conjunction in Hitler's chart. Neptune was in 0°51' Gemini, and Pluto in 4°40' Gemini. I believe this conjunction explains a great deal about the kind of power he exercised over the collective, and the kind of obsession he had about playing a messianic role for his people.

Unaspected planets will always, sooner or later, receive an important aspect from a transiting or progressed planet, or they will be activated through relationship, by the planets in someone else's chart. An unaspected planet doesn't stay unaspected. Life provides aspects for it. A planet may begin as a very unconscious and unconnected point in the horoscope, but the moment one gets involved in a relationship with another person, the planet will start finding avenues of expression in the context of that relationship. Usually, at the beginning, it will be projected onto the other person. When this happens, the relationship may be powerfully affected by the complex reflected by the planet, which contributes a quality of compulsiveness and mythic overtones to the interaction. This can prove disastrous to the relationship. But it can also prove immensely creative, and gives one a chance to get acquainted with what has previously been a deeply unconscious dimension of the psyche.

Complexes exist at varying degrees of depth. The ocean is a good metaphor for the unconscious psyche, which is why dreams about the sea so often refer to the depths of the inner world. Complexes are denizens of the ocean. There are complexes which hang around the harbour, and you can see them under the water. They are not that far down, and there are bits that protrude above the level of the water when the tide is low. Then there are some that you cannot see unless you go out in a boat and bring snorkel equipment. And there are others that lie very, very deep, and they remain undiscovered unless and until they are ready to begin moving toward the surface. There may also be complexes that never come into consciousness in the course of a lifetime. Certainly there are always areas in every horoscope which never seem to be fully lived. Life is just not long enough, and the opportunities may not be there because of external factors such as the society and epoch in which one lives.

When something is ripe for consciousness, a relationship of some kind will often coincide with important transits and progressions, and the synastry between the two charts will trigger whatever is unconscious in both people. Any of you who work with chart comparisons will have noticed that, if one has got a tense configuration in the birth chart, such as a T-cross or a single planet in square to a stellium, one's important relationships will invariably be with people who have similar tense aspects, and whose planets trigger these areas of one's own chart and the complexes they represent. Relationships that don't involve the energy charge of a complex tend to be inexplicably boring, and we seem to get involved with people who in some way mirror our unfinished psychic business. Whether we are dealing with an unaspected planet, or a planet which is inimical to the ego because it collides with other factors in the chart, we do not have to try to force this unconscious issue into awareness. Life will always bring us people who do it for us. We are drawn toward those who can play the required roles in our inner drama because their inner drama is the same. They are then given parts in our play as we are given parts in theirs, and they will act out something which allows us to bring our own undeveloped depths into consciousness.

The theatre as a metaphor of complexes

Audience: I was just thinking about the relief I feel when I go to see a play. Theatre gives a context for this mystery.

Liz: In its earliest form, theatre was religious ritual, and the Greeks dedicated their performances to Dionysos and Apollo. Unlike so much modern theatre, Greek tragedy did not shove political polemics down the throat of the audience. That would have been sacrilege. These plays portray the interaction between humanity and the gods, which is another way of describing the relationship between the individual and the collective unconscious. When we see the archetypal background revealed beneath the personal conflicts of the individual characters, we may experience a sense of great beauty, compassion, and awe, because that is what lies behind our little personal dramas too. We get sidetracked by the personal associations which accrue around a complex, and miss the meaning of the core. We lose contact with the deeper significance of what is compelling us, and then we think that complexes are pathological. Theatre has always been one of the greatest means of connecting us with the deeper levels of reality.

Are any of you familiar with the 16th century Commedia dell' Arte? The characters in the Commedia are stock characters, and no matter what version was performed, the audience always met the same figures, the most important being Arlecchino, the "clown" or trickster. Arlecchino is a Renaissance version of the Greek god Hermes. He is clever, sly, foolish, resourceful, and always facilitates the marriage of the lovers through trickery. The actors had no lines to memorise, as they do now. They were required to understand their roles fully, so that any action they performed would be true to the character. Then they were given the bare bones of the plot – which was one of a limited number of possible "scenarios" – and had to make up the dialogue and surface action as they went along.

So in this week's performance, the old merchant (Pantalone) has got money hidden under the floorboards, his daughter (Flaminia) is in love with a penniless young gentleman (Orazio), his maidservant (Franceschina) is in love with Orazio's servant (Arlecchino), and no one can get married unless someone works out how to steal the money from under the old man's nose. The actors must spontaneously flesh out this plot, and make it funny, emotionally rewarding, and attractive to the audience.[4]

That is what we do too, with more or less talent at making life imitate art. Shakespeare knew this perfectly well when he said, "All the world's a stage and all the men and women merely players." The complexes are the "scenarios", and the different facets of our personalities are the stock characters, many of whom we enlist other people to play. Or, if you like, the planets are the archetypal characters, the signs are the costumes they wear, and the planetary aspects in the chart are the plot. We are given a basic story and then have to make up the dialogue and the action as we go along. Every repeat performance is different, according to the transits and progressions triggering the birth chart at any given time.

The nature of projection

For any of you who are unfamiliar with the term "projection", it can be most easily understood in the context of the transparencies I have been using to put up diagrams. Here is an overhead projector. The actual diagram is not on the screen. You can see an image of the diagram on the screen, but that is not where it is actually located. It is on a transparency placed on the glass plate of the projector, and light is directed through it and bounced onto the screen. That seems to be the way in which unconscious components of the psyche assume a reality for us. We are not aware of their true location within. We see an image in someone or something outside ourselves, and believe that is where it is located. Instead of light, we might think of psychic energy, which bounces the projection onto

[4]For more information on the Commedia dell' Arte, see *The World of Harlequin* by Allardyce Nicoll, Cambridge University Press, 1963. See also Frances Yates, *Theatre of the World* and *The Art of Memory.* In both books she examines the cosmic symbolism used in Italian and English Renaissance theatre, revealing that, during this period, playwrights such as Shakespeare deliberately utilised the analogies between astrology, the archetypal world, psychological dynamics, and the theatre.

the "hook" outside. Or perhaps it is a kind of light – a nascent consciousness, which brings the image out of darkness and projects it into the outer world.

We are not aware of many things in ourselves. In infancy we are aware of hardly anything at all, other than the presence or absence of food, safety, and sensual gratification. Gradually we become aware, as bits of ourselves get projected onto the screen – initially the mother. We look out and say, "Mother is going to devour me," when in fact it is our own hunger which threatens to devour us, or "Mother will always protect me," when in fact it is our own survival instincts which ensure our continuing existence. At first virtually everything is projected on mother, and then, to a lesser extent, on father. We gradually take many of these projections back, although some will remain glued onto the parents throughout one's life. The process of internalising parental projections is an area in which Melanie Klein's work can give us invaluable insights. Initially all our loving and destructive impulses are perceived in the mother, who is alternatively "good breast" and "bad breast". The slow process of internalising both good and bad feelings gradually leads to the formation of an ego capable of experiencing ambivalence – the recognition that we, and others, can be both good and bad at the same time.

Projection as a natural process

Throughout life, as undeveloped components of the psyche enter consciousness, we may discover them first through projection. In fact we do not project these components. They project themselves as a natural process of development. We don't say, "I think I will project my Saturn square Mars on you." It is not a calculated conscious act. The aggressive energy reflected by Mars may be inimical to one's self-image or the expectations of one's parents, as well as to the values of one's Libra Ascendant or Sun conjunct Venus in Pisces. The ego identifies with Saturn's restraint, Libra's courtesy, and Pisces' empathy, and Martial aggression is projected – or projects itself – on a whole succession of apparently aggressive people who always seem to be giving one a hard time whenever something transits over the natal Saturn-Mars square.

If we can understand that projection is a natural process which heralds the beginning of something emerging into the light, we can get a sense of the extraordinary intelligence of the psyche. Every birth chart contains conflicts, and there are always complexes which are slow to emerge because their content seems to threaten our personal reality. We don't allow these archetypal characters a place to live. But everything within us wants life. How can it get this life, if the ego refuses to acknowledge it? It projects itself, as though it is saying, "You are not acknowledging me. So I will appear in the guise of your partner or child or colleague or guru, and then you will realise that I exist." There is a profound intelligence at work in the way people arrive in our lives at precisely the right moment, ready to act out the role which our complexes assign to them.

Projection is not a pathology. Unfortunately it has crept into the vocabulary of the psychologically semi-literate, as have so many other terms, and it is now frequently used as a weapon. If someone says, "You are being really rude and unpleasant. I don't like it when you behave like that to me," we reply, "You are projecting." We use the word in the same manipulative way we use the word "selfish". The term projection can easily be abused. It is important to remember that projection is the natural, appropriate, and creative means by which we gradually come into contact with the whole of ourselves. It is not a voluntary act. It is the way in which complexes make themselves known to the ego, and it gives us a chance to start establishing a relationship with our complexes. Then, hopefully, we may begin to realise that there is as much of us in the "hook" as there is of the other person, and sometimes a great deal more.

Some projections are quite gentle. We can have projections that are comfortable, because the complex behind the projection is not highly charged, and the "hook" may be pleased to carry it for us. We may idealise certain people whom we will never meet and therefore through whom we will never be hurt or disappointed. We may cast certain objects or places or institutions in a particular role, and there is no friction. I spoke about this earlier in relation to places. There is no pain involved, and one may go on like that for a long time. But some projections have an enormous energy charge, and this can generate compulsive behaviour. The intensity of the charge, and the importance of the complex, make us create crises and conflicts, and then it becomes urgent that we face what is really going on.

We can usually recognise a highly charged projection because our emotions and reactions are out of proportion to the situation. In the last few days, for example, we have read about a case of road rage, in which someone was killed. That is what I would call a reaction out of proportion to the situation, and there is great deal of this kind of thing occurring at the moment. The reasons for this eruption of collective anger, toward individuals and particular social and religious groups, may be connected with the inflammation of certain collective complexes, reflected by the still operative Uranus-Neptune conjunction. As this conjunction was exact in Capricorn, we might fruitfully speculate about a collective father-complex on the move, reflected in the external world by certain political, religious and social authorities and hierarchies collapsing.

On the personal level, this high charge is very disturbing. We snap someone's head off because he or she has asked something that touches a raw nerve. Or we get obsessed with a particular person, positively or negatively, and can't get him or her out of our mind, and it is so bad it wakes us up in the middle of the night. These kinds of experiences are what might be called dead giveaways. There is always some unknown piece of oneself involved in such situations, and it is very important to try to look at it honestly. The compulsiveness of a projection is very different from simply disliking someone, or not enjoying their company, or finding them a bit boring. Conscious feelings without a complex fuelling them do not carry the same intense emotional charge as a projection. Projections can be positive or negative, or a mixture of the two. And as I have said, they may fall on things other than individuals. We often don't recognise how much we project onto political issues, or social and racial groups.

It is very interesting to think about these group "hooks" which are favoured or denigrated by our projections. Who are our scapegoats, and why do we choose them? We would all like to believe that, when we look out at the state of the world, we can easily discern who is an evil persecutor and who is a blameless victim, and therefore our political sympathies are of course inarguably right. Some cases of persecutor and victim are indeed screamingly obvious. But some are not so obvious. This is the case when we enter the endless and usually fruitless argument about the "battle of the sexes". Who is really the oppressor? And who is really the oppressed? And might both tyrant and victim be within the individual of either sex? Projections of the political and social kind hurl us into a hall of mirrors, and then we are faced once again with the problem of subjective perception.

Audience: I very much like the comments you have given about projection being natural, because it redeems the negative projections that we have on the word projection itself. I am thinking of the full Moon, that reflects the projection of the Sun's light and brings light to the surface of our world at night. Without projection there wouldn't be any awareness of self and other.

Liz: I suspect there wouldn't be any consciousness at all. Complexes project themselves, and projection leads to conflict, which leads to consciousness, which leads to the complex being incarnated and, potentially, transformed. I think we are once again in very mysterious terrain. There is a school of thought which has been around for many millennia, which teaches that everything we perceive as manifest reality is in fact a projection of the soul, or of an Other.

This is the central tenet of both Buddhist and Hindu teaching, and it is also embedded in Plato's work – everything in this material universe, including the individual ego itself, is a dream dreamt by the One, a projection of the psychic potentials of the One, which otherwise could not be fulfilled. It is essentially an Eastern world-view, although Plato placed great importance on the role of the individual in participating in this process of manifestation, and so did the medieval alchemists. These latter, as I mentioned earlier, believed that God depended on individual human beings to fulfill the purpose of creation through greater consciousness. If we interpret that psychologically, the collective psyche depends upon the individual ego to give shape to the complexes which represent the inner design and development of the collective.

It is possible that, if we take this very mysterious phenomenon of projection to its furthest extreme, we wind up with this central theme of ancient philosophical and religious thought. Projection is a means of fusing subject and object, but it never achieves its goal, because such fusion destroys the integrity of the individual. Therefore a powerful and highly charged projection always generates conflict, sooner or later. In psychoanalytic language, we use the term projective identification. I would have no awareness of you at all unless I projected a bit of myself onto you, and you would not be aware of me unless you projected a little of yourself on me. But in creating this energetic flow and counterflow, we will inevitably force each other to define ourselves in order to survive as individuals. Without projection we would never interact with each other, and we would not only never recognise each other – we would never recognise ourselves. And then we would be truly fated, because we would possess no capacity for choice.

The materialisation of the horoscope through projection

The "psychoid" nature of projection endlessly fascinates me, although I have no answers for the multitude of questions it raises. As I have gone along talking about complexes and projections, I have been describing these dynamics as though they were purely psychological, and dealt mainly with mental and emotional states. But matter itself has a very peculiar way of rearranging itself according to the dictates of complexes. Hence George and his boss find each other at exactly the right moment, even if both have had to travel thousands of miles to arrive at the meeting at the appointed time. Jung referred to the collective unconscious as "psychoid". By this he meant that archetypes, and the complexes which form around them, are both psychic and physical.

It is not as simple as, say, projecting one's Mars and then reacting aggressively to anybody that one perceives as aggressive. One will actually attract Martial types. They come from the ends of the earth and turn up on one's doorstep, and they always have the Sun in Aries or Mars on the Ascendant or the Sun or Moon conjunct Mars. How do they get there? They bypass tube strikes, British Rail disasters, London traffic jams, air traffic controllers' strikes, and French truck drivers' blockades. Nothing keeps them away when the time is right.

Even odder, this projected Mars may manifest in starkly material ways – such as the fire which burns the house down under a progression of Mars square Saturn and Uranus, or the idiot driver who ploughs into the rear of one's car when Chiron transits over one's 3rd house Mars. Somehow or other, physical reality moves itself to fit the shape of our complexes. If someone is going to prang one's car, it will always happen on a day when there is an appropriate transit. If one is going to win the National Lottery, likewise.

When our horoscopes manifest in this way, there is something very strange at work. The material events we experience are like one end of a spectrum, the concrete expressions of an archetypal pattern whose other end is psychic. Both together are the manifestations of a complex. Complexes are psychoid. They are not just psychological. They can materialise through projection. When a complex projects itself, it doesn't only mean that we have an emotional reaction. There may be physical repercussions, expressions in the world of form. If we think simplistically, then all transits and progressions pertain only to material events, or only to psychological ones. But anyone with any experience of inner work knows that no material event is unconnected to the person experiencing the event; and no person is exempt from material experience. If both inner and outer levels are recognised, then the meaning connecting both becomes apparent.

Audience: It is synchronicity.

Liz: Yes, that is the word Jung used to describe the meaningful coincidence of an outer event and an inner state. He called synchronicity an "acausal connecting principle", meaning that the event does not cause the inner state and the inner state does not cause the event. They happen simultaneously because they are both part of the same hidden complex. Many astrologers use this term, but nevertheless find it hard to grasp, because our conscious perceptions do not easily encompass paradoxes. Secretly we still persist in thinking that we have "caused" something to happen due to an inner condition, or that the event has "caused" the inner condition, or that the planets have "caused" both.

Complexes operate on both a psychological and a material level. They are the point where predictive and psychological astrology meet. These perspectives on astrological interpretation are not mutually exclusive, contrary to what some astrologers might think. It simply depends on where the individual astrologer places his or her focus. I am inclined to look at a complex on the inner level first because, if there is such a thing as free will, that is where we will find it. And if there is such a thing as the possibility of transformation, I believe it must begin from within. If we focus only on the physical materialisation of the complex, we may become well versed in prediction, but we have also ensured that we are fated, because there is no consciousness of the energy pattern at work inside, and therefore no chance to make a relationship with it.

Events as symbols

Because chart configurations, both natal and transiting, have a way of manifesting on the concrete level, we may be so distracted by events that it becomes very difficult for us to look at the complex within. Sometimes people even use events to avoid dealing with what is happening inside, because it is easier to assign blame when there is a concrete thing or person "out there" which seems at least partly culpable. It is sometimes very useful to take the events which occur under particular transits and progressions, and treat them as though they were a dream – in other words, symbolically.

I had a client that I worked with in analysis for many years. Initially she seemed quite incapable of thinking symbolically. She didn't dream, or, more accurately, didn't remember any of her dreams. Nothing was real to her except the concrete events which happened around and to her. Her perception of reality was entirely causal and material, with no sense of an inner life. This doesn't give the analyst much room to manoeuvre. So, rather than getting frustrated about this situation, I decided to treat the events of her external life as though they were the events in a dream, and explored them symbolically. After all, who is to say that dream events and physical events are really so very different at core?

When she was knocked off her bicycle one day while riding to her session, we worked with that as though it were a dream. I didn't know her transits. I wanted her to tell me what was happening to her in her language, not mine. What would this event mean if one dreamt it? What colour was the car that hit her, and what associations did she have with that colour? What did the driver look like? Did he remind her of anyone? Was he aggressive, or remorseful, or indifferent? What kind of feelings did she experience once the shock passed? Was she in any way responsible through her own carelessness? Or was she really a victim? Could she remember feeling these feelings before?

Gradually a hidden pattern began to emerge. This was not the first time she had experienced being the victim of a man's aggression. Memories of a violent father began to become more than just "the past", because she recognised that her emotional responses to the incident with the bicycle were the same. One rides a bicycle when one is a child, and one learns to drive when one has grown up. Although many adults enjoy cycling, nevertheless my client's associations circled around herself as a victimised child. And ultimately the issue was not the external violent father, but the internal father-complex which had victimised both her and her father – and, for that matter, her whole family – from within.

This particular lady used to have constant physical disasters. There was always something attacking her from the material world. She would get knocked off her bicycle, or her wallet would get stolen, or her flat would get burgled. The more we worked with the stuff of her material reality as though it were "psychoid", the less the violence manifested, and the more the complex began to express itself through emotions and ideas and beliefs. All kinds of things began to come up from the unconscious. She even began to remember the occasional dream. The realms of psyche and matter are mysteriously bound up together. I don't believe they are really separate things.

Audience: Is the tendency to materialise complexes linked with anything particular in the chart? I was wondering whether it might have to do with a lot of earth, or maybe no earth, or certain aspects.

Liz: I think there are some clues. My client had, and I suppose still has, the Sun, Moon and Mercury in Taurus, square a Mars-Saturn conjunction in Leo in the 8th, with Capricorn rising. The emphasis in earth, and the Mercury-Saturn square, might have something to do with her difficulty in entering the world of the imagination. The hard aspects between planets in earth and fire in a predominantly earthy chart suggest that the Mars-Saturn conjunction would probably be projected. But I would not know from the chart alone that this complex would manifest so literally in a repeating pattern of disastrous physical events. It might have been enacted in a relationship on the emotional and sexual level, or it might have led to physical symptoms of one kind or another. The chart may tell us about the nature of the complex. But it seems that the deciding factor in the end is the degree of relationship one has with the unconscious.

The repetition of experience

Audience: Do you think that, in order to release a complex, the outer world has to become similar to what it was in childhood? We have to go through a period when circumstances are similar to the complex as it was at that time, so that it is no longer an alien energy. Perhaps we have to find ourselves in that same place of unhappiness or sense of loss or whatever it is we had to go through. The outer reality has to be on that level so we can no longer deny the complex.

Liz: Yes, I believe that is often true, if we are talking about the blocking of a complex because of painful associations – although not all complexes are unconscious for that reason. Freud coined the term "repetition compulsion", which suggests something like Pavlov's dog – we keep returning to the same painful place because it is what we are familiar with. But like you, I feel there is a purpose in the compulsive recreating of painful situations. It is as though the complex is trying to tell us something. We can deny the past most of the time, but not when it is also the present. This is what happened to my client when she was knocked off her bicycle. This alignment of past and present happens as a matter of course when the time and the transits are right.

Let me try translating what you are saying into astrological terms. Let's say that a certain kind of mother-complex is represented in the chart by the Moon square Pluto. The archetypal face which mother wears is that of Hekate, goddess of the mysteries, ruler of the underworld and keeper of secrets. Let's say that this is an applying square. The Moon is in 12° Scorpio and Pluto is in 15° Leo. That means the square would have come exact by progressed motion at roughly three months old.

There may be a painful event that we can tie in with this. Or there might have been a particularly turbulent and uncomfortable emotional atmosphere which eroded the child's trust. The mother might have become ill, or had a breakdown, or suffered a severe depression. The father may have had a mistress and the mother found out about it, and couldn't interact with her child because of her own emotional upheaval. She might have turned to the child as the sole source of love and comfort, using emotional blackmail to ensure that the child turned against the treacherous father. Any one of several possible scenarios could be described by that exact progressed square at three months old. But that isn't really what the aspect means at core.

This kind of event may crystallise the negative potential of the complex, because it surrounds the kernel of the complex with layers of dark feelings and associations. Let's say our example is a man. Let's also say that the Moon-Pluto doesn't sit comfortably in his birth chart, which is predominantly airy, with a Sun-Venus conjunction in Libra and Aquarius on the Ascendant. His image of women, and his capacity to engage in deep emotional involvements, may be badly distorted by his raging or manipulative or depressed mother. But the core of the complex is archetypal, and is not "caused" by what happened when he was three months old.

What, then, does Moon square Pluto really describe, if we track it back to the archetypal core? It is not, in itself, saying something intrinsically negative about the mother-principle. The mother-archetype portrayed by Moon-Pluto is a symbol of life's hidden mysteries – the mysteries of death, regeneration, fate, and the inevitability of natural cycles. That is the mythic core of the complex. But this is a square, so the caring, bright, safe dimension of mother and the stern, dark, unsafe dimension are in conflict. This man would have to become both Moon and Pluto himself, rather than projecting it, in order to tap the riches of the aspect. He would have to learn to delve into those mysteries emotionally and intuitively, through experiences of intense passion which transform him and teach him to trust what he cannot see or control. But his early experiences, combined with his refined airy nature, have probably made the hidden side of life frightening or repellent to him.

In order to develop any consciousness of this side of himself, he needs to connect with all the layers around the archetypal core. He may spend a very long time avoiding that, through shallow relationships which don't touch him deeply, or through leaving his Moon-Pluto firmly on his mother's shoulders while he travels to the other side of the world to escape her demands. So the complex may sleep fitfully for many years. Then, one day, transiting Saturn enters Aquarius. Like a Swiss train, it arrives on time. It crosses the Ascendant and squares the Moon, then it reaches the Moon-Pluto midpoint, and then it opposes Pluto. That process may take over two years, because of orbs and because of Saturn's unpleasant inclination to make stations in the worst possible places. During that period, this man will find the right stage set and the right group of actors who will recreate the original emotional situation. He may have married a Plutonian woman years earlier, without noticing what she was really like. And then, when the Saturn transit arrives, he finds that he wishes to leave the marriage, and discovers that he is more like his father than he has ever realised, and has married his raging, depressed, manipulative mother.

Audience: Sometimes we need to recreate a whole childhood.

Liz: Yes, sometimes it can be a whole childhood. We create it, or we are drawn to it, or we make other people create it for us. One way or another, the complex will manifest on a concrete as well as an emotional level, and suddenly it becomes accessible. A single event, such as the death of a pet, can invoke the whole of one's childhood and every painful separation one has ever experienced. And it often happens that something other people would consider small has the power to trigger a complex, because it isn't small for the person experiencing it. There isn't really any point in trying to make this happen prematurely, because it happens when it is ready to happen.

Audience: Our tendency is to run away from these things if we can, but this is where free will comes in.

Liz: I quite agree. We may sense that the original experience is about to be triggered, which is what happens when a transiting planet begins to come within orb of a "hot" configuration in the birth chart. Because we know on some level what is coming, we may erect massive defences against our emotions and our memories. But this rarely works. The complex breaks through anyway. We do have free will in terms of choosing to face what is arising, rather than trying to escape it. That involves asking the right questions.

Audience: So it isn't necessary that the exact scenario is repeated. We recognise particular features of that scenario in a present situation because the transits are right. The same features might have been around six months earlier, but didn't have the same effect.

Liz: The scenario does not have to be the same. How could it be? One is no longer a child, and the world has changed. The costumes of the characters are never the same. But the core meaning is the same because the same chart configuration is being activated. And then light is suddenly cast on the unity of past and present, because we perceive and feel them as the same, even if we don't want to acknowledge it. Then one has access to those deeper levels.

The positive face of the complex

Audience: Can the breaking through of a complex also bring joy? Sometimes I think people only talk about their sadness and pain and grief. I wonder about joy, great moments of joy in childhood. Moments where your father appeared through the door. The complex vitalises this kind of experience, energises it.

Liz: Yes, the archetypal nature of a complex can be reflected in feelings of great joy and being "taken out of oneself" as well as in feelings of pain and conflict. We have looked quite a lot at aspects like progressed Sun applying to conjunct Saturn, or progressed Moon applying to square Pluto. But one might equally have progressed Sun applying to conjunct Venus, or progressed Ascendant conjunct Jupiter. The same joyful feelings will arise later in life when the complex is triggered. This often happens when one falls in love. Projections are not just negative, but can also be positive, and when components of a complex are projected, the same compulsive quality may also apply to ecstatic feelings. But most of the time, when we have an experience of joy, we don't tend to rush to the astrologer or psychotherapist for an appointment. That is why you are not hearing much about joy today. Joyful experiences are not usually the ones that we feel an urgent need to understand.

Audience: I'm sorry to sound cynical, but I wonder whether these experiences of joy in childhood which this lady asked about are real, because they involve projecting something archetypal on the parent. So later on, if we fall in love and put this same projection on the lover, it is not really to do with the person we think we are in love with. Won't the complex be creating an impression of joy, rather than the real thing?

Liz: Perhaps you could tell us just what the real thing is. Lots of us would like to know. Joy, like beauty, is usually in the eyes of the beholder. Is there such a thing as objective joy, recognised by common consensus? Like pain, joy is a subjective state, dependent on the individual personality and the individual moment. It may be that what the ego experiences ordinarily, at the best of times, is contentment or tranquillity. Those powerful emotional highs that we all seek may be connected with the experience of something archetypal intruding on everyday earthly life. Archetypal doesn't mean unreal. It may mean super-real.

It could even be argued that any experience which affects us profoundly, whether painfully or joyfully, has plugged us into the archetypal realm, and is linked with the energy of our complexes. Otherwise, we would merely nod at an experience, register a bland response, and get on with the next thing. Which realm is "real"? Our individual birth charts predispose us to register certain experiences as important, whether they are "good" or "bad" experiences, because these experiences are aligned with the deeper patterns at work beneath the surface of life.

If someone has, say, a Moon-Saturn conjunction in Taurus in the 2nd house, a sense of material and emotional security may be compulsively important to that person. There is a complex at work, involving body and security issues. For such a person, a constantly changing environment in childhood will be experienced as deeply frightening and unpleasant. But another person, with a Moon-Uranus conjunction in Sagittarius in the 2nd, may experience a rush of joy every time the family moves house, because it's so exciting and full of possibilities. Even if there is anxiety, it is more than compensated by the joy of change. The mother-complex reflected by these two very different aspects will contribute very different responses to the same life experience. For Moon-Uranus, confinement in one house, one community and one set of friends may feel painful and suffocating. Joy is experienced in change, and the need for change may be compulsive. Does that make the joy illusory or unreal?

Harmonious aspects in the birth chart may reflect a complex which does not pose a threat to the ego's world-view. There will be some conflict, but it is not of an unbearable kind. Let's say that there is an applying Moon-Jupiter trine, from Cancer to Pisces. That is an especially harmonious aspect, because both planets are in the signs of their dignity. The mother-archetype here is connected with mother as giver of bounty and bringer of joy, and the protector of the traveler on the journey. A powerful transit will trigger this complex, but the complex might not be especially charged with unresolved conflict – although it may conflict with other chart factors. What may be constellated is a recollection of a wise, supportive, generous mother, who is internalised as a deep instinctive faith in life.

If, for example, the transit is from Uranus, there may be a sudden revelation of the inherent order of the cosmos, even if external matters are in a state of chaos. There may be a sense of spiritual homecoming, a transformative realisation that life can be trusted, because mother could be trusted. Some transits can trigger the positive face of a complex. Such experiences provide answers in themselves. One doesn't need an astrologer.

Audience: Could a complex be beautiful and positive and still unconscious?

Liz: I don't think it's quite so clear-cut. Complexes, like the archetypal patterns at their core, are full of ambivalent associations and feelings. Usually there are positive and creative experiences locked up in them, which can sit side by side with painful and disturbing ones. No complex is "just" positive or negative. Even a Moon-Jupiter trine can suggest a mother who is too big, dramatic and overwhelming, even if she is also supportive and generous. One can have too much of a good thing, and one may find it hard to grow up and leave such a mother. Both positive and negative associations may be triggered by an important transit or progression. And not all unconscious issues are unpleasant. Sometimes one finds that perfectly lovely configurations in a chart are very unconscious. The ego might not perceive them as lovely, or one has been taught to see oneself as unlovely. Then some of one's best resources may be hidden away in the darkness.

This latter is known as the wet blanket syndrome. For example, we might see a chart with a lot of planets in Capricorn, an angular Saturn opposition the Sun, and Mercury square Chiron. And along with these placements is a delightful Venus-Jupiter conjunction in Sagittarius, but it's invisible. The person doesn't seem to exhibit the joyful, self-indulgent, and adventurous spirit we associate with the two "benefics". Where has it gone? Most likely it has been suppressed, by both the parents and the ego, and it is being projected. It may be either a positive or a negative projection. There might be a lot of envy toward people who seem to have everything: "It's all right for some, with looks and money and plenty of time to indulge themselves, but the rest of us don't have it so easy." Or the person may perceive the Venus-Jupiter wholly negatively, and stomp around saying, "Irresponsible, self-indulgent people! All society's problems are their fault!" Or the partner may appear as the enchanting, forever elusive *puer* or *puella*. One can hear such scripts everywhere.

But an important transit may trigger this sleeping conjunction into awareness, and the spirit of the *puer* may erupt as something very joyful which totally transforms the personality. It may be the first time that the person has really let go and realised that life can actually be fun, and isn't just a vale of tears and endless investments in one's pension fund. A complex can contain deeply unconscious joyful elements. They may be blocked for reasons which require a lot of painstaking work to unravel, and an honest confrontation with difficult issues from childhood may be required. There will usually be pain involved, although the complex can release joy. Powerful aspects like Venus-Jupiter are not blocked because one has a perverse desire to be miserable. There is always a good reason why we cannot contact that which is joyful within ourselves.

Audience: The next thing I will ask is whether the character of the complex is always compulsive. Or can it be somebody who just takes life terribly easily, and doesn't know why, because he or she is just naturally optimistic? Can that be a complex?

Liz: There is a difference between temperament and a complex. What you are describing is a habitual attitude of the conscious ego. Complexes have dynamic energy, which is why the ego experiences them as compulsive. They seem to have a will of their own. That is why the early psychological researchers perceived their effects as a "divided will". The signs of the zodiac don't have the kind of dynamic energy that the planets and aspects do. I believe the signs tell us a great deal about temperament, while the planetary configurations tell us a great deal about complexes.

Of course the two interweave. If we look at the chart from the perspective of temperament, we might say, "Here is the Sun in Sagittarius and the Moon in Libra, with a Gemini Ascendant. This person is easy-going, sociable, communicative, always views life positively, and looks for the best in people. Lovely personality, great fun to be with, everybody likes him/her." That's not a complex. But if that Sun in Sagittarius is opposition Chiron in Gemini, which in turn conjuncts the Ascendant from the 12th house and trines the Moon, then we are looking at something much more dynamic. We might then fruitfully explore myths such as that of the wounded healer. And we might guess at a deep and compulsive conflict between the Jupiterian sense of being a divine child in a cosmos that resembles an adventure playground, and the bitter experience of isolation and social oppression that comes down through the family inheritance and keeps this person always on the move and strenuously determined never to let anyone get that close.

Audience: All right. But if the temperament is based on the memory of great joy in the early part of life, that leaves a positive energy in the unconscious. I am straining to see something positive in this idea of the complex.

Liz: Perhaps you are straining because you have a complex. Temperament, as I understand it, is not "based" on anything. It is the substance of which the personality is made. Complexes fuel the substance and give it life, movement, and direction. They do not do this because they are inherently negative. They do it because they are the engine which moves the vehicle. I could suggest many analogies. Complexes are like the life-force which animates the physical body, or the evolutionary urge which makes all the species of nature develop new adaptations in order to survive better. Please don't confuse compulsiveness with negativity.

The experience of deep joy, which has an archetypal, consciousness-expanding quality, is not the same thing as being cheerful and easy-going. Joy is something very special. It comes momentarily and it is like a window that opens and lets the sunlight flood in. It is a recognition of something transpersonal embedded in personal life. Astrologically, joy is, in part, connected with Jupiter, and is fundamentally a religious experience. Its roots lie in something bigger than saying to oneself, "I am having a good time." And what we perceive as religious experience is also bound up with complexes, because our encounters with the "objective psyche" reveal a higher or deeper reality than that which the ego perceives.

Complexes and chart configurations

It should be fairly obvious by this time that every configuration in the chart can be viewed from the perspective of complexes. Every planet forms part of a web of interlocked complexes. A person doesn't have just one complex. Each individual has a series of interwoven stories that makes up his or her very special pattern. Some of these complexes are going to be relatively close to the surface and stimulate ego-consciousness in a way which allows a workable relationship. We can have compulsive behaviour that we know is coming from a complex, but it doesn't have to be destructive. We can actually harness it and make positive use of it. This happens regularly in creative work – "something" impels us to create. But some complexes are submerged very deeply, yet constantly kick the underbelly of the ego, and the chart can be very helpful in pointing us in the right direction to understand more about these. The complexes that cause us the most trouble are the ones that are most highly charged but disconnected from consciousness.

Complexes and hard aspects

As you will have worked out by now, hard aspects are one of the first things we should look at. In this I would include minor aspects, since these often link the major hard aspects – such as a square between two planets with a third planet semisquare both, or an opposition with a planet semisquare one end of the opposition and sesquiquadrate the other. The more planets are involved in such a configuration, the more powerful it is. A Mercury-Jupiter square sitting by itself might not necessarily have a lot of charge to it. But a Mercury-Jupiter square embedded in a configuration which also involves the Moon, Pluto, and Saturn is a very big one, and it will reflect one of the major themes that the individual will keep encountering throughout life.

Hard aspects usually make themselves known first through projection. In the main, we tend to identify with one end of the hard aspect and project the other. There are exceptions. These may occur when the planets themselves are friendly, such as Venus opposite Jupiter, or Mercury square Uranus, or Mars square Jupiter. These pairs of planets have so much affinity with each other that it is often possible to express both, albeit somewhat compulsively. Another exception might be planets which are in opposition but also in mutual reception, such as Jupiter in Gemini opposite Mercury in Sagittarius. Then it is not likely that the opposition will contain too compulsive a charge, because even though there is tension, the ego can handle it it. And another exception might be provided by the general tone of the chart in which the hard aspect is embedded. A Saturn-Pluto square, for example, might not be so unconscious or potentially disruptive if the individual has an emphasis in Capricorn and Scorpio, and is therefore predisposed to sympathise with both planets. The tough, suspicious, tenacious qualities which this pair of planets reflects is in keeping with the ego's conscious values.

When there are hard aspects but no planetary or sign affinity, we may get a sense of where some of the powerful complexes lie in the chart. It is these aspects which drive us through life, because there is usually a good deal of unconsciousness and therefore a high charge around the aspect. We don't get this sort of motivating energy from our trines. They reflect gifts and talents and a sense of harmonious relationship between the two planets, but they don't "divide our will", because they don't hurt us. They feel nice, and so we are not driven to become more conscious.

Once again, there are exceptions. Planets which are inimical to each other, like Mars and Neptune, may cause difficulties even in trine, if the rest of the chart is unsympathetic to one planet of the pair. For example, an Aries with Capricorn rising and Sun square Mars may dissociate from Neptune, and a high charge may linger around experiences and people who are "hooks" for Neptune's ineffable world.

The really energetic points in the chart are not usually the trines – they are the hard aspects, amongst which I include certain conjunctions. Many conjunctions act as hard aspects because the two planets may themselves be inimical and don't like being married to each other. Or the conjunction – say, a Mars-Jupiter conjunction in a very earthy chart – sits uncomfortably amidst signs and aspects whose general tone is radically different. But usually trines are much more readily digestible by ego-consciousness, as are sextiles. It is not that these aspects are therefore unconnected with our complexes. But the energy charge is much lower, and we do not struggle against them. Trines may still manifest in concrete form. But it seems that we have a greater range of choices, and are less inclined to fight the archetypal pattern reflected in the complex. In fact we often think it is personally "ours", rather than recognising that it is archetypal.

Complexes and element imbalances

The issue of the element balance of the chart is extremely important if we are exploring complexes. I mentioned just now that signs reflect temperament. When there is an emphasis in fiery signs, for example, the ego is "made" of fiery stuff, and the innate temperament is intuitive, forward-looking, and focused on possibilities rather than concrete facts and objects. When an element is weak or missing, the ego is not naturally aligned with the substance of that element, and this may colour the unconscious tone of the complexes which are highly charged and waiting to emerge into life. They come out wearing the clothing of the missing element.

For example, we might see the Sun in Leo with a great weight of planets in fire signs, along with an angular Jupiter. In direct contrast we may also find Mercury in Virgo in this chart, trine Saturn in Capricorn – the only planets in earth. Even though it is a trine, the person may find it hard to express and acknowledge, because it does not reflect the kind of qualities the ego wishes to be identified with. Mercury trine Saturn in a chart weak in earth may feel boring to a fiery individual who wants to do dramatic and exciting things in life.

Fiery temperaments do not value the virtues of Mercury-Saturn, because it seems so pedestrian and stifling to the imagination and the spirit. The aspect, however fine and constructive the astrologer might deem it, simply doesn't get used. It gets stifled, and it may get projected. This Mercury-Saturn trine, even though it looks like such a helpful, sensible aspect, may in fact be deeply unconscious, and thus it may carry a very high energy charge. Because it will emerge into life wearing earthy clothing, it may manifest as chronic money worries, or a surprising pedantry and obsession with details. Or it may get projected onto academic authorities. The person may have an ongoing and compulsive issue about not having a degree, or not possessing some kind of academic qualification, or not doing the Faculty exam, or not writing the CPA diploma thesis.

Audience: I know that one!

Liz: Well, you could always write your thesis on Mercury-Saturn aspects. Even though this aspect is a trine in our example, it is not easily digestible because of its being embedded in a fiery chart. So it will form an important dimension of an unconscious complex, and we may find other bits of the chart which also feed this complex. When we start looking carefully at the configurations, we may realise that the chart is forming clumps, a bit like clumping cat litter. Are you familiar with clumping cat litter? All right, I won't go any further in describing it. We can get a sense of bits of the chart that start gluing together, forming a kind of unconscious "gunge" which carries a great deal of unconscious energy.

An element imbalance can throw even harmonious aspects into the position of being unacceptable to the ego, and therefore they may begin to accumulate a complicated web of associations on the unconscious level. Sometimes these trines get attached to parents who seem to have qualities we lack, or who apparently expect us to be things we believe we cannot be. The fiery person with an earthy Mercury-Saturn trine may project that trine onto a parent, and say, "My mother had incredibly high academic expectations of me," or, "My father was only interested in practical things, like whether or not I could get a job." Neither of these attitudes is a criminal offence in a parent, and the mother or father who is interested in his or her child's intellectual progress and material well-being is hardly an evil parent. But it is often experienced that way because the individual is fighting these qualities in himself or herself, and there is a high charge around the complex. Parents often have to carry these projected bits, even when they are so-called "good" aspects.

Audience: I have noticed something about the trine. Even if it is part of a complex, it is the thing with which the person identifies most, and it can be a defence mechanism. One gets trapped in inertia.

Liz: There is movement in a trine, but it goes around in a loop and doesn't stray outside its own circuit. Whether trines are conscious or unconscious, they are closed systems. They have their own little world in which things happen because they are supposed to be that way, and there is a strange kind of passivity. Because trines – especially grand trines – reflect gifts, we tend to rely on them to get through life. We sit back and let it all happen because we assume it will happen to our advantage. We don't have to struggle, because everything just seems to fall into place. When trines are unconscious and get projected, the same quality seems to belong to the person or thing on which they are projected. We usually admire these "hooks", but we may feel we cannot get near them. Projected trines seem to represent something that is complete, perfectly formed, and has its own life, and one can't engage with it. There is a very passive feeling to trines. They are not energetic; they don't make us try to resolve conflicts. Trines don't cause pain. Sadly, we may cause ourselves pain by hiding behind our trines to escape the tension and compulsiveness of our hard aspects.

Complexes and angular planets

Let's look now at planets on angles. They are like lightning conductors. They have a very powerful manifesting propensity. We have to express them, although sometimes they are very unconscious. One can have a planet sitting on the Ascendant or the MC with which the ego does not identify. We cannot assume that unconsciousness is limited only to planets on the Descendant or the IC.

The angles have a lot to do with manifestation. They are the cross of matter on which we are incarnated. The MC/IC axis is concerned with our inheritance, and what we are "destined" to work with, inwardly and outwardly, as a family legacy. The Ascendant/Descendant axis is concerned with the nature of the individual, independent of the family inheritance. The cross of horizon and meridian anchors us in the world, in a physical body which has come from a physical mother and father. Planets on angles seem to display a powerful compulsion to manifest, because their angular placement makes them part of this cross of incarnation. They must be expressed in the world. They materialise. Often these angular planets appear as physical characteristics. People look and move like the planets on the angles.

Audience: Do you mean anywhere in the angular house, or do you mean conjuncting the angles even if the planet is in the 9th or 3rd?

Liz: It is the angles themselves, rather than the angular house. This is supported by Gauquelin's work, which revealed the great importance of planets in the cadent houses just behind an angle.

Audience: What about the Descendant? And the IC? I thought these were to do with others, or with roots, not with the world.

Liz: Roots, whether defined as father, family, birthplace, or home, are still the world, and so are our relationships with others. The Descendant and the IC are also concerned with manifestation. Sometimes a planet at the IC is so powerful and obvious in the person's life that others identify him or her with that planet. I was thinking of Rajneesh, who had Neptune conjunct the IC. The four angles of the chart, even if they are habitually projected, nevertheless are evident in the person's interaction with external life.

Audience: What orb would you use – 8°? Or smaller?

Liz: Larger. I usually use $10°$, the same as for a planetary conjunction. Because angular planets have such a strong compulsion to manifest, we remain unconscious of them at our peril. The less connected we are with them, the more chaos they tend to create, internally and externally. We need to provide them with concrete vehicles. If they are on the MC/IC axis, they suggest the presence of a powerful family complex which demands expression in outer life, through one's work or the place one calls "home", or both.

We can have a planet on the Ascendant or the MC, screamingly obvious to everyone else, yet have no idea what it is doing. The ego may not want anything to do with it. Just because it is in such a prominent position doesn't mean that it is part of consciousness, especially if it is an outer planet or a planet inimical to the chart's overall element balance – like Saturn on the Ascendant of a fiery chart, or Uranus on the Ascendant of a watery chart.

For example, there is a particular age group, born between September 1948 and June 1956, which has Uranus in Cancer, and a great many of these people have Uranus rising. How many of this generation group can consciously acknowledge and creatively express the tension of that combination? The planet and the sign are predisposed to quarrel – they are not friends. Uranus in Cancer constitutes a complex in itself, a collective complex concerned with the potential transformation of our definitions of family and roots. This complex is personally relevant to the individual with Uranus rising in Cancer.

I have noticed that many people with Uranus rising in Cancer identify almost wholly with the Cancerian component, especially if this is supported by a chart emphasis in water signs. Uranus is then projected onto the environment and onto relationships, and one can clearly see the complex at work. Personal life is perpetually disrupted. There may be constant moves or relationship breakups. Meanwhile, the poor Cancer Ascendant is saying, "But I just want some security. Why do these things keep happening to me?" In this way a planet on an angle can be deeply unconscious. Just because it is on the Ascendant, the ego will not automatically identify with it.

Saturn and Chiron as complexes

Certain planets are, by their nature, indigestible. The outer planets may carry a high charge because they deal with collective energies which the ego experiences, quite rightly, as inimical to its control. Saturn and Chiron may also be indigestible because they are "hard" planets, in the sense that they often reflect painful feelings and experiences which we do not wish to own. With Saturn this is not always the case. There are many people, especially those with an emphasis in earth – life's realists – who relate well to Saturn and can consciously contain its difficulties, even when the going is tough. But because of the sense of inferiority and woundedness which so often accompanies Saturn's placement – and also Chiron's – these two planets are often disowned, especially by those with a highly idealistic temperament.

Sometimes the complex symbolised by Saturn or Chiron absorbs everything else, and the person identifies almost wholly with his or her wounding. Whenever we see someone who is identified with an archetypal role such as that of the victim, we know that a complex has taken over consciousness. All other facets of the personality feed one's martyrdom, and life's kind face is ignored or never allowed entry. There are people whose lives seems to constantly repeat the theme of hardship and victimisation. It is as though there are five Chirons and six Saturns in the birth chart, and no other planets. One can hear the world-weary voice saying, "I've struggled and suffered all my life," and although we often initially feel compassion, we may eventually be struck by the way in which such a person makes it quite impossible for anyone to offer any help to alleviate the hardship and suffering. The complex perpetuates its own myth, because any good or happy experience is prevented from happening, or interpreted negatively or cynically.

The complex as a "supernatural" power

Audience: When I see a pattern in a chart, I try to explain this pattern to my client in terms of complexes and projection. I see things from a psychological point of view. Usually this is fine. But I have a client who sees everything on a supernatural level. I am confused, because the things which have happened to her are truly very strange. They are not normal, ordinary things. I wonder whether these are really projections, or maybe supernatural after all.

Liz: Why do you assume that projections are always normal and ordinary? The psychoid nature of complexes makes them behave in extremely mysterious ways – they *are* supernatural, in the most profound sense. We all interpret experience according to our complexes, and for some people a supernatural interpretation is the only one possible. The languages may seem very different, but it is not impossible to offer a translation which is acceptable to both of you and helpful to the client. Can you tell us more?

Audience: This woman was badly beaten by her mother. Now she is an invalid, although there is nothing physically wrong. I can say, "Your illness is the reflection of a mother-complex." But she was also recently beaten on the street by a woman whom she had never met. At one point I met her in a pub and had a drink with her. A drunk man sat down near us and started to say abusive, threatening things to her. I saw this for myself. She was terrified. These things just come and meet her. They come after her. How is that projection?

Liz: I sympathise with your discomfort, because I have seen this kind of thing too. It is very strange and disturbing. We have been exploring the deeper level of complexes quite a lot today, and it is clear that complexes possess the power to attract external circumstances in ways which we do not understand. Your client is a little like the client I was describing earlier – everything seems to manifest in outer reality, in a magical and apparently persecutory way. But while my client saw everything as bad luck, yours apparently sees everything as the signature of some supernatural power with punishing intent. And it sounds as though she is infecting you with this complex, or triggering one of your own. Can you tell us something about her chart?

Audience: The Sun is in Virgo in the 3rd house, conjunct Uranus and Pluto, and all three are opposition Saturn in Pisces in the 9th. Mars is in the 12th, conjunct the Ascendant in Leo. There is a Moon-Neptune conjunction in Scorpio, square Mars. She takes the role of the victim-messiah, saying that if people don't beat her, others will suffer.

Liz: If this lady is a one-off client who sees you only infrequently, I am afraid you may not be able to do much for her. I don't mean to discourage you from trying to help. But she may need more than what an astrologer can offer. It sounds as though she has been taken over by her complex, and her ego is not strong enough to mediate it. She has very little freedom because the complex is running the show. But her victimisation also makes her feel important. There is a powerful unconscious inflation here. I am saying this because of what she has told you – that she must be beaten or others will suffer. She is identifying with Christ. She sees herself as a redeemer-victim, which is part of the mythic core of the complex. She was beaten as a child, but this childhood abuse didn't put the planetary configurations in her chart. She was born at a moment when the world around her was violent, and her mother acted out the violence of the collective. This experience has clothed the complex with powerful personal associations of a concrete kind.

Audience: Her mother was beaten by her father during the pregnancy. Is this connected with Mars in the 12th square Moon-Neptune?

Liz: Probably. Is the Moon-Mars a separating square?

Audience: Yes. It was exact during the pregnancy.

Liz: Then the crystallisation of this family complex began even before birth. We can surmise from the Sun-Uranus-Pluto conjunction that there is also a very difficult issue connected with the father, who beat the mother when she was pregnant. It is also connected with the religious background, because Saturn is opposing this triple conjunction from the 9th house. The mother is a mythic victim, the father a dark persecutor. With Mars poorly aspected in the 12th, we can guess that suppressed or misused aggression is part of the family background. Complexes involve more than a layer of individual associations wrapped around an archetypal core. Because we begin our individual development embedded in the family unconscious, we inherit the complexes that have been at work in the family for many generations. If these are highly charged, they will often appear reflected in the chart as planets in the 12th.

One of the dilemmas facing your client is that this is a collective complex which goes right back into the history of the family. It is the driving force of her collective antecedents. It undoubtedly has religious roots, because she is identifying with Christ and because of the 9th house Saturn. I am picking up a distinct odour of medieval Catholicism. Was she raised Catholic?

Audience: During her Saturn return she started to have these victim experiences very strongly, and she became very religious.

Liz: Could I ask again what religion she was brought up in?

Audience: Catholic.

Liz: Thank you. Why were you reluctant to answer? Were you also raised Catholic?

Audience: Yes.

Liz: That is why you are susceptible to her complex. This complex stretches all the way back to a collective religious past. Religions have complexes, or are themselves the expression of a complex. Catholicism emerged from a collective complex which erupted into life at the dawn of the Piscean era, and like other religions, it has its own archetypal themes. Anyone who is bound up with Catholicism through the family background will be affected to a greater or lesser extent by the complexes existing within that religious organism, depending on the individual birth chart. And there are certain themes running through the Catholic world-view which are deeply imbued with victimisation, sin, sacrifice, self-inflicted punishment, and redemption through suffering. These themes have been made personal by your client's personal experience of violence. The archetypal core of the complex and the personal encounter with violence and suffering have become inextricably bound up together. Of course she will interpret what is happening to her from a supernatural perspective. Actually, it is a medieval Catholic perspective. But it is also a complex.

Audience: I could say to her, "Try to integrate your own aggression, because it seems to me that you are living it out through other people." But saying something like that is really difficult for me to communicate on a rational level, because she just gets bored and looks out the window, as if I had said, "It's nice weather out." It means nothing to her.

Liz: It isn't only *her* aggression. It is her parents' aggression, and her grandparents', and the aggression which nourished the Inquisition and the Crusades. Her suffering is her mother's, and her grandmother's, and that of all the thousands of women burned at the stake or doomed to a miserable life of constant childbearing and poverty. Ultimately it is the suffering of Mary, who is also a victim-redeemer. Her struggle is not with a drunk in a pub, or a woman on the street. It is a struggle between good and evil, between God and the Devil, which in Catholic teaching requires the intervention of a divine redeemer. It may be that such language would mean more to her than psychological terminology.

I fear that, as an astrologer, you cannot solve her problem. This lady needs long-term therapeutic work. An astrologer is not going to get very far trying to transform such a massive, pulsing complex. As I said earlier, complexes don't sit down for a cup of tea with us, or listen quietly while we pontificate about the planets. When they have taken possession of the psyche in this way, the most you can hope to achieve is to provide some sort of intellectual framework that might be useful to her later. And you may need to do that in a hybrid language, which is both psychological and religious. You can also offer support and empathy to the woman suffering beneath the compulsions of the complex, and that may go further than you think. But initially she will not believe what you tell her, because the only power she feels she has derives from the archetype. She needs much more than an astrological consultation.

I think we must recognise the limitations of astrology when dealing with complexes that have taken over the personality. The chart can give us insights, and we may be able to communicate some of these so that the client has something to work with. But this lady has a long journey to make. There is no guarantee of success, because this is a family complex which stretches back to her religious and racial roots. She is carrying a collective burden, and she is on her hands and knees under the weight of it. It is not surprising that the ego has said, "I take no responsibility for this." It is only through building a solid ego that she will be able to work through these collective issues and claim an individual identity. Encouraging her to work with someone on an ongoing basis, in combination with the occasional astrological reading, might be a useful suggestion. Perhaps, if she is willing, she might get in touch with an organisation such as the Westminster Pastoral Foundation, which has a register of priests and nuns trained as psychotherapists. They would be versed in speaking her language.

In this kind of situation, however intelligent and intuitive the client is, ego-building must come first. This means slow, careful therapeutic work, so that she can experience a safe parental container. Given a solid enough therapeutic relationship, she might be able to face the savage emotions portrayed by that 12th house Mars. Understandably she is terrified by her own anger, which is global. Not to put too fine a point on it, it is the rage of centuries of wretchedly unhappy women labouring under the yoke of a male clergy which has told them that women must suffer to be redeemed. But it is only through expressing personal anger that she can come to a sense of personal potency. At the moment she is focused entirely on what has and is being done to her, and the archetypal figure of the victim-redeemer gives her the illusion of power and an escape from the rage which she is so frightened of.

Audience: For me, it's a philosophical question. How can people unconsciously make this kind of pattern happen over and over again?

Liz: People don't make the pattern. Complexes make the pattern, because they *are* the pattern. There is a great deal about the nature of reality that we do not understand, because we only measure reality with the crude instruments of modern science. Our present world-view only acknowledges the material level of reality. Complexes are both material and psychic. They manifest synchronously on both an outer and an inner level. I have seen or heard about the kind of thing you have been describing many times. These situations put the astrologer in a difficult moral and philosophical bind.

Some time ago a mother came to see me because her daughter had been raped. She showed me her daughter's chart. There was a Moon-Jupiter conjunction in Scorpio, which transiting Pluto was conjuncting. Transiting Saturn and Mars had also triggered this natal conjunction on the day of the event. The girl was walking down the street in broad daylight, and she was dragged off into the bushes and raped by a complete stranger. The man got away.

By no stretch of the imagination could we think that either mother or daughter "caused" this thing to happen, or that the girl was personally projecting something on the rapist. Yet here is a striking chart configuration, triggered by three powerful transits. What does it mean? In myth, Hades-Pluto is a rapist. So is Zeus-Jupiter, who raped Demeter, Persephone's mother. The Moon is in Pluto's sign, conjunct Jupiter and transited by Pluto. A mythic story has come to life. The Hades-Persephone story is concerned with the ruthless violation of innocence through necessity. Five characters are involved: Zeus, who violates Demeter and fathers Persephone on her; Demeter, who, because of her rage about the rape, protects her daughter's virginity long past its natural time; Aphrodite, goddess of sexual love, who is enraged because of Demeter's refusal to allow her daughter to enter womanhood; Hades, whom

Aphrodite inflames with passion as a vengeance on Demeter; and Persephone, who is an innocent victim, unformed and ripe for life. On the archetypal level we can all nod our heads and imagine that we understand the necessity of this mythic rape. On the personal level it is an utter outrage.

It is hard to talk about such an issue, because our personal feelings will rightly and inevitably be stirred. Whose complex is it anyway? The girl's? Her mother's? The family's? Society's? Perhaps it is all of the above. There is something so ruthlessly impersonal about Pluto. Somehow this young woman met in the outer world something that was in her inner world, although it was not "hers" in the personal sense. How can one help in this situation? From the psychological perspective, before there can be any understanding or healing, the girl must be able to express the rage she feels, within a safe container. To deny it or rationalise it would be destructive to her. To act it out blindly would be destructive not only to her but to others. I believe this is also the case with your client. She is going to have to get very angry before she starts healing. "Father, forgive them, for they know not what they do!" is simply not on as an opening gambit.

Audience: Can rage help her to make the complex conscious?

Liz: Rage can be healing if it is consciously expressed rather than acted out compulsively, because it unhooks the ego from its identification with the complex. This is because one feels rage on behalf of oneself. To shout, "*My* body has been violated!" is an ego statement – it is the voice of Mars. Mars doesn't say, "I rage for humanity." It says, "That bastard hurt me!" That is the ego beginning to speak at last. The moment it can speak, it is not wholly enthralled by the complex.

Audience: So Mars is important for working with complexes.

Liz: All the personal planets are important, because they give the ego strength and definition. Mars is especially important for your client, because it has been castrated by the family and religious background. Once the ego has some strength of its own, it can hold the energy of a complex until some integration is possible. Without a reasonably solid ego, the complex runs the show, and then one gets these magical synchronicities that feel like the intervention of supernatural forces.

Audience: This woman was born under the Uranus-Pluto conjunction in Virgo. That is a collective thing, isn't it?

Liz: Yes, she is one of the children of this extremely important outer planet conjunction which was operative during the 1960s. It is an anarchic, transformative, explosive, and visionary conjunction. A new social and spiritual vision was breaking through, combined with a will to destroy all that had gone before. The changes that happened in the world under this conjunction were very profound. It transformed collective morality and collective social attitudes. The people born under it embody it, and its effects are still going on, because this generation is still engaged on working the conjunction out on the worldly as well as the psychological level.

They have a heavy package to carry, because they must integrate a complex which is not just theirs or their families'. It is a huge collective issue, and it is being enacted in those spheres of life which are associated with Virgo – the health of the planet, attitudes toward the body, the use and abuse of technology, and the orderly workings by which societies and worldly structures operate. Virgo symbolises the interface between the psyche and physical reality. Being mutable, it is one of the signs concerned with integrating two different levels of reality. That is why I said your client has a long journey, and she needs something more than an astrological chart to help her on her way. We can get insight into what kind of complex is at work, but that knowledge is not going to do a lot of good unless the ego can cope with the complex. One needs a strong ego to cope with Sun-Uranus-Pluto, especially when Saturn is thrown in. A high percentage of strong egos is needed in this generation to get the best from the Uranus-Pluto conjunction on the collective level. Those of us who do not have to deal with such powerful outer planet combinations may find it easier to define our personal ground apart from the collective.

Audience: Since we are on the subject of the supernatural, could complexes have anything to do with poltergeist activity?

Liz: That is another area in which the psychoid nature of complexes may be evident. The energy of the complex is operating independent of the individual's physical body. The complex is running loose, autonomous and telekinetic. On a subtler level, the same principle is in operation when someone prangs your car on the day transiting Mars is square your Uranus. The other driver may also have a transit of Mars to Uranus, or a natal Mars-Uranus square. Where has this person come from? How did they wind up just behind you in the traffic queue?

Audience: But poltergeist activity is much more dramatic.

Liz: Yes, but I think it is the same dynamic. The most popular theory about poltergeist activity seems to focus on "disturbed" adolescents, whose powerful emotional energies are in some way connected with the moving objects. No one knows how this happens, but it is generally agreed that there is a young person, often pubescent, at the centre of all the activity. Do any of you remember the film *Carrie*? Sexual energy in an adolescent can be incredibly powerful. If it is totally blocked from consciousness, it may well have the power to affect material objects. I cannot "prove" what I am saying. It is merely speculation. But if anyone has a better suggestion, do let me know.

Audience: Perhaps our mental framework reflects a collective complex which is part of our religious attitude. We have the tendency to split everything into good and evil, and above and below, instead of having a more comprehensive world-view.

Liz: You are echoing what I said earlier – religions have their own complexes, and the religions which arose at the beginning of the Piscean era are dualist in nature. Their complexes involve perceiving a split between spirit and matter. This doesn't apply only to Christianity and Islam, both of which were born under this astrological age, but also to the various redeemer-cults that flourished at the same time Christianity began – Orphism, Mithraism, and the Egyptian mystery religions. All the redeemer-cults of the early Piscean Age have a particular dynamic energy which perceives reality in twos. Spirit and matter are irrevocably split. That is the complex of this particular waning epoch.

Audience: We carry it even if we do not go to Church.

Liz: Yes, it is part of the fabric of the collective psyche. Astrological ages have their own complexes according to the planetary rulers, and so do the great conjunctions which inaugurate particular historical epochs. The institution of the Church has complexes through which reality is perceived. Religious institutions follow the same psychological laws as individuals, because it is individuals who create them. We are imbued with a collective perception of reality. No matter how hard we try, it is very difficult – perhaps even impossible – to step out of the skin of our epoch, however liberated we think we are. We get glimpses of the past and the future, but we are always limited in our perceptions.

Example charts

Complexes in a relationship – Ellen and Franco

Now we can look at two charts which have been given to me by a couple in the group. We can look at how complexes might be expressed in the birth chart, and also how they interact with the complexes of another person. This is the most characteristic way in which we meet our complexes when they are on the move. Would either of you like to tell us what is concerning you?

Ellen: Since it was my idea to give you the charts, I'll go first. Franco doesn't know much about astrology. At the moment, Pluto is conjuncting my Mars, and square Franco's Mars. I suppose I'm a little concerned about what that might mean. Also, Uranus is going over my Jupiter and his Sun, and it will square my Scorpio planets.

Liz: Is this a long-standing relationship?

Ellen: Yes.

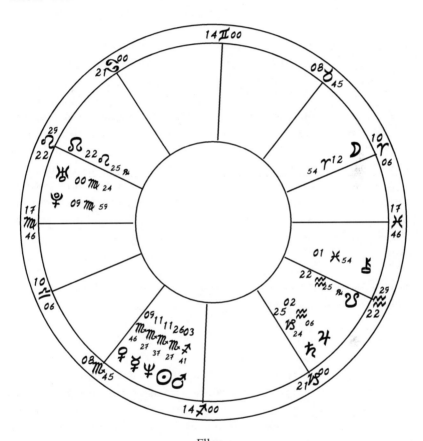

Ellen
[Birth data withheld for reasons of confidentiality]

Liz: The first thing that catches my eye is that there are two areas in the chart where there are very powerful, intense, stressful configurations. That is what I would look at initially, to get a sense of what kind of complexes might be at work, and what kind of story is being unfolded.

Venus, Mercury, and Neptune are conjunct in Scorpio, and all are square Jupiter in Aquarius. Saturn conjuncts Jupiter, although it does not square the Scorpio planets. That is one very important configuration, involving four fixed planets. Then there is the Uranus-Pluto conjunction in Virgo, opposite Chiron in Pisces. All these are in turn square Mars, so this is a very strong, energetic T-cross, involving four mutable planets. The two configurations are linked, by Chiron, which trines the Venus-Mercury-Neptune at the same time that it is involved in the T-cross, and by Jupiter, which sextiles Mars.

First of all, it might be helpful to get a sense of who the characters are in these two stories. Here are two quite different complexes, if you like, which will be interwoven in your life. They are both being triggered at the moment, as you pointed out, and they are also both picked up by issues in Franco's chart, which we will look at next. But briefly, this T-cross of Chiron, Uranus-Neptune and Mars, plugs into Franco's Mars in Pisces opposite Moon in Virgo, and the Venus-Mercury-Neptune square Jupiter squares Franco's Sun in Aquarius.

As with any important relationship, the attraction is partly because of these hard aspect interchanges. Both of you are carrying internal energy dynamics that affect each other. You pull each other into your own drama, which is what happens in all important relationships. Of course, when a transit such as Pluto comes along to set off these mix-and-match configurations, your individual issues get triggered and the energy between you becomes combustible. So, what do these configurations mean? Let's start with Mars square Chiron square Uranus square Pluto. What story is that telling us, and how does it sit with the rest of the chart? You have all gone deadly quiet. I'll nudge you a little bit. Try starting with the personal planet. There are four planets involved in this configuration, but only one – Mars – is personal.

Audience: It's in the 3rd house. I think it is describing a strong urge for freedom. Maybe issues around authority will trigger that very self-willed Mars in fire – to a point which is sometimes really sore.

It could be over-reactive about "my" way of being, "my" way of doing things. It's a strong, independent spirit.

Audience: I see a difference between Mars wanting to study and be enthusiastic in all sorts of intellectual ways, and Chiron, which is much more caring and Piscean, and in the 6th house, wanting to be of service to others. There is a conflict, and because there is an opposition from Chiron to the outer planets, there is a big generation conflict as well as a very personal one.

Liz: I agree. Mars in Sagittarius in the 3rd, which is also conjunct the Sun at the end of Scorpio, reflects a lively, inquiring, restless spirit. The world is full of adventures, and Mars says, "It's really boring around here, let's see what else is out there." It is a natural traveler, explorer, and student. The mind might not work in an academic way, but it is full of curiosity and optimism, eager to learn everything there is to learn, especially if the knowledge is universal. In a way this Mars is a bit naive. The world is a giant Disneyland, where everybody lives happily ever after.

Ellen: All right, I know I'm impossibly romantic.

Liz: There is a wonderfully optimistic spirit here. But it collides with a problematic ancestral inheritance, because Uranus and Pluto are in the twelfth. And Chiron in itself has bearing on the family inheritance, and in Pisces there is a suggestion of a great deal of sacrifice and suffering. So there is some heavy family stuff here, going back over many generations. That may make it hard for Mars to retain its spirit and optimism. This excited, excitable, enthusiastic, childlike Mars keeps crashing into some very unfair aspects of life – wounds in people that are inherited from the past and can't be healed. This will affect Mars' ability to function. The family issues these outer planets symbolise may dampen the spirit and undermine the will. Chiron in the 6th in Pisces can also suggest feelings of obligation – one should look after others. Mars can't be self-willed without a lot of guilt. We are looking at a family complex, which involves the suppression of feelings over many generations – especially self-willed, passionate feelings.

Ellen: There is a lot of pain and anger coming up at the moment about my family. But I also feel a great curiosity about what's really going on.

Liz: Do you feel that you can express Mars?

Ellen: Not very well. I feel very guilty if I do anything just for myself.

Audience: There is a lovely 5th house Jupiter sextile Mars, so that will be a way out.

Liz: On paper it is a way out. In real life it isn't that simple. Let's try to get a feeling of the other characters in the play. This T-cross is embedded in a chart in which the Sun and chart ruler, Mercury, are in Scorpio, a water sign. That suggests a person with deep, enduring feelings and an inclination to make strong, lasting attachments. Venus-Neptune is naturally compassionate and responds immediately to wounded and suffering people. The Virgo Ascendant longs to be useful and bring order to a chaotic and disorderly world. These three characters share certain values in common. They are friends. And they will strongly colour the ego's values and world-view.

Sometimes even "good" aspects can get projected, if they are indigestible to the ego's values. This adventurous 5th house Jupiter, sextile Mars in Jupiter's sign, is indeed a lovely aspect. But Saturn is in Capricorn and also in the 5th, conjunct Jupiter. It is sextile the Sun, bringing a quality of responsibility and self-discipline to the chart. Saturn says to Jupiter, "Where do you think you're going with that suitcase? There are duties to discharge, and people who depend on you." Venus-Neptune in Scorpio says, "But your mother needs you. Actually, the whole world needs you. Don't be so selfish and unfeeling."

Mars sextile Jupiter doesn't get much of a chance to go anywhere. It is sandwiched between other people's need of Ellen and Ellen's need of other people. This aspect is likely to be exteriorised, and projected on someone whose Sun happens to be in

Aquarius and placed just on the cusp of the 9th, Jupiter's natural house.

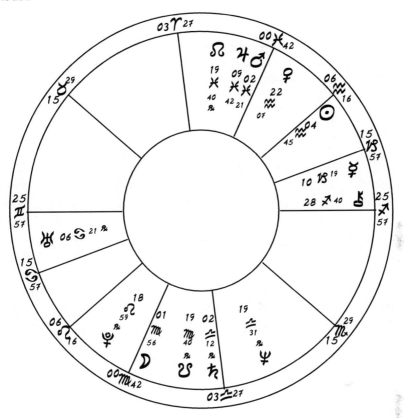

Franco
[Birth data withheld for reasons of confidentiality]

Franco: This is where I come into the play?

Liz: This is where you come into the play. You get to be Jupiter in Aquarius in the 5th, one of whose faces is the *puer aeternus*. Do you understand what I mean by *puer aeternus*?

Franco: Yes. I am the eternal youth for her.

Liz: That is one of the parts in Ellen's drama in which you have been cast. It means that both of you could get a great deal of enrichment from the relationship. Your independent, intellectually inquisitive, detached nature activates Ellen's Jupiter, and shows her a way of getting out from under this burdensome family inheritance. By simply being who you are, you help her to see that she has a right to enjoy life.

Ellen: I am afraid if all my selfishness comes out, it will take my life over.

Liz: It is interesting that you call it selfishness, as though it were something negative. You fear that it will take over. When something is part of an unconscious complex, it may feel threatening to the ego, because the ego is convinced that if one gives it a finger it will bite off one's hand. There is a sense that something compulsive and uncontrollable might burst its bonds if one doesn't keep it carefully chained up. So you have the fantasy that, if you let Jupiter sextile Mars out of prison, you will wind up being one of those dreadfully self-centred, narcissistic types who is so callous and unfeeling. That is a fantasy which I would question. Where does it come from? Whose voice is it? If you persist in seeing this side of yourself so negatively, you may find yourself giving Franco's Sun in Aquarius a very hard time. On the one hand, you find his independence extremely attractive. On the other hand, you may accuse him of being selfish and uncommitted. You may be fighting your own complex within the relationship.

Franco: This is what I keep saying, although I have not used the word "complex". I keep saying she needs the space herself.

Liz: She probably does. There are other powerful cross-aspects which also generate a lot of energy within the relationship, and activate complexes on both sides. Franco, when you express Mars in Pisces, which is a very different side of you – much more sensitive and vulnerable than the elusive *puer* – you run up against Ellen's Chiron in Pisces, as well as her Uranus-Pluto in Virgo and her own Mars in Sagittarius. Your Mars is conjunct Jupiter and opposition

Moon in Virgo, and this configuration speaks of strong feelings and great generosity of heart. This Mars is trine Ellen's Venus. The moment you show your feelings, Ellen responds with both passion and compassion. But at the same time, she may sometimes feel resentful, because her Chiron tells her it is one more person wanting something from her. She may react through her Mars, asserting her own needs in an irritable way that bruises your Moon and ignites friction between you. And you in turn may feel she is trying to dominate or possess you, because you might feel a little overpowered by her Pluto square your Moon. This may stir up all your own parental issues. Your Mars-Jupiter-Moon straddles the meridian of the chart. It reflects a parental inheritance, and a conflict within the parental marriage – in other words, a parental complex.

This issue between the two of you is getting triggered now by the transit of Pluto. Both of you are carrying complexes related to the family inheritance, the wounded world, the suffering of others, and the sense of obligation which such suffering invokes. Both of you probably have a fair amount of anger inside, because both of you have, to some extent, been manipulated or blocked by issues in the early environment. So it is not easy for either of you to express personal wishes and desires without some guilt. To the extent that these issues are projected, they will come out through conflict in your relationship. The core of the shared complex circles around Mars and Jupiter on the one hand, and Neptune and Chiron on the other, and is concerned with autonomy versus merging, independence versus dependency, self-assertion versus emotional need.

This central issue is echoed by another dynamic series of aspects across the charts. As we have seen, Ellen's Jupiter squares her Venus-Mercury-Neptune conjunction. This conjunction is intensely emotional and romantic. Jupiter in the 5th in Aquarius is detached and cerebral. It is tolerant and generous, but prefers not to get too involved. Jupiter in Aquarius values friendship, and sharing intellectual and spiritual values is vastly preferable to heavy emotional scenes. Franco's Sun, because it conjuncts Ellen's Jupiter, also squares her Venus-Mercury-Neptune. The two of you may be constantly engaged in a struggle as to who plays the emotionally needy partner and who plays the one who wants a bit of space.

Audience: I am interested in the way her Mars-Uranus square touches his Moon. Maybe her moments of impulsive anger can help him to overcome that shy Virgo Moon.

Franco: I would not say that I am shy.

Ellen: I would. Not in an obvious way, but underneath. Shy about talking about feelings.

Liz: In order to make sense of Mars-Jupiter opposition the Moon in Franco's chart, we need to know more about his family background and the relationship between his mother and father. Although the Moon at the IC suggests a strong emotional attachment to the father, it can also reflect an unreliable, moody, or periodically absent father. It is possible that the real strength in the family lay with the mother. Also, I have the feeling that she let everyone know she carried everyone, because these 10th house planets are in Pisces. There is a touch of the martyr here. The oppositions describe a conflict which is perceived first between the parents. Because it is the Virgo/Pisces axis, the conflict might be connected with emotionality versus aloofness and self-containment. Moon in Virgo needs its boundaries respected. It is very self-contained – "shy", if you like, not from fear, but from a strong sense of privacy. However deep one's feelings might be, Moon in Virgo doesn't like them splashed all over the walls and ceiling.

But Mars-Jupiter in Pisces is emotional and emotive, and tends to be very impulsive. Here is an archetypal conflict experienced through the parents, and it is also your own complex, Franco. You may be bringing this parental complex into your relationship with Ellen, and you may feel as though you keep getting cast in the role of your father, being accused by your mother of not feeling or giving enough. Your responses to such accusations may also reflect this complex, rather than the actuality of the relationship. How do you feel about what I am saying, Franco? Do you want to comment, or are you just going to sit quietly with that worried look on your face?

Franco: I always look this way when I am listening carefully.

Audience: When I look at this chart and see Sun in Aquarius and Moon in Virgo, and Mercury and Uranus in opposition with Gemini rising and Uranus in the 1st house, it seems to me Franco's mode of operation in life is extremely mental. His mind is very active, to the point that he might suffer from insomnia because he can't stop thinking. But in addition to the Pisces planets, he has a Venus-Pluto opposition, which matches all the Scorpio in Ellen's chart. And Ellen has the Sun square Uranus, and Jupiter in Aquarius, and a Virgo Ascendant, and all those planets in the 3rd house.

Liz: Yes, Ellen and Franco are, in a sense, manifestations of each other's inner world, and mirror each other's complexes. That is why I thought it would be interesting to start with these two charts. Each of you really embodies all the bits of the other one's chart that you don't actually want to own, or find difficult to live with. That could be an incredibly creative dynamic. The only trouble is that, if you don't understand what is happening when this mix-and-match complex setup gets triggered, you may turn on each other and inadvertently recreate both your family backgrounds. This may be happening at the moment, because both Uranus and Pluto are stirring up these cross-aspects.

Yes, this is a very cerebral chart, up to a point. But in addition to Mars-Jupiter in Pisces and the Venus-Pluto opposition, there is also a Venus-Neptune trine to help the insomniac get to sleep, and Neptune is in the 5th house – the house of "love". This is where Ellen's Jupiter-Saturn conjunction is placed. Franco's Saturn is also on the cusp of the 5th; they share this house placement of Saturn in common. Saturn is restrained, while Neptune is intensely romantic. As befits a Gemini Ascendant, there are two people in Franco's chart. One will be lived out freely and easily, and one may be harder to live, and is likely to be projected, at least in part. How long have you been together?

Ellen: Four years.

Liz: Initially you were probably both very happy to carry these things for each other. People usually do, when they first fall in love. You could each vicariously enjoy something unrecognised but extremely important and valuable within yourselves. Complexes have a great deal to do with why we fall in love. They are the hidden force behind any compulsive attraction. They colour what we imagine to be our "objective" taste, and what we find beautiful. All of that is fine, for a while. But over time, you may both want to develop in your own right what has previously been projected. And that might cause difficulty. Neither of you can live the unconscious dimensions of the chart, because the other one has laid claim to them. Franco can't play Pluto, because Ellen has taken that role. Of course he cast her in that part, and she colluded, because that is what she most easily expresses. But it is not the whole of who she is.

Ellen, can you see why your reluctance to be "selfish" and ask for your own space not only keeps your Jupiter squashed, but also makes it difficult for Franco to integrate his Venus-Pluto? He doesn't feel jealous and possessive because you are so busy doing it. So he gets away with pretending that he doesn't feel such things. You are the possessive one. Can you see how he sets you up, and how you set him up to be the uncommitted *puer?*

Franco: I do not set her up. I just allow her to be a Scorpio.

Liz: I know. Butter wouldn't melt in your mouth. For Venus-Pluto, however, one of the driving forces in life is a love that will burn and transform the soul. That is the secret romantic impetus behind this cool and rational nature. It is the urge to be lifted out of yourself through passion. But I think you want your cake and eat it too. You want the transformative experience without getting your fingers burned. One way to do this is to find a Scorpio who will act it out for you. Then you can offer the well-known Aquarian Code of Behaviour in Matters of the Heart. Rule One: one shouldn't try to own another person. Rule Two: one should always be honest, even when unnecessary. Rule Three: one should not have to explain where one is going and what one is doing. Rule Four: one should always discuss things reasonably. Rule Five: one should always stay friends afterward.

He needs you to be Scorpionic, Ellen, because if you stopped acting out Maria Callas on a bad day, he might find himself playing the role himself. If you suddenly started exhibiting that 5th house Jupiter in Aquarius, he might begin to feel deeply, intensely jealous. You have been carrying that bit of the complex for both of you, but now I think you are getting angry and don't want to do it any more. That could be part of what is happening with these transits.

Audience: They have both got Venus-Neptune.

Liz: Yes, they are both romantics who long for a perfect union. They also both have Sun-Uranus – Franco has a quincunx, Ellen a square. There is a great difference in temperament, but a great similarity in the lines along which the complexes are operating. They are participating in the same drama, and the same energies are at work, but they are viewing it from quite different perspectives because the air-water balance is different.

You are both very quiet. Are we on the wrong track, or are you rendered speechless because we are on the right one?

Ellen: Rendered speechless, I think.

Liz: At the moment I hope you will both be very careful with each other. There is a lot of anger about, but it belongs elsewhere. I think you must make the effort not to turn on each other and wound each other. Mars in both charts is being triggered by Pluto. This anger belongs to the complex, and the transit provides an opportunity to bring these issues into consciousness rather than being dominated by them. If you don't bring some awareness into the situation, you could each end up sounding like your mother sounded to your father and your father to your mother. You may find yourself using the same words and expressions. You might wind up acting out your parents' marriages, which would be very sad, because there is obviously a great deal of life and energy in the relationship.

Could I ask about your family background, Franco? I am interested in this Mars-Jupiter-Moon configuration on the meridian.

Franco: It was a traditional Italian family. There weren't any obvious problems. But my mother was very unhappy.

Liz: So your parents stuck together within a traditional framework, but underneath things were not as they seemed. Do you know the source of your mother's unhappiness?

Franco: My father was very unstable. You used the word before. I believe she found it very difficult.

Liz: By "unstable", do you mean he suffered breakdowns? Or just volatile moods?

Franco: Moods. He could sometimes be kind, and sometimes very angry, or very cold and cruel. But he was also unfaithful to her. There were terrible scenes.

Liz: Are these scenes what you fear now?

Franco: Yes. That is what I do not want in this relationship – scenes as my mother and father had.

Liz: So what you fear from Ellen is what your father got from your mother. They both seem to be telling you, "Be more stable. Stay with me. Don't go away. You're hurting me every time you turn your attention elsewhere."

Ellen: It also has to do with sacrificing ourselves to the past. It's as if we have to sacrifice ourselves to each other's past, to redeem something our parents did. I sometimes feel I have to do that for Franco.

Liz: The issue of sacrifice is bound to come up, because of Venus-Neptune trine Chiron in Pisces in your chart, and Venus trine a 5th house Neptune in Franco's chart. But I am not sure, if any sacrifice is required, that it must be the sacrifice of your freedom to live what you are. Trying to become the opposite of Franco's mother by sacrificing your emotional needs is not likely to solve anything. Nor would it be of any help for Franco to sacrifice his Aquarian independence of spirit to compensate for your lack of connection to a Sun-Uranus-Chiron father. Both of you have Venus-Neptune, and this combination often espouses the belief that real love involves suffering, sacrifice and the abnegation of happiness.

With Chiron opposite Uranus-Pluto in your chart, it is clear that you are not going to get off lightly. Not all aspects are fun. But this doesn't mean that the sacrifice of personal happiness is the only way in which the configuration can come out. There may be many possible channels of expression, one of which might be a commitment to a field of work which requires a lot of concentrated effort and tenacity, and the inevitability of disappointment from time to time. But you can't send the configuration back and ask for a grand trine. It is a T-cross involving an outer planet conjunction, and there are certain limitations which you may have to accept about your life – but without becoming a victim.

It is all very well to say, "Mars has to get free. It must be expressed." Yet whatever you do with this complex, Mars will still be square Chiron and Uranus-Pluto. It will never be as free as a Mars which only sextiles Jupiter. You can free it in the sense of being conscious of your needs and wishes and expressing them in an honest rather than a covert way. But much of what Mars in Sagittarius wants from life, you might not be able to have, because of the nature of your family background and the collective into which you were born – and more importantly, because of your own nature.

One of the things that configuration might imply is a powerful sense of obligation, because of Chiron in the 6th in Pisces. There may also be the desire for a tough life, a life which involves many challenges. That includes the kind of relationship you want. You may need something very difficult, where you have to struggle to make it work. That is probably part of your nature. I suspect you would be very bored with a man who gave you everything you wanted. Otherwise you would be sitting there with someone else. This is very different from "sacrifice" in the sense I believe you meant. It has to do with recognising the choices made by your own soul, and electing to cooperate with them, rather than feeling victimised by them.

Audience: What about the two Venuses in square by sign? Is this a problem of conflicting roles?

Liz: I think it is conflicting values rather than conflicting roles. Venus reflects what we value most – what makes us feel happy and contented, and in harmony with the cosmos. Ellen has Venus in Scorpio, so intense emotional exchange – even if this involves battles – will be a high priority. And emotional security matters, because Scorpio is a fixed sign. Venus in Scorpio wants emotional guarantees, and also, because it is in the 3rd house, it wants to speak about feelings. But Venus in Aquarius in the 9th says, "How can you guarantee feelings? That's nonsense. Feelings are irrational. They're too *personal*. How can I promise that I will feel exactly the same in twenty years? What matters is friendship, and a shared world-view."

Ellen has the capacity to appreciate Venus in Aquarius' values, because she has Jupiter in Aquarius and the Sun square Uranus. And Franco has a Venus-Pluto opposition, so if he is prepared to acknowledge it, he can understand something of Venus in Scorpio's world. But at the same time, this Venus-Venus square by sign might sometimes make both of you discontented. What each of you finds beautiful and pleasurable might not be pleasing to the other. It may be hard to share the things which give you the greatest happiness as individuals. You may find it difficult to make each other happy, and neither of you may know what you are doing wrong. This kind of disharmony is not usually destructive in the way that, say, Venus opposition Saturn across the charts might be. It can be accommodated, if the bond is strong, and you can both learn a lot about the intrinsic beauty in things which you might not have noticed before. But you may both feel rather lonely and unappreciated at times.

However, to compensate, Franco's Mars-Jupiter trines Ellen's Venus. So he can make her happy sexually, and also make her more aware of her worth as a woman. But there are going to be times when Ellen may simply have to accept the fact that Franco will not be as emotionally demonstrative as she would like him to be. And he may have to accept the fact that Ellen will not be as self-contained or as wildly enthusiastic about philosophical and political discussions as he might wish. Ellen has a square from Scorpio to Aquarius in her own chart, so the same conflict is inside her, between the mind and the heart. It is her own issue and he has been enlisted to act out the part.

Audience: So you don't fall in love, you fall into each other's complexes?

Liz: Yes, if you like. Loving may be a different matter. But falling in love invariably involves projection and the activation of complexes. Being in love is not a conscious state. It is a state of deep unconsciousness. That is not to say there is something wrong or pathological about it. How could there be, when it is one of life's great joys and transformative agents? Loving is not the same thing, however. It is not compulsive, and one can perceive the other person's reality. The two may, of course, occur together.

Ellen: I am curious about the meaning of Franco's Moon at the IC. It seems to be buried down there. Would there be a problem expressing the Moon?

Liz: It is clearly a problem for you. But no, I would not interpret this Moon placement as a problem in emotional expression. After all, the 4th is the Moon's natural house. The Moon at the IC has a very powerful attachment to roots and family background. It is also best expressed in private, and not necessarily verbally. Moon in Virgo at the IC may have a deep feeling for the land, for nature, for animals, for the country of one's birth. It may be extremely refined and full of delicate and sensuous feeling, but is not inclined to talk about it. Franco, I would expect you to have difficulty in expressing yourself on demand.

Franco: Yes, that is true. That is one of our difficulties.

Liz: This Moon is also trine Mercury and Chiron, and sextile Uranus. The oppositions to Mars and Jupiter may create emotional tension and erratic moods, but the Moon is disposed of by Mercury, which is the chart ruler, so it is not an inaccessible Moon. I am pretty sure that Franco knows what he feels most of the time, except for some of the more odorous Venus-Pluto stuff. And even that may be acknowledged, although unadmitted. But he isn't inclined to tell you what he feels, especially when you start getting insistent and bring Mars in Sagittarius in to hustle the Moon into responding. Mars in Sagittarius wants an immediate response, right now. But Ellen, the more you hammer at the Moon in Virgo, the more silent it gets. Moon in Virgo hates its boundaries being invaded without a prior invitation. It withdraws and becomes extremely rational and very controlled. You might feel that he has trouble expressing his Moon. But it may be that you are not giving him the chance to do it in his own way and time.

Ellen: My Mercury is in Scorpio conjunct Venus and Neptune. You said earlier that I need to talk about my feelings in depth. It's true. But Franco hates all that probing and airing of deep stuff.

Liz: Yes, you are the one, after all, who asked us to look at the charts. You want to talk about the relationship. That is right and appropriate, for you. But Mercury in Capricorn square Saturn is not wildly enthusiastic about doing this, nor is Moon in Virgo. These are not shallow placements, but they are not very happy about airing all the dirty linen, even in private. Despite this, Franco has managed to stay in the room with us, rather than walking out.

Franco: If I had run away I might have missed something.

Audience: I think that for these two people living together, it would be a very exciting life, but not very comfortable. It would be emotionally frustrating all the time.

Liz: From time to time, yes. But if you look at the two charts individually, do you think either of them wants everything to be comfortable all the time?

Audience: If they want to have fun together, yes.

Liz: Fun, like beauty, is in the eyes of the beholder. I remember reading an interview with the American actor, John Malkovich, who said his idea of a fun weekend was staying home and putting wood stain on a table. Ellen has Venus in Scorpio sextile Pluto, and Franco has Venus opposition Pluto. Ellen has the Moon in Aries and Franco has the Moon opposition Mars. Neither of them is going to opt for a nice, comfortable, trouble-free mate who enjoys shopping at Sainsbury's. They want a transformative relationship, and they crave the occasional good fight.

Audience: The problem is, with all that Mars-Moon stuff, the feelings may be very sore, and always on the edge of exploding.

Liz: A lot of the time, yes, but there are powerful mitigating factors. We have been focusing on the complexes, and have not looked at the traditional synastry contacts, which are extremely happy ones. In the end it is a question of balance. Complexes generate tension and difficulty, but also passionate attraction. And Ellen and Franco have a lot to give each other on the side of harmony. Ellen's Jupiter conjuncts Franco's Sun. Her Venus-Mercury-Neptune trines his Mars-Jupiter, and sextiles his Mercury. These aspects are very supportive. And we should not overlook the mutual contacts to the Moon's nodes. Ellen's nodal axis, in 22° Leo/Aquarius, is lined up exactly with Franco's Venus. Franco's nodal axis, in 19° Pisces/Virgo, is lined up within 2° of Ellen's Ascendant. So we might say that each of them triggers a sense of meaning and destiny in the other. They would both feel the relationship is somehow "right" and "meant". Does that seem to fit?

Ellen: Yes.

Franco: I would say so. I don't always feel this, but often.

Liz: With any relationship, it is a question of whether the complexes overwhelm the conscious interaction, or whether both can be contained in a workable balance. And of course there needs to be a basis other than mutual projection. There is enough harmonious synastry here to suggest a good deal of genuine affection and respect. But there is also a powerful shared complex, which will inevitably create an edge. The edge has probably always been there, and it probably always will be. It may be that your complexes and your natures both require it.

I haven't done a composite, so I can't see what the transits to the composite might be at the moment. Relationships have their own complexes, and these are described by the composite chart. Just to give you an idea of how this works, let's consider the composite Mars. There is a square between Mars in Ellen's chart and Mars in Franco's, so the composite Mars will be in semisquare to both – in about 17° Capricorn. Jupiter has recently stationed right on that composite Mars. That is another way of looking at the same thing, since transiting Jupiter at 17° Capricorn is semisquare natal Mars in both charts. Or we might look at the composite Venus, which is in 1° Capricorn. Last month Saturn moved into square to the composite Venus, and it will move back in December and make a station direct there. Throughout this year, the sense of harmony within the relationship is being challenged, perhaps by material difficulties, or perhaps by the necessity of defining separate boundaries.

Audience: Franco has the Sun and Saturn in trine. Ellen has got Saturn and the Ascendant in trine. This gives them both a good structure, to contain all these feelings.

Liz: Yes, there is great staying power in both of you. I believe you both appreciate the importance of sticking with it. Now we will leave you to get on with it.

The dissolving of projections

Audience: If you start to own your projections in a relationship, does that mean the relationship will end?

Liz: Sometimes. This often coincides with a particular transit. It depends on the nature of the projections, and how much actual respect and love there is between the two people. There are relationships which are built on nothing but projection. Usually these occur when a complex is pushing hard at the ego, and the choices one makes in terms of a partner have very little to do with personal taste, values and feelings. Such relationships are extremely compulsive. The whole thing is a hall of mirrors, and yes, it may well collapse when the projections come home – which they tend to do whether we wish it or not. Time and familiarity break apart many projections. Sometimes the beloved is wholly idealised, and when this breaks down, one is left with the sense that one has been deceived.

This kind of idealisation, followed by rage and disappointment, is what Melanie Klein called "splitting". In the stage before a baby begins to learn to handle the reality of mother as both "good" and "bad", nourishing and rejecting, the two are split, and the idealisation alternates starkly with the rage. Gradually this moves into what Klein called the "depressive position". But some people get stuck and never stop splitting. They can never quite allow another person to be lovable and flawed at the same time. The projections on the beloved are initially superhuman and totally idealised. This is, in effect, the divine "good" mother – even if he is male.

Then, when this idealised beloved doesn't provide an unconditional, unchanging supply of milk, he or she becomes the "bad" mother, and the projections become as awful as they were initially wonderful. One says, "How could I possibly have thought I was in love with that horrible person?" Love turns to hate, and the once-beloved is never forgiven for the betrayal. This kind of splitting is dreadfully common in people who are locked into a pattern of successive short-lived relationships. The real partner is never even glimpsed. When one can contain the ambivalent feelings of babyhood, which is another way of saying that one can acknowledge ordinary humanity in oneself and others, idealised projections may still provide the initial rush of attraction. But there is usually also genuine liking and respect for the other person, and that can deepen and sustain the relationship when the idealisation breaks apart through time and familiarity. It depends very much on what kind of projections are involved, and how much inner integration the person possesses.

I have already recommended Ethel Spector Person's book, *Love and Fateful Encounters*,[5] on other seminars. It is especially relevant to this theme. She writes primarily from a psychoanalytic perspective, about the feeling of fatedness that we experience when we fall in love with our idealised projections. She also describes the creative power these projections have on the recipient. When we are the "hook" for someone's positive projections, we feel really good, because we are seeing ourselves through the eyes of someone who perceives us as better than we perceive ourselves. This can be very healing, especially for someone who suffers from feelings of inferiority and woundedness. If someone sees the Sun, Moon and stars in our eyes, we suddenly think, "Yes, I actually have got some lovely qualities!" Positive projections are not just things that should be got rid of. They awaken us to positive aspects of ourselves.

Negative projections can be constructive too. If we are convinced that we can do no wrong, and someone is unloading his or her negative father-complex on us, we may realise that we do indeed have some rather unpleasant qualities which are providing the "hook". That can also be healing, because we come to know ourselves better. We usually have something that provides a hook, however small, when we attract projections from other people – especially if it always seems to be the same projection – unless the other person is completely out of touch with reality, and has been possessed by a complex. But the projector and projectee may place different value judgements on the complex. Remember George? He places a negative value on Saturn. The recipient of his projections might have strong Saturn qualities, but they may be expressed in a positive and constructive way.

Audience: Do you know any fairy tale or story that could help a child understand a little bit about complexes and projections? Obviously you cannot use such terms. But I think there are existential truths that children can understand, if you find the right words.

---

[5]Ethel Spector Person, *Love and Fateful Encounters*, Bloomsbury, London, 1988.

Liz: Every fairy tale portrays the enactment of complexes. Like myths, they describe archetypal patterns. They can be taken at both a parental and an archetypal level. Bruno Bettelheim explores the former in great depth in *The Uses of Enchantment*.[6] Marie-Louise Von Franz explores the latter in her various volumes about fairy tales.[7] Stories which involve the transformation of something ugly into something beautiful portray the breaking down of negative projections. Remember "Beauty and the Beast"? And all the poor princes and princesses who have to be frogs until someone recognises their worth?

Such stories present the resolution of conflicts in a natural and instinctual way. There is room for savagery, because a child's inner world can be extremely savage. There is a natural and timeless morality, not an artificially constructed or fashionable one. Fairy tales don't try to pretend that there is no suffering involved in human development. Suffering takes place. This is why I deeply mistrust what is currently being done to these stories in America. They are being rendered politically correct, which utterly destroys the deep and honest truths they have to teach.

Audience: Do you think political correctness is a collective complex which has taken over?

Liz: Yes.

A somatised complex – Ted's hayfever

Shall we look at another mass of seething complexes? Here is another chart from the group. What did you want us to focus on, Ted?

---

[6]Bruno Bettelheim, *The Uses of Enchantment*, Vintage Books, New York, 1977.
[7]See Marie-Louise von Franz, *Shadow and Evil in Fairytales* (Spring Publications, Zürich, 1974), *The Feminine in Fairytales* (Spring Publications, Zürich, 1972), and *Individuation in Fairytales* (Spring Publications, Zürich, 1977).

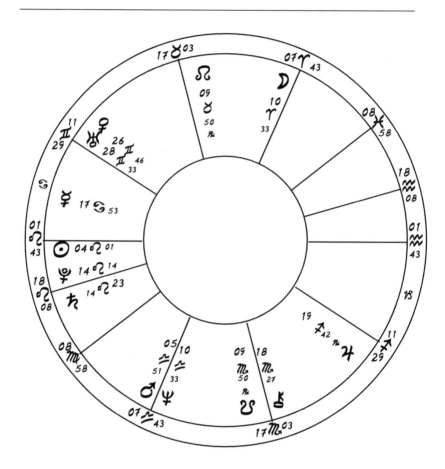

Ted
[Birth data withheld for reasons of confidentiality]

Ted: I wanted to explore the Venus-Uranus conjunction in late Gemini, because I have the impression that it has been pushed to the back of the queue. For the last twenty-five years, every time the Sun transits it, I burst out in hayfever. Transiting Venus is retrograde there at the moment. It hasn't started yet this year, but I'm just waiting. It is quite funny, because my hayfever takes me over for six weeks. I get very wet.

Liz: And you feel this hayfever is connected with a complex?

Ted: Yes. You made the point earlier that complexes may manifest as illnesses or psychosomatic symptoms. I was interested in exploring that, because the "big guns" don't give the idea much of a hearing.

Liz: Let me put up another simplistic diagram, before we begin to go into the chart. I have stolen this one from Marie-Louise Von Franz' book, *Projection and Re-Collection in Jungian Psychology*.[8] I think it is useful to see what importance she gives to the psychosomatic propensities of the complex. The left side of the diagram is concerned with the ancient concept of possession by gods and demons, and the physical suffering which this was understood to cause. I don't want to spend time on this, as it is unlikely that you are possessed by a demon. At least, it is unlikely in the framework of our present world-view, even though we still say, "Bless you!" when someone sneezes, echoing the ancient belief that a sneeze was the expulsion of an evil spirit from the body. Hayfever would suggest a whole crowd of them. But if you look at the right side of the diagram, where the psychological equivalents are listed, you will see that Von Franz has labeled the second level of the triangle "psychosomatic impairment by a constellated archetype". Something as common as hayfever may be viewed from this perspective. The "psychoid" archetypes are the same as the cosmic gods, and the malign intervention of a god in pagan times was usually viewed as the result of a failure to offer that god the "ritual worship" that he or she required.

The constellated archetype which produces "psychosomatic impairment" is therefore an angry deity, who demands greater recognition and relationship on the part of the ego. In Von Franz' thinking, the Christian concept of sin, which is linked to the psychological idea of the shadow and all the feelings of inferiority associated with this, makes it very hard for the ego to grant that archetype the acknowledgement it seeks. Before we can make the required relationship, we need to understand our "sin" differently,

---

[8]Marie-Louise Von Franz, *Projection and Re-Collection in Jungian Psychology*, Open Court, London, 1978, p. 118.

because we perceive the archetype through its lens, and it therefore seems to us evil. Are you with me so far?

Ted: Absolutely.

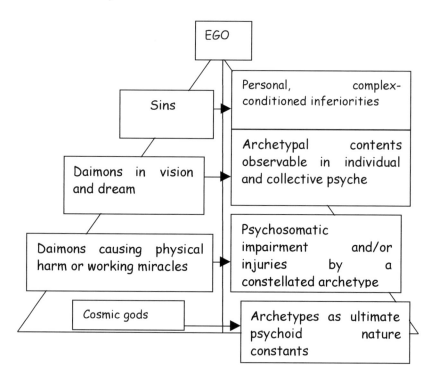

Historical concepts   Psychological equivalents

Liz: Now let's look at the Venus-Uranus conjunction and what sort of aspects it makes. Although technically in the 11th, this conjunction is so close to the cusp that it is pulled into the 12th. It is opposition Jupiter, which is not, I think, a malign opposition – Venus and Jupiter get on quite well, and so do Uranus and Jupiter. Both planets are sextile Saturn, which trines Jupiter. And there is an out-of-sign square from the Venus-Uranus to Mars.

Neptune is a little too far into Libra to be involved in this square, but Venus disposes of the Mars-Neptune conjunction. There is enormous energy in that angular Mars-Neptune, and because it is at the IC, opposition the Moon at the MC and with Mars ruling the MC, the family background is immediately implicated. Venus rules the IC, as well as disposing of the Mars-Neptune conjunction. We therefore need to consider all these planets, not just the Venus-Uranus.

Let's look at the physical qualities of hayfever and try to get a sense of what it might reflect as a symbol. Remember that we can work with concrete events as though they were dreams, and interpret them symbolically. What happens when you get hayfever?

Ted: I get depressed. My eyes get sore. I get headaches, I get problems with my nose, I get catarrh, but basically I get wet and I struggle with breath.

Liz: So you see it as a form of weeping.

Ted: Yes.

Liz: Weeping is basically a reaction to grief or unhappiness, isn't it? So we might say that the hayfever is a reaction to something.

Ted: It is a very explosive reaction. People are terrified of it.

Liz: Hayfever is usually attributed to an allergic reaction to pollen. Try playing around with the image of pollen.

Ted: It fertilises, brings new life.

Liz: Yes, it fertilises. "The flowers that bloom in the spring, tra la!" and so on. The time of nature's greatest fertility provokes a very explosive, even grief-stricken reaction.

Audience: And Mars, the ruler of Aries, is in detriment.

Liz: And the Moon is in Aries...

Audience: ...Which is the sign of spring.

Liz: There is some powerful issue around that rush of energy and potency and life-force that erupts in the spring.

Ted: Unconsciously I am walking round with part of my body saying, "I'm dying of this." And part of my body says, "No way."

Liz: Perhaps we should also remember that Gemini is traditionally the sign associated with breathing, and very often, when a person has chronic respiratory problems, there is an emphasis in Gemini in the chart. Here is a conjunction in Gemini that says, "I am not being expressed, I am not receiving the ritual worship I desire." How do you understand Venus-Uranus?

Ted: I sometimes think that beauty is very important to me. Beauty is a very necessary thing to me. I don't really want to live life without beauty. I think it is essential.

Liz: Yes, I understand. But that is also an important part of being a double Leo with a Mars-Neptune conjunction in Libra sextile the Sun. This combination alone would make you very receptive to beauty and the joy that beauty invokes. What else might Venus-Uranus mean?

Audience: He falls in and out of love all the time.

Liz: I was thinking the same thing. In the ordinary run of things, when the Sun goes over this conjunction each year, you might be inclined to fall in love, instead of going down with hayfever. Venus-Uranus is very susceptible to this kind of sudden joyful rush, which subsides equally suddenly when the object becomes too real.

Ted: I am susceptible. But my Leonine loyalty is very well established.

Liz: Now we are getting closer to the conflict inherent in the complex. Your basic temperament is very steady and very intense. Here is Saturn in Leo in the 2nd. It is loyal, devoted, and deeply responsible. What it has, it holds. The last thing in the world this

Saturn is going to be is flighty. Saturn is sextile the Venus-Uranus, so it curtails the wandering propensities of the conjunction. Aphrodite Urania is kept locked up, and allowed out for brief walks, heavily veiled and under supervision.

Here is Chiron in Scorpio in the 5th, square Saturn. Matters of love are taken with incredible seriousness.   Attachment is forever, and you can be deeply wounded if there is any fluctuation in a close emotional bond. There is tremendous loyalty and constancy reflected by many points in the chart. But then we have Venus-Uranus, and to add insult to injury, they are opposed by Jupiter in Sagittarius in the 5th. "Loyalty?" says Jupiter. "How do you spell that?" There is another man in this chart, perhaps one not unlike your father, because Venus rules the 4th; and he is not being lived. There seems to be a family conflict here, circling around themes of infidelity, fickleness, flightiness, abandonment, and inconstancy. Here is the "sin" in von Franz' diagram. It is a family complex, and you are mobilising very strong fixed attributes to keep it quiet – possibly because there is a great deal of pain behind it. But it is likely to be projected as well as somatised, and other people may act it out for you. You may chose partners who suddenly go away and leave you.

Ted: Yes. That has happened more than once. The worst was when Uranus opposed my Uranus.

Liz: So other people are carrying this Venus-Uranus for you, but it is actually yours.

Ted: It's mine. It has got that unconscious feel that just gets up my nose. That's all I know about it.

Liz: Up your nose? What an interesting turn of phrase. We are back to the ubiquitous "Bless you!" to ensure that the bad spirit, once expelled, doesn't re-enter. What is so frightening about that Venus-Uranus? Who got to play it in your childhood?

Ted: I guess it was my father. He was the one who quit.
Liz: He went off?

Ted: Yes. He served in the RAF during the war, but he was only demobbed for a while before he rejoined.

Liz: So he flew away literally as well as metaphorically.

Ted: Yes, he did.

Liz: And what happened to him?

Ted: He died in an air crash three months before I was born.

Liz: Here is the family background which has put flesh on the archetypal bones of the complex.

Ted: There's not another link to my father, is there? I thought I had got them all mapped out!

Liz: You might well have mapped out many of the personal issues. But there is always an archetypal background to a complex, and we need to look at it more carefully. Your father is a kind of stand-in for an archetypal image. Because you never knew him, he was never "humanised" in the way parents are when we experience them in their ordinariness day after day, and gradually begin to discern the gap between the archetype and the person. Unconsciously, your father remains a magical, superhuman figure, stuck in a timeless place. And your perceptions of him may also be heavily coloured by how your mother felt, which has probably made it harder for you to build a bridge to the real man.

If we look at the mythic level of that Venus-Uranus conjunction, what have we got? We have Aphrodite Urania, a deity who is by nature inconstant, and for whom love exists as a state of mind and spirit. Actual people don't matter; it is the perfect ideal that matters. Friendships are important, but constant falling in and out of love is inevitable because no love object can ever match the perfect ideal. Venus-Uranus in Gemini holds a vision of a cosmos which is full of light, movement and joy. If life begins to look too much like a burden, it flies away to look for a brighter world. This conjunction is a *puella* in the most creative sense – it is a butterfly, it is the messenger between heaven and earth, bringing visions of beauty and joy. Whether it is portrayed as male or female, the energy is the same. Perhaps we should think of Aphrodite Urania in a male form, because I believe it describes the archetypal level of your father-complex. It is the winged Eros, the beautiful but elusive mover of the wheels of the cosmos.

It may be that this tragedy in the family background strikes chords which go back long before your father, and all your associations with that dimension of life are therefore perceived as destructive or "sinful". There are a lot of questions I would like to ask, about your mother and her relationship to your father, and about why he rejoined the RAF after he was demobbed. Was he trying to escape something? What was he really like? But probably this isn't the time or place to go into such personal material. And no doubt you have asked all the questions yourself.

Audience: I keep looking at that 4th house Neptune and Mars. Mars makes him explode with sneezing and Neptune makes his eyes water. I wonder if there is something Ted is not touching, some deep *in utero* memory of his father going away.

Liz: That is an interesting observation. What time of year did he go?

Ted: He went at the end of April.

Liz: So your hayfever always coincides with the anniversary of his departure.

Ted: Yes, you are right.

Liz: It may not be only your personal father for whom you are grieving. Think of the time of year when your hayfever usually begins. T. S. Eliot wrote that "April is the cruelest month." Christ is crucified and resurrected, Attis is castrated, dies, and is reborn, Tammuz and Adonis die and are reborn – the spirit of nature, the beautiful *puer aeternus*, dies and is reborn. This is the time when the vernal equinox marks the death of the old year and the beginning of the new one, and in ancient times, for two weeks after the Aries-Libra full Moon following the equinox, they celebrated the rites of the suffering, death and resurrection of the god. There is a terrible sadness at this death of the old spirit which dies in the last degree of Pisces. There is a time of mourning, and then it is reborn. But your father was never reborn. He went away, but there was no resurrection. For a man with the Sun in Leo, attuned to the imagery of the divine child, beloved of the divine father and redeemer of the old, sick Grail King, this resurrection is desperately important, because it is Leo's spiritual regeneration.

Beneath the personal level of the father who flies away, there is the huge mythic backdrop of what this time of year symbolises. The youthful *puer* spirit can be reflected by Venus-Uranus; this conjunction is neither "masculine" nor "feminine", but a combination of the two. The youthful god comes and goes. He is a beautiful, ethereal, unstable and deeply melancholy mythic image. He never stays alive long enough to mature into full manhood. He is androgynous and winged; he is Adonis, Attis, Tammuz and Osiris. He is one of the ancient lineage of beautiful youths who die and are resurrected, and represent the fragile spirit of nature that comes alive in the spring with the flowers that make the pollen that gives you hayfever. So your father is not just your father. He is also a symbolic carrier of beauty and immortality. But somehow you haven't come to the resurrection yet. The deeper level of this complex is mythic.

Ted: Yes, because we both suffered in the same way. He didn't have a boyhood and neither did I. He flew away without returning. I tied myself to fathering to compensate. Neither of us was resurrected.

Liz: I think a question remains which none of us can really answer, which is, "Great, nice mythic stuff, but what do you do about it?" If your hayfever starts again, it should be pretty soon, shouldn't it?

Ted: Yes, it is imminent.

Liz: It may be useful to use your imagination to enter into that depressed, grief-stricken place that you are somatising, and start writing about it – not analytically, but poetically. What kind of images are invoked in this place? What kind of images does your body give you when it is in that state? Try to ignore whatever controls your rational consciousness tries to place on these images, because your body seems to be expressing something which at present can't come out in any other way. Maybe you have to grieve for the god who dies, who is also your father. Perhaps you haven't really grieved properly.

Audience: I think he has tried to be very responsible.

Ted: That is very true. I became a father myself when I was only twenty-two.

Liz: You have been determined to become what your father wasn't. It's a kind of compensation for the "sin".

Ted: That's right.

Liz: And in the process you have stifled what your father is in you. You have compensated for his inability to be there by being there steadfastly for your own child, and you have proven something to yourself about your own strength and loyalty in the process. But in doing it with such intensity, you have, as the ancients might have put it, angered the deity represented by Venus-Uranus in the 12th.

Audience: There is a lot of activity going on in the chart right now. It's not only the transiting Venus.

Liz: Yes, it seems that all hell is breaking loose. Or perhaps all heaven might be a better term. Transiting Uranus is exactly opposite the Sun at the moment, which suggests a breaking open, a freeing of the sense of individuality. Uranus is also trine Mars in 5° Libra, and semisquare Jupiter at 19° Sagittarius. This may encourage more healthy self-centredness, and temper that excessive sense of duty.

Saturn is opposing Mars, trine the Sun, and approaching a conjunction to the Moon and the MC. This could help affirm your bond with your father through some kind of inner separation from the mother. The Moon at the MC suggests that you have always been deeply identified with her feelings, and this may have made it hard for you to see your father as anything other than the man who willfully abandoned you both. Transiting Chiron is meanwhile at the IC, going over Mars-Neptune. Issues around the father are likely to rise to the surface, perhaps initially in a painful way but ultimately giving you much deeper insight.

Meanwhile, transiting Pluto is trine the Sun and Ascendant. All these transits are going to continue through next spring, at which time transiting Jupiter will join the fun and form an opposition to the Sun and a trine to Mars, and transiting Mars will go stationary retrograde in early Libra right on its own place. I doubt that all these aspects are concerned only with your hayfever. Saturn at the MC suggests that there are big changes underway in your work and your direction, and Uranus transiting through the 7th may bring some surprising revelations, inner or outer, in your personal life. But all these things are bound up together, and the same complex underpins it all.

Audience: Most people do outgrow hayfever.

Ted: I can't get much older!

Audience: There are some who get it very young.

Ted: It started when I was around twenty-one.

Liz: In other words, just before you got married.

Ted: Yes. I started messing with women and drugs at twenty-one.

Liz: At that time transiting Uranus would have been square Venus and square its own place. We all have this Uranus-Uranus square at that age. So you started acting out your Venus-Uranus conjunction, and the hayfever arrived right on cue, like a kind of punishment. Then, at twenty-two, Saturn squared its own place, and you married. This is very interesting. Because of the clustering of important transits at the moment, I would suggest that, if you do get hayfever again this year, you try to explore it more imaginatively. It might not be enough to just endure it or analyse it. Try to give voice to the feelings which accompany it. Physical symptoms always provoke feelings and fantasies. Let them loose, and then see what happens.

Audience: I was wondering if there is a subtle blaming of the mother who drove the father away, and an inability to forgive her.

Ted: No, I don't feel that. I was much more involved with redeeming my mother, because I was the reason she lived. She once said to me that when my father was killed, she would have thrown herself under a bus had it not been for me.

Liz: What a very helpful thing to tell a child. So you had to be responsible for her. You had to be there for her, or else she would have destroyed herself. No wonder it is a "sin" to be Venus-Uranus.

Ted: I worked very hard to be there for her.

Liz: Your mother's need to turn you into a surrogate Saturnian husband landed on fertile soil. I would not see this as a situation where the mother is the "culprit". She wanted something which your own nature was ready to give, because that is how you are made and that is the nature of your complex. You yourself were predisposed to pit your capacity for loyalty against the dangerous fluidity of the *puer's* spirit. From the very beginning, something in you evidently said, "Yes, all right, I will carry this burden." Another child might not have done so, but you took it on. And another child might not have perceived the archetypal figure you perceived in your vanished father. Once again, this is what I meant when I said that our complexes are our fate.

Thank you for being so open about yourself, Ted. I am afraid we will have to end now; we have run out of time. Thank you all for coming and participating.

Bibliography

Bettelheim, Bruno, *The Uses of Enchantment*, Vintage Books, New York, 1977.

Ellenberger, Henri F., *The Discovery of the Unconscious*, Basic Books, Inc., New York, 1970.

Jung, C. G., "Answer to Job", in *Psychology and Religion, Collected Works, Vol. 11*, Routledge & Kegan Paul, London, 1973.

Nicoll, Allardyce, *The World of Harlequin*, Cambridge University Press, 1963.

Person, Ethel Spector, *Love and Fateful Encounters*, Bloomsbury, London, 1988.

Von Franz, Marie-Louise, *Individuation in Fairytales*, Spring Publications, Zürich, 1977.

Von Franz, Marie-Louise, *Projection and Re-Collection in Jungian Psychology*, Open Court, London, 1978.

Von Franz, Marie-Louise, *Shadow and Evil in Fairytales*, Spring Publications, Zürich, 1974,

Von Franz, Marie-Louise, *The Feminine in Fairytales*, Spring Publications, Zürich, 1972.

Part Two: A Psychological Approach to Transits and Progressions

This seminar was given on 8 June, 1996 at Regents College, London as part of the Spring Term of the seminar programme of the Centre for Psychological Astrology.

Introduction: the nature of prediction

We have a challenging theme to explore today. How do we interpret transits and progressions from a psychological perspective? I would like to begin by saying that, although the internal nature of our exploration should be clear to all of you, I am not in any way denying the value and long tradition of predictive work in astrology. But the two are not mutually exclusive. "Psychological" does not mean only "inner". Too many of us have had experience of accurate prognostications of a specific and concrete kind to pretend that the planets are not related to the outer as well as the inner world, or that it is impossible to predict certain kinds of events in certain situations.

Many years ago I gave a seminar for the Wrekin Trust, which was then transcribed, edited and turned into a book called *The Outer Planets and Their Cycles.*[9] In passing, while examining the birth chart of the Soviet Union, I made a prediction about its future. It was really a kind of throwaway, as I did not have much knowledge at the time about the subtleties of mundane astrology. My rather naive prediction was based on the fact that Pluto would creep up to conjunct the Soviet Union's natal Sun in seven years' time. I had observed that every time a powerful transit hit this natal Sun in Scorpio, the Soviet leadership changed. In mundane terms, this is a fairly obvious and simple conclusion, since the Sun in a national chart reflects, amongst other things, the nation's leadership.

---

[9]Liz Greene, *The Outer Planets and Their Cycles*, CRCS, Reno, Nevada, 1983.

The reason I expected a collapse rather than yet another typical struggle for the leadership was because Pluto is rather more all-encompassing than the other outer planets. It tends to wipe everything clean, and nothing remains of the original form or structure. There were other transits – for example, the Uranus-Neptune-Saturn conjunction in the first decanate of Capricorn, approaching the Soviet Union's Venus in the 4th house – that suggested that this imminent collapse was going to be like a marriage breakup. It would be a disintegration from within rather than from without, and all the various satellite countries would start asking for a divorce. This was how I read it at the time, and there was no indication in 1982 of the events to come. A new leader was certainly on the cards; but a total collapse was unthinkable. In the subsequent seven years, therefore, I didn't think about it. Then everything came to pass as predicted. So every now and then, astrologers can make accurate prognostications. I am sure that many of you have had this experience.

However, focusing solely on the predictive side of astrology is like a medical doctor focusing solely on a bodily symptom, rather than considering the whole individual and the interrelationship of body and psyche. Over the years, I have come to believe that a great deal of what we assume to be fated, in terms of transits and progressions, is not fate at all – it is our unconscious complexes at work. As individuals and as a collective, we unwittingly contribute to, create, or are drawn into situations which enact internal issues – either because we have been avoiding these issues in the past, or because they are simply ripe and the *kairos,* the right moment, has arrived.

It would be very foolish to imagine that all life situations are the individual's creation, because many are not. One cannot say that six million individual Jews had particular transiting or progressed aspects which meant that they would be taken away to the concentration camps. It is sheer lunacy to suggest such a thing, as well as an avoidance of our unconscious collusion when such acts of brutality occur on a mass level. There are collective movements and upheavals, as well as "natural" disasters such as floods and earthquakes, which may supersede individual choice, complexes, and will. There may be other, deeper spiritual factors as well, about which I am not in any position to comment.

Many people in the astrological world believe in karma. I am not a disbeliever. But I feel it is a lot more complicated than what someone once called the "ding-dong theory" – one was nice or naughty in one's last life and therefore one is rewarded or punished in this one. As morality is such a deeply subjective and relative thing, I find little value in such simplistic approaches to the realm of the spirit. But there may well be something that continues through and beyond a single mortal incarnation, which accrues "substance" according to the choices made in each lifetime, and which acts as a magnet for the kind of experiences we attract. This may be a factor above and beyond one lifetime's efforts at consciousness. Those of you who attended the seminar on complexes might remember that we discussed this issue then.

There may also be factors in the family inheritance over which we have no control. However unfair it may seem, we are the inheritors of family conflicts and complexes that have crystallised over many generations, and these often act as a kind of fate. If such conflicts have remained largely unresolved, we may lack the mobility to choose or avoid certain events, and any individual undoubtedly possesses greater freedom of choice if there is not a heavy backlog of accrued psychological inheritance. Thus there are many factors other than individual consciousness which determine how transits and progressions are going to be expressed. Nevertheless, a great deal of what we assume to be predictable may not be predictable at all, once individual consciousness has begun to expand the levels at which we experience reality. For this reason I believe we need to try to live as though we have the freedom to work with our transits and progressions on a psychological level. We may then have room to transform or alter future events, or deal more creatively with anything that is our own creation due to the workings of unconscious complexes. As for those things about which we truly have no choice, we will find out soon enough, and can hopefully learn to accept and live with our necessity in a more tranquil spirit.

One of my main objectives in exploring today's theme is to suggest that we may have more freedom than we think, on levels of which we might not initially be aware. If we can learn to work with the planetary movements with more insight and less of a literal, "Uranus is going over whatnot and therefore such-and-such will happen" approach, we might discover what Pico della Mirandola meant when he said that human beings are co-creators with God.

Literal-mindedness doesn't do us justice as astrologers. It can also be downright destructive, because there is, of course, such a thing as a self-fulfilling prophecy. Because our perceptions are invariably distorted by our individual complexes, we are inclined to interpret transits and progressions not according to what they might mean, but according to what our complexes tell us they will "do" to us. Even the most orthodox "traditional" astrologer is not really able to be objective when it comes to predicting events. We cannot even be certain what an "event" really is, since so much depends on how and when the person registers what has happened. Our assumptions about the future are just as heavily coloured by our own psyches as our assumptions about the present.

A psychological approach to transits and progressions is more challenging than a literal one, because it involves taking responsibility for what is symbolised by the configurations in one's birth chart. It also necessitates learning to work with traditional predictive techniques on more than one level. It doesn't mean that there is no value in trying to get a sense of how a planetary movement is likely to come out on a material level. It is as foolish to ignore this dimension of life as it is to ignore the psyche. If one has the progressed Sun square a 2nd house Neptune while transiting Saturn is conjuncting that natal Neptune, it may not be a good idea to go into a business partnership with someone whose background and credentials one knows little about. The concrete application of astrological principles can be of great value to us. But without the background of psychological understanding preceding any literal interpretation, I think we may, much of the time, create our own fate, manifest our own predictions, and generate considerable suffering when it may not be at all necessary to do so.

Levels of expression

Now I would like to examine the different levels on which transits and progressions are likely to be expressed. Many of you will have heard me talk about this at other seminars, but at the risk of boring you I will repeat it, because it seems to me such a fundamental part of understanding planetary movements. We can explore the differences between transits and progressions as we go along.

Meaning or teleology

There are three main levels on which transits and progressions seem to operate. Some of you may think of more than three. But as a general overview, I have found this division quite useful. The first level is the one which is likely to be of greatest concern to the spiritually inclined astrologer – the deeper meaning of a particular transit or progressed aspect. By "meaning", I am referring to its teleology – its ultimate purpose in terms of the evolution of the personality, the soul, or both. Those of us who have a religious or spiritual bent assume that the cosmos has some kind of purpose, and that there is meaning in the experiences which occur in an individual life. Events therefore have a hidden design, a teaching function, and if we can grow because of what happens to us, we are fulfilling some greater spiritual or evolutionary design.

Whether such a cosmic design really exists is an arguable issue. However certain we might be about the objective existence of such a deeper pattern – which is another way of saying that God, or the gods, exist – none of us is in a position to prove it. We may, in fact, project a highly personal perception of meaning onto an utterly arbitrary and unconnected universe. But even if this were the case, a great many people experience life as containing an innate meaning and purpose, and this conviction, whether projection or not, can be life-sustaining. It is psychologically and spiritually creative even if it is not "true" in any scientific sense.

When we view transits and progressions from this perspective, we ask ourselves, "What am I meant to be learning from this conjunction of transiting Saturn to my Sun? What is this progression of Venus square natal Pluto meant to be teaching me? What can I discover while transiting Uranus is opposition my Moon? What is the positive potential of this progressed Mars sextile Chiron?" This approach is an extremely important dimension of any transit or progressed aspect. Although I have used the term "spiritual", it is as psychological as an exploration of parental complexes, because we are considering the planetary movements in terms of the evolution of the psyche. We might see this view as belonging to transpersonal or archetypal psychology, rather than reductive psychology. But it is psychological nevertheless. Without this perspective we are treating astrology, and ourselves, as merely mechanical.

Some astrologers focus almost entirely on this level, and consider other levels too negative or materialistic. They will look at transiting Pluto over natal Chiron, or progressed Venus square Saturn, and they will talk primarily about what is on offer in terms of growth. Let's say transiting Saturn is coming up to oppose one's natal Sun in the 5th house. If we approach this transit from a teleological perspective, we may talk about a developing sense of who one is as an individual. Out of this transit one could get a stronger sense of identity, a clearer sense of purpose, and a realisation of one's creative talents. The challenges of the material world might hurt, but they can ultimately result in a deeper commitment to a particular vocational direction. Any events which occur, however difficult, are "meant" to make one more aware of oneself.

The teleological approach on its own is often sufficient with nice transits and progressions, like transiting Jupiter trine the Moon, or progressed Sun sextile Uranus. When we experience harmonious planetary movements, we tend to "plug into" a sense of cosmic purpose and goodness, and such interpretations fit how we feel at the time. The meaning and the emotional response at the time of the transit or progressed aspect seem to be in accord. When less attractive planetary movements come along, one can still interpret them in terms of potential. Often such an approach can be wonderfully healing in the midst of turmoil, stress and pain.

We may see a veritable planetary nightmare coming along, and we need to ask ourselves what potential for growth might be hidden beneath all the stress. It is very important that we keep this in mind, and are able to communicate it. But we may also need to remember that, however profound and positive the meaning, the individual experiencing such transits and progressions may not be in any condition to listen to evolutionary possibilities. For many people, particularly those who have been accustomed to viewing reality from a purely material or extraverted perspective, the deeper meaning and potential of a difficult transit or progressed aspect may not be accessible until long afterwards. While they are going through it, they may be aware of, and able to hear about, nothing except their conflict and pain.

Emotional stuff

Transits and progressed aspects also involve an emotional level of expression. This too is psychological, but it is more concerned with the individual's responses, both on the feeling level and in terms of the unconscious complexes which are being activated. The past as well as the present is usually involved. Our emotional responses at the time of a transit or progressed aspect are extremely complicated, and a lot depends on how much self–understanding we have achieved, how strong the ego is, what kind of containment we can bring to the feelings which are activated, and how much we know about our parental complexes.

Past experiences are almost invariably activated by any important transit or progression, especially if a similar transit or progression has occurred in the past, and we need to consider what sort of memories and associations we have accrued under successive planetary movements to a particular natal placement. Also, an experience which may be ultimately positive and productive in meaning may, by its very nature, require suffering as part of its process. All these factors lie on the emotional level, and because of this, the emotional response to a transit may be wildly different from its teleology.

There may appear to be absolutely no relationship between the meaning of a transit or progressed aspect and how one actually feels and behaves at the time. The astrologer, not to mention the client, can get extremely confused by this. I have seen wonderful transits of Jupiter come along which feel anything but wonderful at the time. We tend to sit and wait hopefully for Jupiter, thinking, "Oh, how splendid, something fantastic is going to come my way when Jupiter conjuncts my Sun." Something wonderful may indeed happen from the teleological perspective, but what happens in actual life may be an emotional nightmare.

If one is a very earthy person, for example, with lots of planets in Taurus and a strong Saturn and a powerful need for structure and stability, and one has been faithfully married for twenty-three years and has three children, two cars, a safe job, and a mortgage on a large house, and progressed Venus arrives on natal Jupiter in the 5th house, what ensues may be anything but wonderful on the emotional and material level. We astrologers may know that the opening up of the heart which such a progression reflects may ultimately be just what the person needs. But meanwhile, what is he going to tell his wife? And can he afford to pay the court costs?

Much depends on how one has been living one's life, and whether one is in touch with all the different configurations in one's birth chart. It is unlikely that any of us can claim we are totally in touch with everything within ourselves, so it is a question of the degree of unconsciousness. If a person has married early for security or social reasons, and the potential excesses of a 5th house Jupiter have been ruthlessly suppressed, such a progressed aspect may unleash a great deal of conflict and suffering. The person may fall in love with someone other than his or her spouse, and must then face the consequences. Sometimes it is the spouse who acts out the renegade Jupiter. Perhaps some of you have seen this kind of apparently vicarious experience in the charts of clients, or in your own charts. One sits waiting for Prince or Princess Charming to arrive when transiting Uranus goes over natal Venus, and one's partner runs off instead. Why are we so reluctant to understand how powerfully the unconscious psyche affects the manner in which a transit or progression is expressed?

Sometimes there may be an experience of great depression with an apparently happy transit. I have seen this very often when the so-called Benefics are involved. Jupiter arrives on one's natal Sun, or progressed Sun conjuncts Venus, and the astrologer assumes that a time of happiness and fulfillment has arrived. Instead, the person plunges into a black hole. Conflicts may be activated by a happy experience, reflecting deep-rooted feelings of guilt linked with the parents. Or it may be that Jupiter makes us aware of unlived potentials, which can exacerbate feelings of failure. If we are so cemented into a rigid structure that we have cut off all the bridges to future possibilities, we may ask ourselves, "What is the point of life?" Jupiter can be connected with deep depression because the gap between our potentials and our present situation may be revealed in a blinding moment of painful truth, and this gap may make us feel ashamed of how we have been wasting our lives.

So the emotional response to a transit or progressed aspect may be very different from its meaning. We need to be able to communicate with a client who is in the throes of an emotional state which bears little resemblance to what we understand as the teleology of the transit or progression. We may be so full of what a particular planetary movement means that we forget that the person may not feel that way at all. He or she may be very frightened by what is happening, even if on a teleological level it is going to be transformative. We may know that the end result will be positive, but the client may not feel it. And if we cannot relate to the immediate emotional situation of the client, and explore any personal psychological issues which could help him or her to find a way through to the deeper meaning, then all our enlightened interpretations will wind up sounding like a load of waffle.

One level without the other is incomplete. It is extremely important to understand how people feel under difficult transits. Many transits are very painful, and it is stupid and shortsighted to pretend that they are not, or that one "ought" to feel optimistic. If somebody with progressed Venus square natal Chiron is sitting there saying, "I'm miserable!" we cannot very well respond by saying, "Nonsense, you should be feeling positive and enthusiastic, because this is a time of healing." We can certainly talk about healing, but we also need to empathise with the sense of isolation, inferiority and unfair treatment which the person is likely to be experiencing, so that we can make intelligent comments about *why* he or she is feeling this way. We may also need to talk about the past, especially those times when Chiron was activated by other important transits or progressed aspects. The emotions which accompany profound inner change are often extremely uncomfortable.

I will be spending quite a lot of time looking at this emotional level of transits and progressions during the course of the day. In some ways it is the most complex of the three levels of expression, because we are confronted with the mystery of individual consciousness. Emotional reality is the glue binding the level of meaning with the level of manifestation, and it is also the area in which we have some opportunity to exercise individual freedom of choice. By the time a psychological issue is so solidified that it must be expressed in concrete form, we can only plan for the future, but we cannot undo what has been knit into the reality of the present. This is really the ground which Jung and Hillman call the soul, and it is the mediator between spirit and matter.

The person with transiting Saturn opposition natal Sun, who has, in terms of teleology, such a superb opportunity for a greater sense of personal identity, may be deeply depressed and insecure. He or she may feel like a failure, and all the achievements of the past may seem worthless. Parental issues may rise to the surface, particularly those connected with the father and the father-complex. The challenges of this transit may not be perceived as challenges, but as victimisation. Questions about the basis of personal identity may have to be raised, and many attitudes and assumptions about life may need to be cleared away before a healthier world-view can grow in their place. The relationship with the masculine – within oneself and with the men in one's life – may have to undergo a complete re-evaluation. There are a lot of things that people can feel under the transit of Saturn opposition the Sun that are not very pleasant, and when people feel bad, they want to know that the astrologer can recognise their unhappiness and help them to understand its basis. The more spiritually inclined astrologer may need some experience of psychotherapy to work on this level.

Materialisation

The third level of transits and progressions is the level of materialisation. It is in this sphere that many, although not all, older astrological approaches have their focus. Working on this level, the astrologer is primarily concerned with what will happen in the material world under a particular transit or progressed aspect. This may seem a simple approach, but it is actually extremely complex. There are many issues, inner and outer, that may affect whether a planetary movement will materialise on a concrete level, and in what way. One important factor is the individual's complexes, which have a tendency to materialise if they are highly charged and dissociated from ego-consciousness. If there is such a thing as karma, that may also be a factor; and the family inheritance, genetic and psychological, is also relevant. And we should not neglect the importance of the environment, especially the prevailing social attitudes and world-view, because the individual is always circumscribed, to a greater or lesser extent, by the collective.

There may also be a destiny in every life – something that the soul or Self may wish to accomplish in a particular lifetime. In Greek philosophical thought there were two kinds of fate affecting the individual, *erinyes* and *daimon*. The former might roughly be equated with ancestral inheritance, and the latter with the soul's destiny or purpose. And there may be a collective fate as well – entire nations or peoples may have a specific destiny in terms of human evolution, and a specific ancestral inheritance. As individuals we are sometimes caught in movements that are bigger than we are, because we are part of a larger humanity which is itself attuned to planetary cycles. Therefore we share in the vicissitudes of this larger humanity, and may have to cope with the psychological baggage we inherit from our racial, religious, social and national background.

These are philosophical questions about which each of you will have your own individual beliefs and convictions. I am mentioning them because they may be factors in the materialisation of transits and progressions. Of all these areas I have touched on, the only one where we can be really effective as individuals is the sphere of our unconscious complexes. Our ability to recognise, contain, work with and transform these may ultimately affect the collective of which we are a part. It may even affect our "karma". Behind the prediction of any event there is always an individual or a group of individuals. In the end we are forced back into our own gardens to contemplate what is growing there, if we wish to understand why and what kind of events are likely to happen to us.

When does an event occur?

There is another important issue about the materialisation of transits and progressions and the prediction of events. The moment we consider what is going to "happen", we enter the fraught area of what constitutes an event, and we are in very mysterious terrain. I will give you an example of how complicated it can be.

Recently I had a second session with a client who first came to see me several years ago. I had heard nothing from her in the intervening years. I noticed that transiting Pluto was now approaching her 4th house Chiron in 5° Sagittarius. It transpired that, a few years earlier, her father had died. My client told me that when he died, it hadn't meant anything to her. It was apparently a non-event. She had not had a close relationship with him. She believed that she felt little for him, and therefore when he died it was as though nothing had happened, because he had never been there to start with. This is how she put it. We had discussed her relationship with her father during our first session, and her perceptions had not changed since then. I am not inclined to view Chiron's placement as an area of life where the individual feels nothing. But my client was convinced that this was so, and that was where the discussion about her father ended.

The reason she came to see me for a second session was that she had become very upset about her brother-in-law, who was ill.

He had been developing small malignant growths, and although the doctors kept operating and removing these, new ones kept growing, and she feared that he would die. What she couldn't understand was that, although she was not close to this brother-in-law, the idea of his dying filled her with blind terror. Contemplating the death of anyone else, including her husband (she had married since I had last seen her), evoked no such drastic response.

For some reason the role this brother-in-law played in her life was far greater than she had thought. She saw very little of him. They had a friendly relationship, but she wasn't close to the sister who had married him, nor had she ever entertained erotic fantasies about him. She couldn't understand why she was now in a state of extreme anxiety about the mere idea that this man might leave her life. She called her state "an irrational obsession", which indeed it was. We should also note that, along with transiting Pluto conjunct Chiron, transiting Neptune was crossing and re-crossing her natal Sun.

Gradually it became apparent that the real event which underpinned her anxiety was the death of her father. This may sound strange, because he had already died, but on the inner level he had not died at all. There was no grief, no emotional separation, and no sense of loss at the time of the actual death. Yet the presence of Chiron in the 4th, combined with a Sun-Jupiter trine, suggested to me that there were highly ambivalent feelings about this father, extremely positive as well as extremely painful, which had been totally suppressed. This lady was in the habit of suppressing virtually all feeling. Although extremely intelligent, she had a curious blankness, as though there were no one home.

The real death seemed to be coincident with transiting Pluto coming up to natal Chiron, four or five years after the father's physical death. My client's brother-in-law had fulfilled the role of father for her. His Saturn, at 22° Cancer, was exactly opposite her natal Sun at 22° Capricorn. He evidently felt deeply responsible for her, although he saw little of her, and she responded to his Saturnian qualities as a daughter might. She took him for granted; he made her feel safe. He was always there in the background. He was extremely stable. She knew that if she ever got into any trouble she could go to him, financially and emotionally. She had never exercised this option, but she knew he would be there if she needed him. She had allocated to him unconscious feelings of a childlike kind which were bound up with her actual father, with whom she had clearly had a very painful and complicated relationship that she had been denying for most of her adult life.

If we were to try to predict the events suggested by this transit of Pluto over Chiron in the 4th, we might say, "She is going to move house, or emigrate. Or perhaps she will divorce." Or, if we are a little braver, we might say, "Here is the death of a parent, and it may raise some very painful and confusing feelings." The death of the father is certainly a likely expression of this transit, especially if we take into account the conjunction of transiting Neptune to the natal Sun. But how can the father die if he is already dead?

For my client, the event of her father's death is taking place now. That is her reality, although it may not be yours or mine. This death and all its painful accompanying feelings have nothing to do with the flesh-and-blood father being popped into his coffin. Now, for the first time, my client is facing the fear and panic and grief which she denied when the actual parent made his exit. She has focused these feelings on a man who is not really the person she is feeling the feelings about. Her brother-in-law is a surrogate, a hook for her unconscious father-complex. Whether or not the brother-in-law will die is not made clear by the transit. In a sense it is not even relevant. It is the possibility of his death which has invoked such a powerful reaction. We might say that his possible death is synchronous with the ripening of a father-complex which is now ready to become conscious.

This kind of dislocation of inner and outer events upsets our notions of what we define as reality. An event, in the sense that it reflects a transit or progressed aspect, may not be quite what we think it is, because the time when concrete things happen to a person may not be a true reflection of when they happen inside. Our emotional recognition of and involvement with the occurrences of our lives are what make an event real. We remember what has impact on us, and the impact may not come at the time of the physical occurrence. The brief example I have given is not uncommon. The time that things happen is not always the same as the time that they physically occur. This is why material events may pass with an inexplicable lack of relevant transits and progressions, even if we expect something important to show up in the chart.

As another example, let's consider the end of a relationship. When does this happen? When the two people physically part? This is obviously not always the case, not even when it is death which has caused the separation. For many people that relationship is still alive and powerful years after the physical separation, and one partner may still be angry, grief-stricken, and unable to get over the loss even though the other partner has long since gone. This is particularly tragic and poignant when a parent loses a child, and cannot process the loss. The child's room may be preserved like a kind of museum, with nothing moved or changed, as though he or she were expected to return at any moment. This can also happen with divorcing couples. The ex-partner's photograph is never removed from the mantelpiece, and no new love is allowed to sit in the old love's favourite chair.

Often people are quite unconscious of this, and are then shocked by their own violent reactions when, sometimes many years later, the ex-wife or ex-husband remarries. All hell breaks loose, as though the vanished partner has been put on ice in a secret compartment of the soul. Even though he or she has gone physically, the beloved presence has still been there internally, and when the ex-partner makes a commitment elsewhere, all the grief and pain are experienced as though the separation has only just happened. In fact it *has* only just happened, although it may have happened on the concrete level years before. And that may be when we see progressed Venus conjunct Pluto, or transiting Saturn over Venus, or transiting Uranus opposition the Moon in the 7th house.

When relationships end, they may end for only one of the two people. Also, relationships sometimes end long before they actually end. A couple may remain living together all their lives, but the life left the relationship two or ten or thirty years before. This also may be reflected by the relevant transit or progressed aspect, even though there is no physical event. Movements in the chart may describe the end of something, but there may be no visible end, no concrete event. Or the relevant transit or progressed aspect may describe the end of something long after everyone else says, "Oh, it ended years ago." Endings, like beginnings, are a highly individual business. Different people take different lengths of time to process events. Some events mean nothing to one person, and a great deal to another. Death itself means different things to different people, and one person may be full of anger and terror and deny his or her mortal illness to the very last, while another is peacefully resigned to death as a rite of passage years before the actual passing.

The perception of an event – its timing, its significance, and the interpretation we give it – is described by the synchronous transit or progression, and thus the real "events" described by planetary movements are those occurring in the psyche. An external event itself may or may not be relevant to the individual. If one has a powerful transit or progressed aspect, an event may have great significance and can completely overturn one's life; but if the same event occurs at another time, when there is not such a powerful concordance of aspects, it is experienced entirely differently and may not be felt as "major". The event itself is not that important as an objective entity. But what one experiences internally attaches importance and meaning to the event, according to the transit or progression coincident with it.

I know this is a difficult thing to grasp, because our habitual way of interpreting reality is that anything happening "out there" is objective. The physical manifestation may be objective (although that too is open to question), but the way we perceive it is not. It is very disturbing to explore the ways in which our perceptions colour what is "out there". And our perceptions are what the horoscope describes, including the transits and progressions over natal placements. When transiting Saturn is on the Moon, we are predisposed to perceive and respond to situations in a certain way, which is likely to be more realistic, and more negative, than when transiting Neptune is on the Moon. When transiting Uranus is on Mercury we perceive truths different from the ones we perceive when transiting Chiron is on Mercury. When transiting Jupiter is on Venus, we experience people differently from when transiting Pluto is on Venus. Is it the people that have changed, or is it ourselves? And if it is indeed the people, might our changing perceptions influence the kind of people we attract, as well as the attitudes they show to us?

If a separation occurs during a transit of Uranus trine Venus, it will have a completely different feeling from one which occurs under a transit of Pluto opposition Venus. In the eyes of others, the event may look the same. Joe Bloggs leaves his wife and runs off with his eighteen-year-old secretary. But if Joe's wife has Uranus trine Venus at the time, she will probably heave a great sigh of relief to be rid of him and free at last. If she has Pluto opposition Venus, the most bitter thing about the whole situation is the betrayal. If progressed Venus opposes Neptune, she may feel victimised. If transiting Saturn squares Venus, she may be preoccupied with material survival and a gnawing sense of inferiority in the face of a humiliating rejection.

We should never underestimate the importance of the subjective dimension of events. How an event feels, how it is understood and perceived, and when it really registers as a reality will be totally different according to the prevailing astrological "weather" as well as the natal chart, because the individual is receiving the event in an individual way. This complicates our definitions of what constitutes an event. The level can vary enormously, and so can the timing. And the event reflected by a particular planetary movement may or may not be connected with a physical happening.

Things become even more complicated when we consider the heavy planets. They may hang about forming particular aspects to the birth chart for two or three years, or, in the case of Pluto, even longer, moving back and forth as they make their stations direct and retrograde. A whole series of apparently unconnected events may occur during the time of these outer planet transits, and all these events will be perceived through a lens coloured by the particular tint of the transit. Thus all the events that occur during such a period seem to carry a similar feeling or meaning.

If those same events happened at any other time, they would not be experienced in the same way. They would seem random. We would not say, "Ah, there is a connection here between my father's death two years ago, the fight I had with my employer last year, and the new love affair I just started this month; it is all part of the same package." It is the transit or progression which reflects this sense of concurrence, not the events themselves. We tend, in the main, to remember periods of our lives, rather than one specific item after another, and this sense of a period, a specific time span coloured by certain kinds of happenings, is deeply subjective and linked with the presiding transits and progressions of the time.

We have to be extremely careful when we try to define an event, because the more closely we look, the more subjective it becomes. Have any of you ever examined a death astrologically? By this I mean not only the aspects occurring in the chart of the person who dies, but also those occurring in the charts of those close to the dead person. We might think that death is such a terribly specific event, which occurs at a particular moment, and we can set up a chart for that precise moment. But no astrologer has successfully come up with a typical "death signature" – it looks different in every chart. And the aspects which are building up, sometimes for several years, may be as relevant as those occurring at the precise moment.

Trying to make sense of the materialisation of transits and progressions means that we need to try to keep in mind all three levels of expression, including the emotional and teleological levels. These latter two have a direct bearing on the actuality of events. Not only are all three levels relevant, but it is also wise to remember all the complexities of each of these levels. Only when we have got a bigger picture of what is going on can we responsibly say, "There is a likelihood that such-and-such will happen." Without this rounded picture, we are throwing darts with a blindfold on. We might get a bulls-eye, but we might also hit someone in the eye.

The repetition of events

Audience: I can validate what you are saying on a personal level. In my mid–forties I finally processed my father leaving when I was a child. What triggered it was something that happened on a mountain climb with my husband. I was suddenly terrified to look up, because I was sure he was going to fall and die, and I realised in the middle of my panic that this is what I felt in childhood.

Liz: How many years were there between the two experiences?

Audience: About forty years.

Liz: It is a good illustration of the way in which events which seem totally disparate can be linked by a similar emotion and meaning. Do you know the transits and progressions on either occasion?

Audience: On the mountain climb, transiting Pluto was in 25° Scorpio, just coming up to my IC. It had been in 25° Leo, conjuncting my progressed Sun and square my IC, at the time my father left.

Liz: So not only the feeling and the meaning, but also the transiting planet and the vulnerable point in the birth chart, were the same – although the events appear to be unconnected. I am, of course, assuming that your husband didn't fall off the mountain.

The triggering of complexes

Before we look at specific transits and progressions, I wanted to emphasise the importance of complexes. A transiting or progressed planet aspecting a natal planet describes the triggering of a fundamental pattern within us. Many of you came to the seminar on complexes, where we looked at this in detail. I don't want to spend much time going over this material again, but I felt it would be of value to mention it.

When we look at a birth chart, we are looking at a set of characters in a play. Not only the characters, but the rudimentary outlines of a plot, are described by the natal placements and aspects. But we must make up the dialogue as we go along, and this is reflected by the transits and progressed aspects, which designate when each act is due to begin and when each character has his or her cue to enter the stage and get involved with the action. The characters and plot are the archetypal patterns, the basic bones of the chart, which in psychological terms are called complexes. More circumspect astrologers like to use the word "potentials", although in earlier times we simply called these patterns fate. The characters sit about backstage, and smoke and drink and play cards and talk amongst themselves. Any time a transit or progressed aspect triggers the birth chart, it is like a cue. The stage manager says, "Get out on stage. You have a speech to make and certain things you have to do; they are waiting for you; get moving!"

During the course of a lifetime, every point in the birth chart will receive transiting and progressed aspects many, many times. When we think of transits and progressions, we usually think of the next big one that is coming along. We think about Pluto going over something, or Uranus, or Saturn. We may forget that the transiting Moon conjuncts every planet once a month, and the transiting Sun conjuncts every planet once a year. In order to understand the impact of the big transits, we may need to spend some time considering the impact of the little ones over a long period of time. The characters who enter the stage under the big movements are not new; we have met them all before. They have been there since our birth. But the degree of consciousness and experience that we have accrued since the last time they were on stage affects how they deliver their lines. And there are memories attached to each successive entrance, because the placements in the natal chart act as containers of experience. Each time something moves over a natal position, our experiences feed a sort of memory pool of emotional associations and images. This is what is meant by a complex – an aggregate of associated experiences, feelings, ideas, and images clustered around a central archetypal core.

Specific transits

Transiting Pluto and powerlessness

Let's go back to your comment earlier. What was happening in your family when your father left?

Audience: Well, I think my father realised he had done the wrong thing when he married my Mum. He hadn't known she was pregnant with me at the time they married, and neither did she. I was just about conceived. I think once he knew, he probably realised he had made a grave mistake. He married on impulse, and then I think he felt trapped.

Liz: How old were you when he left?

Audience: I was three.

Liz: Can you tell us more about your transits and progressions at that age? You mentioned transiting Pluto square the IC and conjuncting the progressed Sun.

Audience: Yes, the progressed Sun was at 25° Leo, which is a sensitive degree that runs down through the generations of the family. My IC is 25° Scorpio, and my natal Sun is 22° 30'Leo. When my progressed Sun hit that 25° point, he left.

Liz: Any other transits or progressed aspects?

Audience: I'm not sure. I haven't thought it through enough. When I was born Pluto was in 13° Leo, and my Sun is in 22° Leo. And I have a Venus-Moon conjunction at the end of Leo, around 26°. I suppose transiting Pluto was also conjuncting the Venus-Moon.

Liz: This gives us a fuller picture of how you must have felt at the time. I think it is important to examine the planetary movements at such times very carefully – it is how we really learn astrology. So in adulthood transiting Pluto came along again, and at the time of the mountain climbing expedition it formed a square to the Venus-Moon instead of a conjunction, and a conjunction to the IC instead of a square.

Audience: Looking back, I think the anxiety about my husband was building up for a few years. But I wasn't really aware of it at the time. My mother died in 1992, when Pluto was square the Sun. I think it may have started then. In fact my husband went off on one of his climbing trips the day my mother died. Pretty good, eh?

Liz: Sometimes I marvel at how people unconsciously work these things out so precisely. The idea of natal planets having memories can be very illuminating. During the course of your childhood, Pluto gradually moved over your stellium of Leo planets. When your father left it had arrived at the Venus-Moon conjunction. Let's look at this transit from the point of view of its meaning, as well as its emotional repercussions on a child.

Audience: I don't remember feeling much at the time. I remember my mother being very upset. But I don't think I really processed it at all.

Liz: This is what I mean by the emotional level of a transit. Pluto moving over the Moon-Venus describes certain feelings of a very powerful kind. But your reaction, to both the event and the feelings, seems to have been dissociation. Your father's departure was a non-event on the conscious level, although clearly, from the importance of the transit, it was anything but a non-event on deeper levels. The age of three is the period Freud referred to as Oedipal, because the attachment to the parent of the opposite sex is extremely strong at this time. But the feelings got pushed into the unconscious, because they were probably too painful and frightening for a child to carry. There is no conscious memory of these feelings until they are raised to the surface by a trigger in adult life, forty years later. What does it feel like to have Pluto go over a Venus-Moon conjunction? All of you have had transiting Pluto aspecting one or other of these planets at some time.

Audience: Well, I was very frightened when Pluto squared the Moon-Venus and I faced the possibility of the loss of my husband. I became very depressed afterward. I also felt a lot of anger at the abandonment I experienced every time he went off on one of his trips. But at another level I was aware, because I was working with my chart. I knew, up to a point, what was going on. So he and I were able to create a container within the relationship, and eventually the result was that he gave me my freedom and I gave him his. So I come down to London to the CPA seminars, and he goes off with his friends on another climb.

Liz: Perhaps it comes to the same thing.

Audience: It's exactly what is happening. He's up a mountain and I'm down here in London.

Liz: You have described anger at being abandoned, and a fear of loss. But these are emotional reactions to something else. We have still not got to the fundamental underlying feeling which triggers this anger and fear of loss. We need to look even deeper. What is it that makes people suddenly say, "Oh my God, everything is going to be ripped away from me!"? What is it that we experience?

Audience: It is powerlessness.

Liz: Yes, the underlying feeling is powerlessness, which makes us rage at our impotence and cower in terror before what might be done to us. When we encounter Pluto, we feel we are facing vast, invisible forces over which we have no control. Once we understand that core response as one of the chief emotional signatures of Pluto, we can see that any Pluto transit, even if not to the same planet, will reflect an activation of the same feeling. We are facing that which we cannot master. We are confronted by the forces of life and death. We are flattened by something hugely impersonal, cyclical and instinctual – a force of nature beyond the ego's ability to categorise and control.

Audience: But it isn't enough to sit with feelings of powerlessness. Eventually we have got to do something about it.

Liz: What does "do something" mean? Sometimes it is impossible for the ego to act decisively during the course of a Pluto transit. It is a peculiar characteristic of this planet to reflect situations in which nothing can be done, or, whatever we do, it won't be what we want. Pluto often calls upon us to learn how to wait gracefully. The "doing something" may involve developing a particular attitude, rather than taking action. There are many responses we can have to feelings of powerlessness. Rage is one. Passive victimisation and the accruing of resentment and self-pity are another. A quiet acceptance of a deeper purpose is a third. A strenuous effort to re-establish ego-control is a fourth. There are many more. Each of these responses can lead to particular consequences.

Feelings of powerlessness are one of the characteristic emotional accompaniments to transiting and progressed aspects involving Pluto, especially the hard aspects – although I have seen the same thing with trines and sextiles. Powerlessness is not the meaning of the transit. It is one of the most typical emotional states which accompanies the transit. If we wish to explore the meaning, we must ask the question: What can powerlessness teach us? What are the most creative responses to it? What can Pluto offer us, as distinct from how it feels? What can such a transit show us, and what kind of positive qualities could it inspire within us?

Audience: The ability to let go.

Liz: Yes, we can learn humility, which is really what letting go is about. We can find the means to accept with grace and trust what we cannot change, and we can discover how to let go when we must, rather than trying to control life. We can learn to put our faith in something we cannot see. And we can learn to endure because there is nothing else we can do. Through enduring we lose our false pride, and discover that which is indestructible within us. We learn how to survive and how to wait. We may also release blocked energy, or clear away poisons which belong to the family past. If we cannot or will not learn these lessons, we may develop bitterness, spite, vindictiveness, and a deep rage toward life. "No one is ever going to put me in that position again," we say to ourselves. Then our relationships become power-battles, and in trying to manipulate and control other people we create the very betrayal or abandonment we are trying to avoid. And then, if we are very silly, we blame the planet for our fate.

Audience: I think it was awareness of this that enabled my husband and I to create a container in the relationship and sort it out subsequently.

Liz: What you have done, in effect, is become conscious of the deeper potential of the transit as well as its emotional repercussions. Because of this effort, you seem to have altered the level on which the transit expressed itself. If you had not tried to contain your feelings and make connections with an earlier experience of abandonment, you might have made life very difficult for your husband, and he may have responded by rejecting you, leaving you feeling even more powerless and resentful.

Audience: Well, I didn't stamp down on my feelings. I let them out. I tried not to subject him to all the emotions. But I didn't pretend that I wasn't afraid. I think it is dangerous to suppress that kind of energy.

Liz: I agree with you, because if Plutonian feelings are cut off from consciousness they will build up over time and find an indirect and more destructive outlet. But people feel powerless in the face of what they cannot see or understand, and they often try to suppress the emotions that rise up during Pluto transits and progressions. Powerlessness makes us feel like infants, and erodes our pride and self-respect. Rage is a very natural human reaction to feelings of powerlessness. One can see it in every infant. Behind the baby's tantrum is a dreadful feeling of total dependency and helplessness. It is extremely unpleasant to be completely out of control, and to feel other people are running the show. It is even more unpleasant when one's own primitive emotions are running the show. A great deal depends on character. If there are a lot of "heroic" configurations in the birth chart – a dominant Mars, a lot of Leo, Scorpio, or Aries, a strong and well-aspected Saturn – feelings of powerlessness are likely to be especially unacceptable, and rage is a very natural response.

This is an area where we do have a choice. We can choose to be honest with ourselves, and admit that we are frightened and bewildered by what we are facing. Or we can pretend to be what we are not, and wear a brave mask to impress others and ourselves with our toughness and strength. That can sometimes be a bad mistake when dealing with Pluto. The kind of strength we may need is a quieter, less showy strength – patience and slowly achieved insight, rather than an attempt to be superhuman. It is not a good idea to suppress the kind of rage that tends to come up around a transit like this, because much of it is the rage of a young child. The later situation is a trigger for the earlier one. A sense of powerlessness must have been one of the chief feelings you experienced at the age of three, because there was nothing you could do to make your father stay. The events going on around you were totally out of your control, and probably beyond your understanding as well. You could scream and shout, you could plead, you could cry, you could get sick, you could do anything you liked – but you couldn't make him stay once he had made up his mind to go.

All the rage and fear of the three-year-old quietly waited until the square of Pluto to the Venus-Moon conjunction forty years later. To try to stifle it again, when it was already stifled the first time, would be asking for trouble. Sometimes this kind of suppression can produce physical problems. It is one of the reasons why we often manifest difficult transits through illnesses. We have repeatedly blocked our feelings every time something has hit a sensitive point in the chart, and all the emotions and memories build up until the body can't take the stress any longer. The feelings are then somatised, because it is the only way these feelings can make themselves known. It is possible that we have more choice than we realise in affecting the future course of transits over the same point in the chart. How we deal with our memories of earlier transits is very important. If we don't know that there are such memories, we may not deal with them very gracefully.

Thank you for giving us your experience as an example, because it illustrates a number of important points. When we see Pluto going over a planet in our own chart or a client's chart, it is a good idea to try to learn something about the planet's memories before we interpret the transit. Has Pluto ever made a major aspect to this point before? Does the natal planet aspect Pluto? What else does it aspect? What other powerful transits or progressed aspects have hit it in the early part of life? Every planet has its own memory system, built up through time and experience. When did transiting Saturn aspect it? Or Uranus, or Neptune, or Chiron? What kinds of things happened, and how did one feel at the time?

On the practical level we obviously cannot do this with every client. We may have neither the time or the inclination to wade through the whole of the life history of a person we are going to meet once for a two-hour session. But before the client arrives, we can make a note of really big and obvious planetary movements in early life. Then we know that the present transit will trigger a particular period of childhood during which important issues may have occurred. And we can ask the client about that period in early life. More importantly, we can learn something about the way planets "remember" by reviewing our own charts. We can sift through our own life histories in order to understand the characteristic feelings that go with each planet, which will be triggered by subsequent transits and progressions.

Pluto and betrayal

Audience: Can I give you my own example? In 1989 Pluto conjuncted my Venus. I lost my job in Germany, I lost my German nationality, and I lost most of my friends. But I survived. Today I am here. Pluto is now trine Pluto. I had to learn to let go. When these things happened, that is what I knew intellectually, even if it was hard emotionally.

Liz: Can you tell us more about the circumstances?

Audience: My aunt, who was nearly ninety, left her house to my brother. She had promised it to me, for myself and my children. We went to visit her not long before she died, and I went away feeling my future was secure. Then she rang me at 9.00 in the morning on my birthday, to tell me that she had decided to leave the house to my brother. He had visited her in the meantime. I don't know what he said to her. She died very soon after.

Liz: This sounds like the beginning of an Agatha Christie plot. Presumably no one was murdered? So you were, in effect, facing forces over which you had no control, in the form of a brother who coveted your inheritance, and an aunt who had no loyalty to you.

Audience: Yes, exactly. And there is also something else. Venus is in Scorpio in the 2nd house in my birth chart, opposition Uranus. So Pluto not only conjuncted Venus but also opposed Uranus in the 8th house, which is the house of legacies.

Liz: That would be the literal interpretation of the aspect. But I think we should look deeper. What are the roots of this situation?

Audience: She was my mother's sister. My mother had died.

Liz: Your assumption was that she would be true to her word and leave you her property. Yet it would appear she bore you some ill-will, since she told you on your birthday that you could expect nothing. That is a deliberately cruel thing to do; it smacks of malice. But it seems you had no inkling of this undercurrent in your relationship with her. It would probably take us all day to explore this situation in depth, so we won't. But it might be worth asking why you should have relied on these rather questionable relatives to ensure your security, rather than building it for yourself. Did you never have any feeling or intuition that they were not on your side?

Audience: It was written in the will.

Liz: That doesn't always mean a lot. Many people change their wills just before death, because the fear of death brings emotions to the surface that they haven't acknowledged earlier. A realist would have said to you long ago that it is not a good idea to count your chickens until they hatch, especially where legacies are concerned.

Audience: It still hurts.

Liz: Of course it still hurts. It was a terrible betrayal. Did it teach you anything?

Audience: It taught me to let go.

Liz: It may also have taught you something about your own naivete. This is another important dimension of the meaning of Pluto transits and progressions. Pluto teaches us that we cannot afford to remain children if we wish to survive in life. Human beings are not always honourable. Just because they are your relatives, they are not automatically going to be devoid of the common human attributes of avarice and envy – and perhaps *because* they are your relatives, they may display more of these attributes to you than they might to friends or strangers. Very nice people sometimes get very difficult when it comes to the inheritance of money and property.

Your Venus is in the 2nd house, with Uranus in the 8th. There is a lesson in nonattachment suggested here, and also perhaps a need to discover your value and worth through your own resources. With such a natal aspect, you need to rely on what is within you, rather than on what an aunt says she is going to give you. You cannot look to the family to give you security in life, and you have learned a very hard, painful lesson through betrayal.

This is another dimension of Pluto's emotional expression. A sense of betrayal is often part of Pluto's process, and through this betrayal a complex is triggered and brought to light. What is betrayal? We expect or assume something from another person, and then the person turns out not to be what we expected or assumed. We are lied to, humiliated, or deceived. We feel an oath, promise or vow has been broken – even if no such oath was made in the first place. Our expectation of others is somehow not in accord with their reality; otherwise we would not be so surprised. I am sure many of you here would be somewhat suspicious if an elderly relative began talking about which one of two siblings would be the beneficiary of her estate. It is a very manipulative thing to do, since it is guaranteed to trigger rivalry and anxiety.

James Hillman wrote an essay on betrayal[10] which is well worth reading. He tells the story of a father who encourages his son to jump off the top of the staircase. Each time the son jumps, he catches him. Then, one day, he deliberately steps out of the way, and the boy falls and hurts himself. The father says, "That will teach you – never trust anyone, even if it's your own father." Ultimately that little bit of mistrust, born out of hard experience, makes us say to ourselves, "Well, they mean well, and they love me, but they are human. No one knows what another person will do under pressure. I could be let down." We lose what Hillman calls "primal trust". This means we must learn to look after ourselves if we have to. That is Pluto's survival gift. Too much of it leads to paranoia and corrosive mistrust. But a little of it is vitally necessary.

The experience of betrayal is often the way in which we become adults. There is no guarantee that we will deal with it creatively. But if we can avoid spite and vindictiveness, we may gain a great deal. Hillman goes on to point out that it is often the experience of betrayal that makes us real. All the anger, rage, impotence, humiliation, and sense of victimisation make us recognise life and human nature as they are, rather than as we want them to be.

Audience: I have a Mars-Pluto-Sun aspect in my chart, and I remember the moment when I realised that I was ultimately alone. At first it was very painful, but quite soon after that I thought, "Well, it is actually very comforting to come to terms with that."

Liz: What you say is very important. The experience of aloneness is both an emotional concomitant of Pluto and a key to its deeper meaning. Here the emotional and teleological levels come together, and often so do the circumstances. Why do we rage at being abandoned? Because we are lonely, and are made aware of our aloneness. We are forced to be alone when we don't want to be. We feel we shouldn't have to be alone, and we fear it; and when we are coerced into experiencing it, we may also experience enormous rage.

---

[10]James Hillman, "Betrayal", in *Loose Ends,* Spring Publications, Zürich, 1975, pp. 63-81.

But without a capacity to survive alone, we must always look to others for our survival, and then we may resent them because they have power over us.

As far as your example goes, could one have predicted that your family would behave in this way? Possibly. If one knew the people involved, and knew the charts and looked at the synastry, it is very likely that an astrologer could have said to you, "Don't count on this. Be pleasantly surprised if you get the house as promised, but don't build your future expectations on what your aunt has told you she will give you – especially when you are clearly being played off against your brother." A 2nd house Venus may reflect something within you which needs to discover its own resources, and one way or another this need will probably be fulfilled – if not by choice, then by someone else's choice.

Audience: With Uranus in the 8th opposite Venus in the 2nd, some kind of loss with regard to money or inheritance is predictable.

Liz: It is predictable in the sense that a certain kind of attitude, combined with a certain kind of external situation, will produce a certain kind of chemical reaction when the right transit or progressed aspect comes along. The external situation may be unavoidable. Your aunt, before her death, did exactly as she pleased, and what pleased her took no account of earlier promises. That was unavoidable. But the attitude is something which lies within the individual, and the more conscious we are of our expectations and assumptions about life and other people, the less inevitable the outcome will be.

The issue of predictability, with a transit like this one, is subtler than you seem to be suggesting. If one has adopted attitudes that are in some way a denial of, or contrary to, what the chart describes, the likelihood is that the transit or progressed aspect will serve as a kind of trigger to an unconscious complex, which will then blow up in a predictable fashion. So if one is sitting with a 2nd house Venus opposite Uranus in the 8th, and one is busy opening bank accounts in preparation for the family inheritance, then one may be setting oneself up for a big surprise when Pluto comes along.

It might be argued that attitude reflects character, and is therefore inevitable. But here, with a natal opposition, the attitude is split. The ego seems to have been aligned solely with Venus, and what Uranus signifies has been ignored or suppressed. We are therefore dealing with an unconscious complex. Freedom from family attachments and obligations, especially on the material level, may be "fated" in the sense that it is part of the teleology of the chart. But the means by which that freedom is achieved is perhaps not so fated.

Families behave like this all the time. Someone says, "Oh, I've changed my will. I'm leaving all my worldly possessions to so-and-so." Innumerable clever solicitors have grown rich because families, when it comes to legacies, are often the least trustworthy of all natural organisms. You experienced this unreliability during a Pluto transit. So to you it was a life-shattering betrayal, because that was your emotional response to the event. The transit doesn't describe the event itself as an inevitable, preordained fate.

No astrologer could say, based on this transit alone, "Ah, Pluto is going over Venus, and therefore your aunt is going to change her will in favour of your brother before she dies." That is not what the transit describes. A fuller knowledge of your aunt's chart and your brother's, combined with your own, might have suggested the sort of behaviour that you encountered. Then we would be in the realm of relationship and family dynamics, and we might be able to put the whole picture together. But the transit of Pluto does not, in itself, make any such statement. It seems to describe a period which lasts for quite a long time, several years in fact, during which you are likely to become aware, sometimes painfully, of what you have not yet developed in terms of self-sufficiency and self-worth. It is a 2nd house Venus that is receiving the transit. It also describes a time when your definitions of love and relationship might be subject to some very important changes, which would ultimately deepen you and leave you more realistic and mature.

Audience: I keep getting the feeling that you are suggesting she could have acted differently, and that what happened was due to her own decisions.

Liz: No, that is not what I am suggesting. I just said a moment ago that the aunt's behaviour was probably unavoidable. There is no way in which we can control other people's actions and decisions, other than threatening them at gunpoint, and sometimes even that doesn't work. But there was an expectation that, because a family member promised something, it was carved in stone like the Ten Commandments. This kind of expectation is bound to exacerbate, if it did not actually create, the terrible sense of shock and betrayal which made this experience so difficult to bear.

Audience: But don't you think that natal Pluto on my MC means I would be fated to experience loss or upheaval in the world? I lost my nationality.

Liz: The MC tells us a lot about the persona, the role one plays on the world's stage. Nationality means different things to different people. To the extent that it provides you with your role in the world, it is part of your persona. Pluto at the MC, apart from what it might tell us about your experience of your mother, also suggests that there is a profound need to find your place in life without the conventional external props that give so many people their sense of worldly security. With Pluto placed there, it is not always a good idea to depend upon formal structures or collectively acceptable labels to make one's way in the world. If one does, sooner or later there may be a backlash – but not necessarily through losing one's nationality.

No transit or progressed aspect can put into a chart what is not already in it. The planetary movements will only invoke what is already an inherent, *a priori* part of the individual's life pattern – whether or not he or she is conscious of it. Venus in the 2nd house opposition Uranus in the 8th seems to convey a message about travelling light. Whatever your values are, and whatever you perceive as your resources, your relationships with other people have to be flexible enough to allow you to let go when necessary. It is important that you develop a sense of security based on your individual talents, skills and values, because if you try to depend on other people for a sense of safety in life, they may let you down or go away. This doesn't mean that you can't have trustworthy relationships. But you cannot expect others to provide you with security. If they do so, well and good; but if they don't, you need to know that you can manage on your own.

Another way of reading this is that you need to remain open and flexible rather than defining yourself and your place in life in too rigid and sharply defined a fashion. We are back to the meaning of the transit, rather than what event might occur. The Venus-Uranus opposition, combined with Pluto at the MC, seems to be saying, "Be flexible enough not to identify yourself solely as German, Danish, British, or whatever. Then, if you should have to give up the label of a specific nationality, you will still know who and what you are." There is something here that suggests a requirement of your own soul. When we go against these deeper requirements – which we inevitably do, especially when young – we may have to face external circumstances which remind us of the path we need to be on.

Audience: My Venus resists this requirement! I don't want to have to be that flexible!

Liz: I am sure you don't. None of us finds the outer planets infallibly congenial when it comes to having our personal wishes fulfilled. But some of your feeling of resistance may be because you didn't choose what happened to you. It was forced on you. Therefore your pride has been injured, as well as your feelings, and it all seems very unfair. But was this truly forced on you? If you had the opportunity now to go back in time and alter the sequence of events according to what you now know about life and yourself, would you really have wanted your aunt's house?

Audience: I don't know. It is a very difficult question to answer. I would not be where I am now, if I had inherited the house and stayed there. My life would have been entirely different, and with hindsight I do not believe it would have been better. You are asking if I accept the life I have, and what I am, because if I do accept it then I would not want to change what happened.

Liz: Yes, in the end that is the question we are always left with.

The unfolding process of successive transits

Audience: She said that Pluto was now trine her Pluto. Would that be a release and an easing of the pain?

Liz: It might be. With all transiting and progressed aspects, we need to think about what we have accrued from the past, because that will be reflected in the way the current transit or progressed aspect is expressed. If, under previous aspects to and from Pluto, there has been a willingness to learn something from experiences of betrayal and powerlessness, then a transiting trine might well reflect a time when inner serenity and acceptance are possible. One discovers one's indestructibility, and one can forgive and let go of the past. But not everyone is willing to learn from experience. Some people go through the same routine over and over again, and they just get more bitter or try to find another scapegoat. Hopefully there is just enough willingness to ask, "What can I learn from this?" It is rather like Parsifal when he has his vision of the Grail. He has to ask the right question: "Whom does the Grail serve?" We might ask this about a transit. Whom and what does this transit really serve?

If we can ask these questions, then with each successive planetary movement we can add a bit more wisdom to our fund of experience about a particular archetypal pattern in life. Then, yes, I think that under a transit such as Pluto trine Pluto one can say, "Now I understand why it was all necessary. I have got something really solid and worthwhile out of all that pain." But if there is a continuing refusal to look more deeply at the inner level of the experience, then a trine can be just as upsetting as a square or an opposition. The textbook benignity of a trine is not always to be trusted. On the level of meaning, it may reflect release and harmony. But one may feel quite differently at the time, because of a backlog of unresolved conflict and anger. If one is determined not to be released, and holds on stubbornly to one's grievances, then the invitation to relax and come to terms may provoke a lot of anger.

Audience: So a transiting quincunx could mean a coming to fruition.

Liz: Any transiting aspect can reflect something coming to fruition. I don't feel happy about categorising the aspects quite so sharply, because consciousness affects how we experience them. It is the natal planet and its situation which make the real statement, not the specific nature of the aspect made by the transiting planet – although it is important. Successive transits reflect an ongoing, cumulative process of increasing consciousness of our birth chart configurations. With all transits and progressions, we need to have a sense of what we have done with that natal planet, up until now. Our own attitudes have an enormous effect on whether the time of a transit feels like yet another episode of the same horrible mess, or a resolution or coming to fruition of something.

Whatever planetary movements are going on, no natal planet exists in isolation. It is usually embedded in aspect configurations to other planets, and even if unaspected, it has a house and sign placement. When Pluto goes over Venus, it will aspect everything Venus is aspecting natally – in this case, an opposition to Uranus. This natal configuration describes a complex, a fundamental energy pattern within the individual. Before the advent of transiting Pluto, there were many transits over this same natal configuration, including new and full Moons and innumerable aspects from transiting Mercury, Venus and Mars. The progressed Moon will have made major aspects to the Venus-Uranus many times, some hard and some easy.

It is therefore useful to ask, "What have I done with this Venus-Uranus in the past? Am I living it? Can I connect with it? Do I understand it? Can I express it, or is just a blank? Have I split it in half? Do I think Uranus is other people? Is it something I am convinced belongs to my partner or my aunt or my brother, or a particular social or racial group? Where is it in me?" Whatever the transiting aspect, in the end what matters is the natal configuration and how conscious we are of it. This natal opposition was triggered by a transit of Pluto. That is the cue for this pair of actors to come out on stage. They have been on stage many times before, but perhaps they were not so important to the unfolding of the plot on earlier occasions. Now they have a critical piece of the action. How equipped the actors are to cope creatively with this important bit of the play depends on how much past experience they have acquired, and how much intelligent directing the ego has been able to offer.

Audience: Going back to my husband's mountain climbing, I certainly feel that issues of separation will come up again when Pluto is in late Sagittarius and trines my Venus-Moon conjunction. But the fact that we were able to work out the square makes me think I don't need to be afraid of the next aspect.

Liz: I am sure you are right. But being afraid of an aspect isn't very helpful in any event. It isn't the aspect which makes things happen; it is the human psyche in combination with external circumstances. The birth chart is certainly our fate, since we can't send it back and order another one. Birth aspects are not going to go away. When Venus is opposition Uranus, one can't white Uranus out with Typex. It will always be there. Every time something transits or progresses over this configuration, the underlying tension and high energy charge will come to the surface, and the issue will emerge into consciousness and into life. It will keep on emerging for as long as one is alive. It may keep on emerging even after one's death, and I don't mean only in terms of family inheritance. Do any of you know the film which was made about Napoleon during the 1930's? It was a wonderful epic. It was made when transiting Neptune was exactly on Napoleon's natal Sun in Leo. Even though the man had died over a century earlier, nevertheless the transit was still operative. Although dead, he had yet another moment of glamour and fame. When Neptune went over his Sun he became a film star. Perhaps one's chart, which reflects one's fate during incarnation, also reflects the fate of the person one was, even after the incarnation has finished.

Maybe these things are not limited to the brief span of our lives. Why should they be? All transits are cycles, and some cycles, such as those of Neptune and Pluto, take longer than a lifetime to complete. Certainly the same issues will keep arising throughout our lifetimes. Each time, there is a connecting thread of meaning which links the present with the past, so every planetary movement to a natal point recapitulates on the last planetary movement to that point. Without grasping this, we cannot get a real sense of how these movements work. All we are doing then is trying to get a cookbook perspective: "Here is a transit. It means X." But unless it is embedded in the life of the person, its meaning eludes us, and we are wandering blind when it comes to sensible, constructive attempts at prediction.

The nature of individual identity

Audience: I was just thinking – are the birth chart aspects really us, or are they the clothes we wear?

Liz: It depends on how you define "us". If we view life through the perspective of something eternal which incarnates and expresses through the birth chart and the body, then the chart portrays the clothes we wear in a given incarnation. That doesn't make it less real or important when one is alive. The belief that it is our clothing may help in terms of getting a more objective perspective, but I don't think it is very helpful to use that belief as a way of avoiding the psychological impact of a transit. We are asking for a lot of trouble if we try.

Audience: Yes, but doesn't the existence of something beyond the personality mean that we should work to detach ourselves from the emotional level of a transit?

Liz: This is a question which is perpetually raised by astrologers. I can't answer it, because it depends on one's personal belief system. If natal configurations are the signature for the role we are playing in a given lifetime, and transits and progressed aspects connote the cues which tell us when different parts of the play are beginning and ending, then we are not that role – we are simply playing it for a given incarnation. This perspective may give some breathing space, which allows us to contain our emotional responses in a more detached way. There is a lot to be said for such containment.

But denial of the reality of our feelings, and of the value of the personal ego, may be a very grave mistake, because personal and transpersonal are not mutually exclusive. The reality of one does not render the other unimportant or of less value. I am always struck by the beauty and resonance of the alchemists' belief that God needs the individual to complete the work of creation. If there is indeed some eternal spirit which reincarnates through a whole sequence of birth charts, then perhaps it needs the ego to give it form and experience in each incarnation, just as the ego needs it to find meaning. Too strenuous a state of detachment, which might also be termed dissociation, can be a powerful and even pathological defence system, mobilised to avoid the emotional level of transits by claiming that they are not happening to the "real" me – they are happening to a transient and illusory entity.

This question arises from the ancient split between spirit and matter which has permeated astrology since the dawn of the Christian era. For the last two millennia we have lived with a dualist world-view, and when we find our own natures painful or difficult, we retreat into transcendence in the hope that life will hurt less. This looks wonderful on paper. But unfortunately in practise, people who espouse such a split often materialise or somatise their difficult transits and progressions, because they have lost touch with the unity of inner and outer worlds. They leap from the level of the spirit to the level of materialisation without dealing with the psyche in the middle. I am not suggesting that inner work is always a solution to external difficulties. Some circumstances may be truly unavoidable. And inner work, like everything else, is limited by the perspective and capacities of the person doing it. But I do have a question about the extent to which we may make our transits materialise because we allow them no other level of expression. I have a deep suspicion that in many cases we are helping to create what comes to pass.

If we believe that our emotional responses are not "us" and should therefore be suppressed or ignored, the unconscious psyche tends to come and hunt us down. I doubt that anything helpful can be gained by pretending that life is nothing but an illusion. Perhaps such an approach works in the East. It is the philosophical basis on which Buddhism and Hinduism rest. But in the West our world-view and culture, in which every one of us is steeped, are rooted in the value of the individual as a co-creator in the cosmos. This is why our chief forms of worship have always been solar – ego-consciousness is important for our development. We cannot afford to throw the ego away. We may often overvalue it, and deny the existence of other levels of reality, and this is dangerous in a different way. But whether the individual psyche is real from the cosmic perspective is not the point. We have to live as though it is.

In adulthood we often translate the forgotten emotional suffering connected with difficult transits and progressions in childhood into fears and patterns of failure on a material level, or into illnesses. When our worst fears happen, we can say, "It is karma," or, "I need to go through this because it is good for the evolution of the soul." But none of us is in a position to know categorically what the soul does or doesn't need. And when one sees someone in great pain, it may be a very stupid thing for the astrologer to say. It encourages passivity and the perpetuation of a cycle of suffering which might be avoided. We disown the individual personality at our peril. We may get into a great deal of trouble if we believe our responses to transits are not "us", because there seems to be a direct relationship between the manifestation of transits and progressions and the degree of responsibility the individual takes for his or her own psyche. I am not sure of the extent of this relationship. There are some things over which we don't appear to have any control. But we will never know what those are unless we try to find out where our true limits lie.

Transits and bodily memory

Audience: I have been reading in the paper recently about tissue memory, and I am pretty excited by that. It seems to support what you say about birth chart placements having a memory.

Liz: The body and the psyche are not separate things – they are aspects of the same entity. Complexes are "psychoid" – they have a physical as well as a psychic level of expression. If one goes through certain physical and emotional experiences, one's later bodily and emotional responses will recapitulate what one has experienced on earlier occasions. It is not only the experiences themselves which are remembered, but the interpretation we have placed on them. It may even be that illnesses are the somatised memory of certain emotions and experiences, because people tend to be prone to the same kinds of illnesses during the course of a lifetime. Traditional medical astrology assigns particular organs in the body to particular signs and planets, and in practise this seems to work. Where a pattern of illness occurs, these ancient correlations are always reflected in the chart. What we do not yet understand is why, in one person, a particular configuration will reflect only emotional conflicts, while in another, a physical ailment is manifested. But chart configurations describe something that is inner as well as corporeal, and if we remember an experience on the emotional level, we are going to remember physically as well.

All these planetary movements are programmed from birth. Transits aren't random. This is an obvious statement, but often we don't think about it. From the moment of birth, the time it takes for Saturn to transit from its birth position to oppose the Sun is already given, because Saturn doesn't change its speed. And the time it takes for Saturn to move on and oppose the progressed Sun is also already given, because the rate at which the progressed Sun is moving is equally fixed. The timing of transits and progressed aspects isn't flexible or subject to our human intervention, because we are part of a self-regulating system which has its own inbuilt timing. The timing of our development as individuals is our fate.

We might think of successive transiting and progressed aspects as a series of developments which give life and substance to a basic theme. The birth chart starts off as a kind of skeleton, a structure of bare bones. It is an archetypal pattern of development which, at birth, has no flesh on it. Every day of one's life, some transit or progressed aspect is triggering one or other placement in the chart, so flesh gradually accumulates on those bones, both physically and psychologically. By the time we reach mid-life, a whole memory system has formed, the core of which is the basic pattern. But the nature and quality of the flesh depend on the kind of circumstances that have happened to anchor the archetypal pattern in life, and the degree of consciousness we bring to each successive layering.

There is a constant reworking and reemergence of the same life-themes. In this sense nothing new ever happens, from the moment of birth. That is why transits do not impose anything which is not already within us. Everything is already there. The feeling of newness comes from the variability of material circumstances, and from changes in the way we perceive those circumstances – in other words, changes in consciousness. It is exactly like a seed. Contained within an apple seed is the whole development programme of the apple tree, although if we shred the seed there is no physical apple tree yet to be seen. Soil conditions, climate, and the intelligent care of the gardener may alter the quality of the fruit which is produced. But an apple seed isn't going to produce a plum tree, no matter what we do to it.

Differences between transits and progressions

Transits: the cosmos impinging on the individual

Transits and progressions tell us about the timing of the unfoldment of this basic pattern. They are not the same in terms of what they mean and how they work. Transits seem to describe the cosmos impinging on us. Planetary cycles go on with or without us – they are not dependent on our birth charts. These cycles were occurring before we were born and will continue to do so after we die. When the transiting planets align with something in the birth chart, the greater system symbolised by these cycles makes an impact on the individual.

We cannot claim that anything astrological is "real" in the objective sense, because the zodiac is an image of the ecliptic, the *apparent* path of the Sun around the Earth. The Sun, as hopefully you all know, does *not* orbit around the Earth, and the zodiac is a purely geocentric perception. The planetary orbits as we plot them are likewise geocentric, and would be entirely different if one were born on Jupiter. A heliocentric perspective is no more objective than a geocentric one; it is merely different. And if one were born on a planet orbiting around Antares, the whole thing would be entirely irrelevant. Our astrological system only exists from the perspective of the Earth.

But since we live within a geocentric perspective, the cosmos we perceive is real to us, physically and psychologically, and the transits, like the truth in *The X–Files,* are out there. The cyclical patterns of our solar system impinge on the individual from the larger whole of which we are a part. Each individual chart is really a transit pattern frozen in time. And each time a transit cycle impinges on us, something is triggered inside us, and a bit of flesh is added to the bone structure through our encounters with the larger world. We cannot ever get away from the world because we exist within it.

The symbolic nature of progressions

Progressions are symbolic – or more symbolic than transits. They are completely dependent on the individual chart, and do not apply to anyone else. If Jupiter is transiting at 12° Capricorn, it will impinge on everyone who has a planet in 12° Capricorn, but if it is progressed to 12° Capricorn, that is unique to the individual chart. There are many different systems of progressing a chart, and all of them have something valid to tell us. Secondary progressions move the planets forward from their birth positions at the symbolic equivalent of one day of planetary motion (which varies according to the planet) equaling one year of life. Solar arc progressions move all the planets forward at the same rate that the Sun is moving, at the symbolic equivalent of one day of solar motion equaling one year of life.

There are a great many ways of symbolically moving planetary placements forward in time. I would recommend that you experiment with at least two of them, because they all give a slightly different perspective on the individual's development. Systems of progression also reflect astrological fashion. Solar arc progressions, for example, are favoured amongst many German astrologers who work with midpoints. All these different systems appear to have in common a representation of the internal development programme of the individual, independent of the world outside. They do not describe the world impinging on us.

If I go back to the hackneyed analogy of the apple seed, progressions tell us the natural life-cycle which is built into the seed – when the tree will flower, what colour the flowers will be, and when its fruit will be ripe. All these things can be affected by external factors, but the programme of growth is innate. But transits tell us how much rain will fall in a particular season, how much sunshine is available for the ripening of the fruit, when a plague of aphids is on the way, and when a goat decides to come and eat the young shoots. The ego is like the gardener, who hopefully understands that the right combination of nature and nurture will produce the best apples. The intelligent gardener respects the innate growth pattern of the tree, but takes steps to deal with the lack of rain, the aphids, and the goat. About the sunshine he or she can do nothing.

Both transits and progressions seem to operate on teleological, emotional, and material levels. Although progressions are more "symbolic", they too can be reflected in external circumstances – although usually the individual's psychological pattern is more obviously involved when they manifest. Nevertheless, both transits and progressed aspects have a meaning, a set of emotional responses, and the potential of manifesting in concrete form.

Example chart 1

Now it might be useful to look at both transits and progressions in an example chart. Although I have made a distinction between the two, in practice they work together. Because progressed aspects, with the exception of the progressed Moon, tend to hang about for a long time, a fast-moving transit or the transiting station of a heavy planet may "trigger" the external expression of the progression. The most important life junctures seem to involve a clustering of both transits and progressed aspects around the same natal planets.

I will omit the name of the male owner of this chart for the moment. If any of you recognise the chart, please keep quiet about it.

I am curious to see whether you can piece together the identity of the individual from what is happening in his chart. I would like to call your attention first to two transiting planets and one progressed aspect which are presently triggering the birth chart. It would be very interesting if you tried to get a sense of the meaning and emotional level of these planetary movements. Then we can consider what sort of events might manifest.

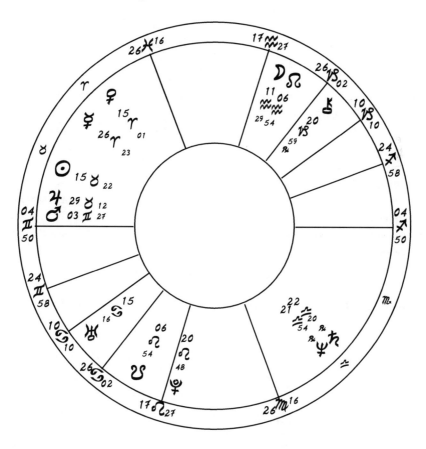

Tony Blair
6 May 1953, 6.10 am, Edinburgh

The natal ascendant is at 4° 50' Gemini, with Mars rising at 3° 27'. Transiting Pluto is perched right on the Descendant at the moment, at 4° Sagittarius. It already made a station in this degree earlier in the year. Now it is retrograde, and will move back across the Descendant at the beginning of 1997. Natal Mars conjuncts Jupiter at 29° 12' Taurus in the 12th. Although Pluto will not go back into exact opposition with Jupiter, it is still well within orb, and will continue to oppose Mars for quite a while longer. This long transit of Pluto over the Descendant and opposition Mars-Jupiter is the first of the transits I would like you to consider.

In the birth chart Saturn and Neptune conjunct in the 6th house at 21–22° Libra. This conjunction opposes Mercury at 26° Aries and Venus at 15° Aries. The MC is at 26° Capricorn, square Saturn–Neptune and also exactly square Mercury. Natal Chiron is at 20° Capricorn, conjuncting the MC from the 9th and square both Venus-Mercury and Saturn-Neptune. Finally, natal Uranus is at 15° Cancer, completing a grand cardinal cross with Venus, Chiron, and Saturn-Neptune. Transiting Neptune is currently at the MC, setting off the Saturn-Neptune opposition Mercury. Although it has moved past Venus, Uranus, and Chiron, Neptune is still activating the natal grand cross, as well as crossing and recrossing the MC. That is the second transit I would like you to think about. Just in case you get bored contemplating these two transits, you might also bear in mind that, in the first part of next year, transiting Uranus and Jupiter, will cross the Moon-node conjunction in Aquarius in the 10th. Uranus will spend a lot of time here over the next year or two. Also during next year, Saturn will move into the second decanate of Aries and trigger the natal grand cross, opposing its own place in the process.

Working with the progressed chart

In the progressed chart, which is set for today, the progressed Ascendant is at 16° Cancer, and has just cleared natal Uranus, which is at 15° Cancer in the 3rd house. When you work out progressed charts, I would suggest that you set up the whole chart, as I have done here, rather than putting in the progressed planets

piecemeal around the natal chart. This way you wind up with an
entirely new chart, including not only the progressed angles and
planets, but also all the progressed house cusps.

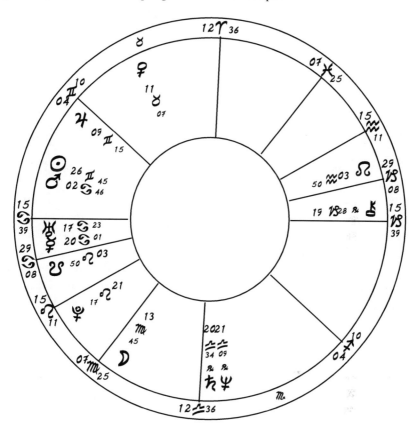

Tony Blair
Progressed chart set for 8 June 1996

Don't neglect the progressed placements of the slow-moving
planets. Even if they creep along, their exact position becomes
important when another progressed planet or a progressed angle
catches up. Visually, you can see these progressed to progressed
positions more easily if you have the whole progressed chart in
front of you. Here progressed Uranus is in 17° Cancer. Although the
progressed Ascendant has already passed natal Uranus, this man

hasn't finished with Uranian issues yet, because it still has to go over progressed Uranus next year. When you look at the whole progressed chart, this hits you straight away. You might otherwise say, "Oh, the progressed Ascendant is finished with Uranus," but it hasn't. It is still very much operative.

Audience: Is there any principle by which you can differentiate a transit to a natal position from a transit to a progressed position, particularly a transit to the progressed outer planets, which can take many, many years to move only a degree? What is the difference in interpretation?

Liz: The natal chart gives us the basic story, the essential psychic structure. It is the play we are called upon to perform in a given lifetime. The progressed chart tells us how things are developing at a specific point in time. Where has that essential blueprint progressed to? Which characters are now out on stage? What point in the plot have we reached? I cannot think of a better analogy than the theatre. Let's say you are familiar with Shakespeare's *Macbeth*. You know the plot and the characters. But you have arrived late for a particular performance, and walk in after the play has begun. That is what we do when we calculate progressions for a particular time.

You come in, and there on the stage you see Macbeth being confronted by the witches, and one of them is telling him he will be "King hereafter". On his face you can read perplexity, fear, and calculation. You have arrived at a critical point in the play, when Macbeth is being confronted by all his unacknowledged ambitions. His progressed chart tells you that these unacknowledged ambitions are now ripe for consciousness. But he might not do anything about it, other than realise what he actually wants. However, his transits tell you that the time has arrived for him to actualise what he is; the world is impinging The transits to the natal chart reflect the moment the witches voice the words and he thinks, "Yes, I would like to be King of Scotland." The transits to the progressed planets reflect the completion of this – his murder of King Duncan.

When a transit hits a natal planet, the wider world impinges on something innate in us. This innate "something" –

whether we call it a complex, an archetypal pattern, a character quality – has always been there, and it is a fundamental life-issue. When it is triggered, a process begins of incarnating something that was previously unborn or incomplete. When a transit aspects the same planet progressed, what is being activated is not the essential pattern, but rather, the completion of the incarnating process which was begun when the natal planet was triggered.

That is why we should always look at the progressed position of the natal planet which is being aspected by a particular transit. This gives us a time frame for the process of development. Don't look only at transiting Saturn conjunct your Sun. Look also at its transit over the progressed Sun, which reflects the completion of what was begun at the time of the conjunction to natal Sun. If you are thirty years old, transiting Saturn will conjunct the progressed Sun roughly two and a half years after it conjuncts the natal Sun, because it will take that long to move 30°. If we consider our example chart, we should look at transiting Pluto over the natal Descendant and then over the progressed Descendant at 16° Capricorn. Pluto, of course, is very slow, and this process will take around twenty years. We might not see much in the way of obvious Plutonian experiences between now and then. But this transit will have a very long development time.

With the outer planets there is no difference in this basic approach. But in their terms, who you are in the present and who you are innately are virtually the same, because their progressed motion is too slow for an individual to have moved very much. The outer planets are generation markers. In their world, the individual hardly progresses at all, because he or she is part of a much larger unit. A transit will aspect progressed Uranus very soon after natal Uranus, or, if Uranus is retrograde, it may reach progressed Uranus first. If the transit is a slow one, one doesn't notice anything different, because the transit is within orb of both during the entire period. If the transit is a quick one – say, transiting Mars – then it may be apparent, through a gap of a couple of days, that one is facing two chapters in the same story.

Let's go back to working out the progressed chart. You should wind up with a new chart, which in our example will have a 16° Cancer Ascendant. The natal MC has progressed from 26°

Capricorn to 8° Pisces, so that is the MC for the new chart. All the other house cusps have progressed as well. The 2nd house cusp has moved from 24° Gemini and is now at 0° Leo. The whole chart has moved, carrying the progressed planets with it. Progressed Uranus is now in the progressed 1st house (in the natal chart it's in the 3rd), and progressed Mercury is at 20° Cancer (opposition natal Chiron), also in the progressed 1st (in the natal chart it was in the 12th).

Don't panic, but when we read transits to progressed planets, we should look at them in the context of the progressed as well as the natal house. Around five years ago, the transiting conjunction of Uranus and Neptune through mid-Capricorn moved across this man's natal Uranus, Venus and Chiron, and the natal houses affected were the 12th, 9th, and 3rd. But this transiting conjunction also went over the progressed Descendant and opposed progressed Uranus and progressed Mercury in the progressed 1st house, while transiting through the progressed 7th house. This tells us that, although the basic pattern activated by that transiting conjunction affected the cadent houses, a great deal of the action five years ago took place in a more public arena.

At the moment transiting Jupiter is stationary in mid-Capricorn, opposite natal Uranus. This implicates the natal 3rd and 9th houses. But it is also a 1st house issue, because progressed Ascendant and progressed Uranus are together, and Jupiter has made its station at the progressed Descendant, opposite them both. It is wise to keep an eye on both areas. Both are likely to be highlighted in this man's life. The station of transiting Jupiter in the natal 9th will trigger his ideals and his urgent need to communicate them. But because Jupiter's station involves the progressed 1st/7th axis, he is likely to do this in the public arena, where everyone can see what is going on.

Diurnal secondary progressions

Audience: I have never understood why, in secondary progressions, we use a method very similar to solar arc progressions for the angles, and another for the planets. If secondary progressions really involve moving every point in the chart at its own rate of motion with the equation of a day for a year, then the angles would progress at roughly one degree per day, since they make a complete revolution of 360° in twenty-four hours.

Liz: You are right, but the angles *are* progressed according to their own rate of motion. As you say, they go around in a complete revolution in the course of twenty-four hours, which means that, at the end of a day, they are back more or less where they started, but have moved forward slightly – around 1° a day, or, in symbolic terms, around 1° a year, depending on whether it is a sign of slow or fast ascension. This is because we always use the same birth time for the progressed chart, so we get the progressed Ascendant at the point of its diurnal return each day.

There is a system called diurnal secondary progressions, which calculates the exact degree of the progressed Ascendant and the other angles for any day during the course of the year, depending on the time of day – or, in other words, the symbolic time of year – for which the progressed chart is calculated. The progressed planets are the same as in standard secondary progressions, but the progressed angles and house cusps are moving very quickly, and over the course of a year they make a complete revolution, taking the progressed planets with them. I have sometimes found this useful in shedding light on important issues, because the diurnally progressed Ascendant or MC will often be on or opposite a progressed planet at such times.

Audience: So in the example, the Uranus-Mercury conjunction in the progressed chart would actually move right around the chart during the year, and three months after his birthday it would be at the progressed MC. Then three months later it would be at the progressed Descendant, and three months after that at the progressed IC, and then on his birthday a year later it would be back on the Ascendant.

Liz: Exactly.

Audience: So you could pinpoint the times during the year when the effects of the conjunction would be most powerful.

Liz: Yes, up to a point. But we also have to take transits into account. The most powerful activation, in my experience, is when a transit is conjuncting or opposing a progressed planet, the progressed planet is on a natal planet, and all three have reached a progressed angle in the diurnal secondary progressed chart. But that doesn't happen very often. And by the time we have worked all this out, whatever is going to happen has already happened, and we are still throwing bits of paper about and madly pounding computer keys. I think it is wiser to keep things simple, spend less time worrying about pinpointing the hour when the event will occur, and give more energy to what is happening inside. The quality of one's life definitely deteriorates if all one's time is spent on working out what kind of day it is going to be.

Transiting Pluto opposite Ascendant and Mars

Audience: I would like to go back to the transit of Pluto in this chart. It is in the 5th at birth. Does this mean the transit carries a 5th house significance?

Liz: Yes, it will carry the associations of its natal house with it. We are really looking at a segment of Pluto's cycle. It starts in the 5th, it has crept through the 6th, and it has now arrived at the Descendant, bringing the pride and passion of a 5th house Pluto in Leo into the sphere of the public. But we are in danger of losing the forest for the trees. Let's first try to understand transiting Pluto opposition Ascendant and Mars – its meaning, how it might feel, what complexes are being triggered, and how it might manifest.

Audience: It has something to do with power over how resources are used.

Audience: It may mean the death or loss of someone, which may affect his sense of joy in life.

Liz: Those are possibilities. What else? Don't ignore the obvious. This is transiting Pluto on the Descendant, opposite a rising Mars.

Audience: Relationships.

Liz: What about them?

Audience: A battle of wills, involving the need to be the centre of attention, someone very special.

Audience: And a battle of ideas, because of the Gemini Ascendant.

Liz: Yes, one way of reading the teleology of this transit is that, through power battles, conflicts, or compulsive or "fated" experiences with other people, this man's Geminian outlook and attitudes are going to be forced to change radically. A phase of his life has come to an end, and nothing will ever feel the same again. We don't know yet what circumstances might provide the external trigger. All that we know is that something is challenging an individual who, with Mars rising in Gemini, is accustomed to getting his own way through charm, intellectual ability, and a flexible approach to life. He is being forced to deepen, to commit himself, to recognise forces in life over which he might not have control.

Audience: Also, Pluto is crossing into the upper hemisphere. He is trying to give birth to what he perceives as his creative purpose in the world. He could become immensely powerful.

Liz: Yes, there is also the issue of purpose or "fate", which is related to power. Relationships as reflected by the 7th house are not only personal. The 7th also describes one's relationship with the outside world, the "public" as it is euphemistically known in astrology texts. The Ascendant-Descendant axis divides the houses concerned with personal development from the houses concerned with involvement with others. What kinds of possible scenarios might this transit describe?

Audience: Conflict. With a partner, or with colleagues, or with the public. Powerful enemies.

Audience: Pluto on the Descendant will teach him about his dark side, through encountering it in other people.

Liz: There is a potential for a deepening of his Geminian outlook through finding out what it's like to live in the jungle. Gemini is essentially an idealistic sign. Basic personality characteristics are relevant here. Gemini is clever, versatile, flexible with ideas, communicative, and full of ideals. Pluto, moving through the house of the horoscope concerned with others, is going to test that outlook, temper it, and put it through the fire. Any glibness or superficiality is likely to be burned away. Any ideals which are left after the battle are likely to be deeply held and will form the core of a profound life commitment.

Audience: He will be able to take a particular ideology and really promote it.

Liz: The gift of promoting ideas and ideals belongs to Gemini, and especially to Mars in Gemini, which is often a crusader on the ideological level. Pluto will probably burn away all the dross, and sharpen the focus of those ideals.

Audience: Jupiter conjuncts Mars natally, and Pluto opposed it before it reached Mars. I think he can be very excessive in what he believes in. It's a sort of religious mission. Jupiter rules the 7th house. So he has the capacity to be a teacher, or even a preacher.

Liz: You are suggesting religious or ideological fanaticism.

Audience: My impression is that he believes he is absolutely right. He might present himself as a flexible person, but really, he isn't flexible at all where his ideals are concerned. Also, he has the Sun square Pluto. His natural tendency would be to avoid dealing with Pluto. Maybe he would project it. He has got the Moon in Aquarius opposition Pluto as well. He prefers to stay up there in the sky, so probably the manifestation of the transit would be through an eruption of something that he hasn't been able to acknowledge yet.

Liz: In other words, the real enemy is within. That gets us more deeply into the psychological dimension of the transit. Whatever power battles he encounters in the world outside, he has to face his own power issues, which probably, as you say, have not been dealt with fully. He may use his ideals to mask a hidden power-drive. Then, when other people sense how driven he is, they will oppose him, and he may not understand that it is not his ideals they are attacking – it is his methods and deeper motives, of which he may be quite unconscious. This transit of Pluto could be enormously valuable in deepening him, and fostering a profound sense of destiny. So much for the teleology. How is all this is going to feel?

Audience: Dreadful. I think he will have a very hard time.

Liz: Have any of you had transiting Pluto opposition Mars?

Audience: Yes. It was horrible. It is a place of knowing what you would rather not know about your feelings. Instead of intellectualising things, you feel them in the centre of your stomach. Reality hits you. It is not very nice. I felt a great deal of anger.

Liz: Anger at what?

Audience: The environment. Not being in control.

Liz: We are back to theme of powerlessness, which is one of the major challenges of transiting Pluto to Mars. One's personal will isn't as big and potent as one thought. That is the message Pluto gives to Mars. There are forces in life stronger than oneself, and one may have to compromise or accept the unacceptable. Anger at powerlessness is a characteristic theme of Pluto-Mars transits. What is his reaction likely to be? You have already noted that this is not a Plutonian nature. There is a lot of lively mental activity and idealism, but there is not much in the element of water. The Sun is in Taurus, the sign opposite Pluto's sign. And, as you have observed, Pluto squares the Sun in the natal chart.

Audience: He could be angry at others, because he feels so powerless. He would blame them.

Liz: Yes, he may feel he is being attacked by evil people, and he is likely to retaliate quite savagely (remember the Sun square Pluto). The enemy, the shadow, is "out there". Evil and corruption are out in the world and must be fought. This makes a crusader, a missionary battling against something dark or evil in the world.

Audience: It's a dragon-fight.

Liz: Yes, I think this archetypal theme is relevant. The natal square describes a complex, and one of the mythic images associated with this complex is the solar hero battling the underworld dragon. As is usual with complexes, the disagreeable half – the dragon – is likely to be projected outside. Because the Sun is in the 12th house at birth, this man is very sensitive to the collective psyche, and would therefore be likely to feel this dragon-fight as something he must do for society, for other people.

Transiting Neptune conjunct the MC

Now, what about transiting Neptune at the MC? When two transits occur within the same time frame, they will be connected by meaning and by feeling, because the individual will inevitably associate one with the other, and interpret the experiences of one in the light of the other.

Audience: That transit has been going on for a couple of years. He has had transiting Pluto opposing all the 12th house planets, plus both Uranus and Neptune transiting over his MC. I feel that, having been through all that, what's left is the last push.

Liz: Yes, after spending a very long time transiting through the 6th house and opposing the 12th house planets, Pluto is finally coming out of the closet, as it were, so all the behind-the-scenes breaking down and rebuilding is now culminating in a confrontation with the world.

Likewise we can look at the long transit of Neptune and Uranus through the 9th house and see that, when Uranus crossed the MC, certain changes might have occurred in his goals and worldly position. Now that Neptune has arrived, it remains for him to place these changes in the context of a broader sense of mission.

Audience: Could Neptune at the MC mean media attention?

Liz: On the manifestation level, it can reflect some kind of notoriety, prominence, or involvement with "the masses". But sometimes the effects are far quieter. They may pertain to the relationship with the mother, or to changes which the world does not hear about. Not everyone becomes a celebrity when Neptune crosses the MC. We need to look first at what natal Neptune is doing. It is in the 6th, so it is carrying the meaning of the 6th house into the 10th. What might this involve?

Audience: He has lost his direction. He doesn't know where he is going. He might feel confusion about his objectives. Neptune breaks down boundaries.

Liz: Transiting Neptune in Capricorn may break down certain hierarchical structures, and this can result in a more fluid response to the world. Where earlier he might have thought he knew his "place" in accordance with the society in which he moves, now he may feel his real "place" has unlimited possibilities. It may also reflect his perception of a world trapped in hierarchical structures and in need of being redeemed. This is the messianic spirit, which projects Capricorn onto the world and identifies with Neptune as the redeemer. And, of course, it can mean boundless ambition.

It is also a parting of the ways from the mother, the past, and the family background. There would inevitably be emotional repercussions with such a process. Why do we get confused about objectives? Because old objectives are disintegrating, and it hurts. It is a kind of loss, a relinquishing of something safe and secure. But it is also a kind of freedom, and anything seems possible. Under Neptune transits, we may believe we have glimpsed the pot of gold at the end of the rainbow. We can have and do anything. God is on our side. It is as if the heavens have suddenly opened and revealed our true destiny. But Neptune is prone to excessive idealising, and can confuse boundless vision with what is actually possible.

Audience: Maybe he will lose his job.

Liz: That is a possibility. But the opposite is also possible. Sometimes Neptune at the MC can seem to make all one's wishes come true – although there is usually a high price to be paid, of which one is generally unconscious at the time.

Audience: He should be in films, if he isn't already. The MC is the way you look at the world. When Neptune goes over the angles, it colours the world with glamour. And he would appear glamorous to other people.

Liz: All of this is sound astrology. But we seem to have become bogged down in what might "happen". I would like to look more deeply at the meaning of this transit. None of you have mentioned Chiron, which is conjunct the MC from the 9th. Before Neptune reached the MC – and the exact square to Mercury, which, likewise, none of you have commented on – it conjuncted Chiron. We have to take it all together. It is not just Neptune over the MC; it is Neptune over Chiron-MC and square Mercury and Saturn-Neptune. We must look at the whole configuration. Otherwise we can speculate forever about whether he should be an actor, whether he will lose his job, or whether he will rob a bank and get caught. And we will be no closer to understanding him. Neptune is taking many years to trigger the most powerful configuration in the birth chart. What does this grand cardinal cross tell us? What kind of complex is described?

Audience: I find grand crosses very difficult to read. There are too many planets involved!

Liz: Try getting a sense of who is friends with whom. Planets are like people – when they are bound together in a group, each planet will make alliances with others according to natural affinity.

Audience: I think he is afraid of Neptune. Neptune is the odd one.

Liz: Yes, I am inclined to agree with you. Saturn is exalted in Libra, and Saturn and Mercury can get along. Venus is relatively comfortable with Saturn because Saturn is in Venus' sign. Chiron is in Saturn's sign. Uranus has affinity with both Mercury and Chiron; and temperamentally this man can relate to both Uranus and Saturn through his Moon in Aquarius. All these planets can turn their faces toward the intellectual side of life and find a means of working together creatively, despite the so-called "bad" aspects between them. Emotional restraint, intellectual energy, self-discipline, detachment, hard concentration, and practical idealism would come out of the combination. This is a restrained, thoughtful, controlled and serious-minded group of planets. But Neptune is, indeed, the odd one out. It is passive, irrational, romantic, and self-abnegating. He is afraid of losing himself, in his personal relationships as well as in the path he pursues in life.

He may hold Neptune at bay through a rigorous morality reflected by the 9th house Chiron, which is disposed of by Saturn. He may also maintain a rigid set of structures in his everyday life (Saturn in the 6th) which help him to feel he is holding it all together. He may be frightened by his propensity to dissolve, to be victimised, to lose his way. He has a very busy 12th house, which echoes the strong but uncomfortable Neptune. But the 12th house planets are in earth and air signs, which don't like swimming underwater. He may secretly feel that, whatever he is trying to build, it is going to continually be dissolved or mysteriously taken away from him. Much of his energy may be directed toward putting order into chaos. But it is like trying to maintain a sand castle while the tides keep washing it away.

Audience: I think that is a very astute observation, that he is always trying to grapple with the forces of chaos. He has two very powerful weapons to use against chaos. One is the very sharp Geminian mind, with its clarity and its ability to deal with ideas. The other is his ability to control himself and others, because there is a powerful Saturn-Capricorn influence there. He is an earth sign. Saturn disposes of the MC and Chiron. Chiron has a lot of Saturn in it. It is in the 9th, which is morality. I think this man has a very, very strong moral code. There are probably wounds connected with his religious background, his religious and moral upbringing. Those wounds are all the time being buffeted whenever he feels there is chaos around. It has also got to do with mother and the background of the maternal line. So as Neptune reaches that point in the chart, a lot of personal issues are going to be translated into work and collective issues.

Liz: Yes, that was very well put. And with transiting Neptune square Mercury, he is in great danger of deceiving himself about what he is really capable of, and also of being deceived by the projections others place on him.

Audience: Might he have a breakdown?

Liz: He might, if there were a propensity for it. But despite the intensity of the conflict, I don't think so. This is a well-knit chart, and a well-grounded personality. He is more likely to translate internal conflicts into ideological issues than to be torn apart from within. Unconscious complexes may erupt into consciousness, but they will appear dressed in the clothing of the outer world. Pluto transiting across the Descendant is also inclined to be expressed in external conflicts. The "breakdown" may occur around him, rather than within him. The deeper meaning behind these transits involves highly personal issues of individual development. But with so many cardinal signs, and with powerful transits at the Descendant and MC, he is likely to act out his complexes on the public stage.

There is also the generation marker of Saturn conjunct Neptune in Libra. Everyone born between 1951 and 1953 is presently experiencing transiting Neptune square natal Saturn-Neptune, and is grappling with disillusionment, inner and outer chaos, and the challenge of bringing ideals into form. He might become a public exponent of a battle which is not only his own, but that of his age group as well – a collective complex, constellated on the worldly level every time Saturn and Neptune make powerful aspects in the heavens. It is worth remembering that many important political and social reform movements have been born, reached a crisis point, died or transformed under the cyclical transits of Saturn to Neptune. He was born under the conjunction. Neptune's dream of an ideal world is challenged by Saturn's demand for making the dream real. Powerful political inclinations of a reforming, utopian kind are typical, although not the only way the conjunction can be expressed. Looking at his chart in this way tells us a lot about what really motivates him.

Audience: I think he is swept along by a vision of saving the world.

Liz: Yes, there is a messianic element, natally as well as by transit.

Audience: Then he has got to be a political figure.

Liz: It does look that way, doesn't it? For those of you who haven't yet worked it out, this gentleman might or might not be our next Prime Minister. This is the chart of Tony Blair.

Audience: So that is how Neptune at the MC is working itself out! And Neptune is also trine natal Jupiter.

Liz: Yes, the sense of mission and the longing to redeem the chaos in the world around him are likely to be extremely intense.

Audience: I keep looking at that Neptune-Mercury square. It is there natally and also by transit. He might misinterpret what other people are doing, and he might do things himself that aren't quite open – even though that is his main argument against the opposition.

Liz: Yes, the sense of enemies "out there", with transiting Pluto at the Descendant, is likely to be pervasive and highly uncomfortable. He might justify using means which, despite his strong morality, are a little questionable.

Audience: If anybody in his own party disagrees with him, he gets rid of them.

Liz: Sun square Pluto can sometimes display that propensity. There is a certain irony in the fact that Margaret Thatcher also has a Sun-Pluto square, and displayed the same propensity during her time as Prime Minister. Although these two people are on opposite sides of the political fence, they share the same deep sense of the mythic dragon-fight. They are engaged in battling heroically against what they perceive as the darkness in the world, and their manner and methods may sometimes be more akin than many people would care to acknowledge. It is a bit of a standing joke in political circles that Tony Blair is Maggie Thatcher's true successor.

My object in using this chart as an illustration is not to get a political discussion going, but to look at the ways in which individual psychology and individual transits and progressions create the reality we perceive, and create, in the world. It is important to try to put aside one's personal ideology as much as possible, to understand an individual like Tony Blair. Whether or not we agree with his politics, we need to know who he is. Otherwise, we cannot know what we are voting for or against.

Audience: Jupiter and Uranus will come up to his Moon-node conjunction in the 10th next year. When is the next election?

Liz: The exact conjunction of Jupiter and Uranus in 5° Aquarius occurs in February 1997. That may be a little early for an election, but it is possible that something happens, overt or subtle, which, in a sense, "fates" the outcome of the election later. This takes us back to what I was discussing earlier. When is the real election? The day that people vote, or the time when the tide has turned on a collective psychological level? Pluto will be at Tony Blair's Descendant and opposition Mars throughout the spring. Saturn will be sextile/trine his nodal axis, and so will Pluto. Just to get you going, take a quick look at the other relevant chart.

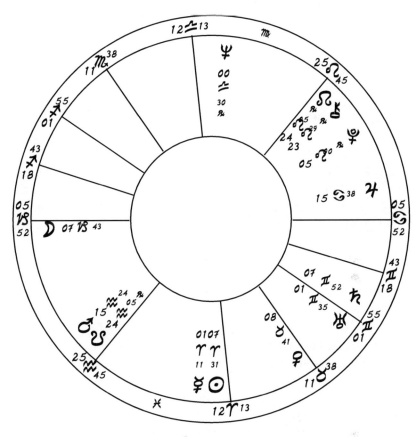

John Major
29 March 1943, 3.15 am, London

At the same time that Jupiter and Uranus will be conjunct Tony Blair's node in the 10th, in February 1997, they will be opposition John Major's Pluto in 5° Leo in his 7th house. Saturn will be in 5° Aries, square John Major's Ascendant, although trine his Pluto. By mid-March Saturn will have reached 7° Aries, and will be exactly on his Sun and square his Moon. Saturn stations in this degree of Aries next month, and will be hanging about the Sun-Mercury for the rest of the year, so March 1997 will reflect the resolution or crystallisation of this long transit of Saturn, which can't have been much fun for him. The usual time for an election would be in May 1997, by which time Saturn will have moved to around 16° Aries, setting off Tony Blair's grand cross. Pluto will still be in 4° Sagittarius in May, and still on Tony Blair's Ascendant. Saturn triggering Mr. Blair's grand cross may seem negative. But it could catapult him to power. It is the greatest challenge of his life.

Creating reality

Who makes the decision about when an election takes place? John Major would make it in ordinary circumstances, and although I doubt that he is getting astrological advice, the aspects look better in May than they do earlier. But some crisis or deep change in public attitude could occur under Jupiter-Uranus which even helpful aspects in May cannot undo, and who would be responsible for such an occurrence? With transiting Saturn on his Sun, Mr. Major might be capable of behaving in a very defensive and even self-destructive fashion over a long period of time. He may polarise with his own party, and in the end they may bring him down.

Although we may be sure what will "happen" next spring, it is equally interesting to look at what is happening to these two men internally. When the last election occurred between John Major and Neil Kinnock, the general consensus was that Labour would get in. The general consensus was proved wrong. I am not well versed in mundane astrology, and I would not attempt to predict an election result on the basis of mundane principles. Nor am I convinced that such events are invariably "fated", because they are in the making all the time, every minute, and all we can map out are likelihoods, not certainties. More importantly, there are individuals involved, with an individual psychology and the capacity to exercise choice – or to be unconscious of what they are doing. And the individual chart may tell us more, and in greater depth, than we might think.

I had a cursory look at Neil Kinnock's chart before the election, and I saw transiting Saturn exactly conjunct his natal Moon in the 2nd house on the day of voting. I didn't bother to look at anything else. I thought to myself, "If I had just been made Prime Minister after such a long time of desperate effort and waiting, would I feel like Saturn on the Moon?" On the basis of that, I said to a few friends, "He will lose the election, because this transit is the signature of a very unhappy person. It describes feelings of deep rejection and failure. Here is the Moon in Aquarius, the lover of the people, feeling depressed, restricted, unwanted, and betrayed. This is not the signature of somebody who has been trying to get into power for years and has finally achieved his fondest wish." However, this transit was operative for a long time before the actual election. Do you think it might tell us anything psychologically about why he didn't win the election?

Audience: You wouldn't expect the Moon to be involved.

Liz: Why not? You have commented on Tony Blair's Moon in Aquarius, about to be transited by Jupiter and Uranus. And the Moon may tell us a good deal about the emotional basis from which a person acts and makes decisions. We feel the way the Moon feels under a particular transit, and we behave accordingly, and others respond to us accordingly. And therein lies the key. The transit of Saturn conjunct Neil Kinnock's Moon at 15° Aquarius had been building up for some time. As I keep saying, transits have orbs. They have a long period of slow and often unconscious development, because they reflect a process, not an event. The event, if any, is only the tip of the iceberg. Now, if someone has an aspect like this going on, what does the person experience inwardly? Have any of you experienced transiting Saturn conjunct the Moon? How did you feel?

Audience: World-weary.

Audience: Serious.

Audience: I kept finding animals that needed help.

Audience: Defeated.

Audience: Lonely.

Liz: All right. If you are in a Saturn-Moon emotional state while you are preoccupied with something as important as planning an election campaign, how are you likely to deal with things? What kind of image are you likely to present to others? What feeling-tone will others pick up from you? Your decisions and judgements will be powerfully coloured by your emotional state. They will not be the same decisions and judgements you might make under some other transit. You will make them from a place of expecting defeat, on some unconscious level. Your sense of defensiveness and isolation, whether conscious or not, will communicate itself to others, and they will not feel in sympathy with you, no matter what you say or how hard you try to be congenial and friendly.

Many people cannot understand why Neil Kinnock lost that election. The country seemed poised to welcome a change of government. But before the actual day, when things seemed to be going so well, some bright person decided to stage a premature victory rally. And it was ill-conceived. It was so like the Nürnberg rallies that it put the fear of God into people who, up to that time, were planning to vote Labour. At the very last moment, a critical mistake was made in relation to "the people" – the Moon. If it was suggested by a slick promoter, Mr. Kinnock still had to give it his approval. Ultimately the responsibility rests with him. Why did he do it? Do any of you remember this rally? A great many people looked at the goings-on and thought, "Oh dear, we are back in 1939." Whether the truth was revealed, or whether it was simply a very poor choice of media presentation, I leave to you to decide. It was a bad mistake, and many people panicked and decided to stay with the devil they knew rather than vote for the devil which appeared on their television screens that night.

Audience: Apparently he knew it was wrong and over the top. He said he had that feeling.

Liz: Perhaps he did. But perhaps Saturn on the Moon reflected a reluctance to listen to the feeling. He didn't do anything about canceling the rally, or reorganising it to tone it down. An element of self-architected defeat is apparent here. Those who live their lives in the public arena are no different from any of us, in terms of psychological dynamics. What they are going through inside is what they broadcast to people outside. When we see Neptune going over Tony Blair's MC, this not only describes how he is feeling. It also describes how he is going to act and project himself to us, and how we are likely to perceive him, unless we look more deeply. We see Neptune on the MC, and we see either the messiah or the advent of chaos, depending on what political stance we hold.

Audience: John Major had a particularly strong Jupiter transit during the last election. I predicted the result based on that.

Liz: You saw the winner's exuberance and I saw the loser's misery. Both transits were "true", psychologically as well as literally. At the moment, John Major has transiting Saturn sitting on the Sun and square the Moon. Any decisions he makes under that transit are going to be coloured by the transit. His perceptions reflect the transit, so he will feel and act accordingly. He keeps generating conflict around him, because a natal conflict between Sun and Moon is being triggered. If he follows his heart, he goes against his conscious goals. If he follows his conscious goals, he goes against his heart. He is burdened by the responsibilities he carries, and gets no help from his friends. His sense of isolation projects itself to others, and they feel no sympathy for him.

Audience: He must be very scared.

Audience: Do you mean that all his decisions are going to be based on the fear principle?

Liz: Saturn may not always reflect fear. But it may be rigid and intractable, and feel misunderstood. Saturn can be very dogged and stubborn at the wrong moment, because one feels weak and undermined, and tries to compensate by being tough and strong.

Audience: One thing I see you are implying is, "How do we create our own reality?"

Liz: Yes, that is what I am implying. Any decisions John Major is making at the moment will spring from the feeling-tone and perceptions described by the transits and progressions which are affecting his natal planets. Transiting Saturn sits on a natal Sun-Mercury conjunction, square natal Moon. Transiting Pluto is exactly on the midpoint of the Saturn-Uranus conjunction in Gemini. Saturn-Uranus, like Saturn-Neptune, often espouses deeply and sincerely held political and ideological convictions, and these can sometimes be quite rigid. Pluto is ploughing into this conjunction, and forcing change. And it will go on doing its ploughing right through next spring.

Audience: His natal Sun is sextile Saturn, so the transit of Saturn will also sextile its own place. That doesn't sound so bad.

Liz: Yes, there is a sextile between the two in the birth chart, and he may respond to the challenge of the conjunction with great perspicacity and discipline – if he is sufficiently conscious. But this transit could also reflect his downfall. One of the problems many people have perceived in John Major's style of leadership is that it is too wobbly, too much a "politics of expediency". The public does not believe he is strong enough to hold together his own party, let alone lead the country. Saturn over the Sun may bring out his strength; or it may bring out a dogged obstinacy which defeats him.

Let's look at transiting Pluto opposition the Saturn-Uranus conjunction. It is just crossing into the 11th house. As with Tony Blair, the enemy is likely to appear "out there". Who is the enemy? Apart from Mr. Blair himself, the enemy is his own party, his 11th house "group". The decisions Mr. Major is making at the moment are based on transits of Saturn and Pluto respectively to a natal Sun-Moon square and a natal Saturn-Uranus conjunction. So he is alienating a lot of people right now, because his decisions reflect two planets which are by their nature isolationist and defensive. Although he is a highly intelligent man, I do not think he is very psychologically aware, and therefore he can't really act otherwise under those transits, any more than Tony Blair can stop acting like a messiah with transiting Neptune at his MC. How could Mr. Blair act any differently, when that is how he feels inside? He is, at the moment, convinced that he is here to redeem us all. John Major is, at the moment, convinced that the world is against him. That is their subjective perception, and they will create their own reality –

which, fortunately or unfortunately, becomes our reality because of the position these men hold in the world.

Audience: Don't we create our reality because of the natal chart?

Liz: Yes, you are quite right; our birth charts are our perceptions of reality. But the birth chart contains many contradictions, and we do not knit it together all at once. Sometimes we look through one lens and sometimes through another, and only over time do we realise that they are lenses, and not the Absolute Truth. Transits and progressions highlight which lens we look through at any given time, or, to put it another way, which complex is activated and in what way. Fate and soul are two names for the same principle. But it would appear that the soul is a very complicated thing, and we seem to discover it bit by bit over the course of a lifetime. Our reality unfolds piecemeal through the triggering of birth chart configurations by transits and progressed aspects.

Watching the reality created by politicians is rather like watching a play. In many ways they are the same, although our lives are not circumstantially affected by what happens on stage, since once the performance is finished we can go home and do something else. With political figures we *are* circumstantially affected, because these people absorb us into their own archetypal dramas. However, as we put them in office to begin with, we generally get the government we deserve. Behind the surface issues lie the mythic stories, and it is sometimes difficult to tell the difference between an actor and a politician. One of you suggested, before you knew whose chart it was, that Tony Blair should be an actor. He was once, and I suppose still is. It's all theatre in the end. The reality we are now seeing is the one that John Major and Tony Blair have, step by step, been creating for themselves. Transiting Neptune at the MC and transiting Pluto at the Descendant are the culmination of inner processes. Whether Mr. Blair wins or loses the next election is not the point. Through his inner necessity he has put himself in his present position, and it is not by chance.

Audience: His father wanted to be an MP. Tony Blair's Sun conjuncts Pluto in the Tory party chart, in the same degree. All the charts interlock. The Tory Party chart, and the Labour Party, and the chart of the UK, and...

Liz: Yes, there are connections between all these charts. The same transits that are triggering one will trigger the others. What this tells us is that we are all interconnected. What else is new?

Audience: Perhaps Tony Blair is acting out a family complex, if his father had political ambitions.

Liz: I am sure that is part of it. But all of us are what we are partly because of our family inheritance. The father-son inheritance may also be glimpsed in Mr. Blair's relationship with John Smith, and there were many striking configurations occurring when John Smith died and Tony Blair became head of the Labour Party. For example, there was a lunar eclipse in mid-Taurus/Scorpio which landed on John Smith's Uranus in Taurus in the 6th house and also fell across Tony Blair's Sun. Once we start playing with these connections, we can wind up totally absorbed in abstractions, and lose touch with the individual's psychology and potential for choice. This is why I don't want to follow that path at the moment, fascinating though it is.

The reality of a person's life starts with the birth chart and its unfoldment over time through transits and progressions. Whatever connections that individual makes with other individuals, groups, organisations, and national charts, he or she will ultimately be impelled by inner necessity, and the timing of that necessity is governed by the transits and the progressions. The eclipse that occurred at the time of John Smith's death might certainly be interpreted as a herald of change, and of the emergence of hidden potentials. But John Smith *chose* to work extremely hard despite his doctor's warnings, and Tony Blair *chose* to say yes or no when offered the leadership.

Audience: Transiting Pluto will be making a grand trine in John Major's chart, to his Sun-Mercury and also his natal Pluto. Wouldn't that mean we can predict he will win?

Liz: It is very difficult to interpret grand trines on the level of manifestation. They are the trickiest configurations we can encounter. They seem so easy, but because of their ease they can make us passive, and we can become the resigned recipients of things over which we have given away our control. Transiting Pluto trine the Sun suggests a profound shift, the end of a chapter of life and the beginning of a new one, and also a change in one's self-image, values and goals. The fact that it is a trine does not mean "winning" as opposed to "losing" – we don't know how he might feel if he experiences defeat. He may interpret it as an act of fate, and accept it with dignity. The Sun is trine Pluto in the birth chart, and transiting Pluto will trigger this natal trine. I expect, if he loses, that he will heave a huge sigh of relief and go away thinking, "Thank God that's over."

Progressed new and full Moons

Audience: I find it interesting that they were both born under a last quarter Moon. They both have this thing about giving something to the collective. I wondered whether the progressed Moon is about to go into the first waxing square to the progressed Sun.

Liz: It will do so in late summer 1997, when the progressed Moon is in 28° Virgo and the progressed Sun in 28° Gemini.

Audience: I wonder what internal decision he may have taken about six years ago, at the time of the progressed new Moon, that the present striving for power may be reflecting.

Liz: The progressed new Moon six years ago was in $20°$ Gemini, and fell in the 1st house. It was trine Saturn-Neptune in Libra, and also widely trine the natal Moon. So this progressed new Moon formed a grand trine with natal Moon and Saturn-Neptune, and activated all his idealism and need to anchor his ideals through service to the public. As you say, what we are seeing now is the unfolding of all this.

Let's look more carefully at the progressed Moon's phases. Progressed new Moons occur roughly every thirty years, with a progressed full Moon roughly fifteen years after the last new Moon. The timing of the first progressed new Moon after birth depends on the phase of the Moon under which you were born.

Let's say that you were born under a new Moon, with the Sun in 10° Taurus and the Moon in 15° Taurus. The Moon will make its progressed return at roughly twenty-eight years old. It will first conjunct the natal Sun, and then five months later it will conjunct its own place. But the Sun will have moved roughly 28° further by progressed motion in those twenty-eight years, and will be in around 8° Gemini. In order to form a progressed new Moon, the progressed Moon has got to catch up with the progressed Sun. We can then work out how long it will take the progressed Moon to get from 15° Taurus to 8° Gemini. This would be just under two years. In those two years the Sun will have moved another 2° by progressed motion, so the new Moon will in fact fall in 10° Gemini, roughly thirty years after the new Moon which occurred at birth.

Let's say the Sun is at 10° Taurus and the Moon at 15° Virgo. Your first progressed new Moon will not occur thirty years after your birth. The progressed Moon will, as usual, take roughly twenty-eight years to return to its own place in Virgo. But it will arrive at the degree of the progressed Sun sooner than that – it has to move 240° to reach the natal Sun in Taurus, which will take around twenty years, since the progressed motion of the Moon is around 1° per month. At twenty years old the progressed Sun will be at 0° Gemini. The Moon then has to move another 20° past the natal Sun to catch up with the progressed Sun, which will take another twenty months, during which time the Sun will have moved almost two degrees further, so the progressed Moon will occur at roughly twenty-three years of age. The progressed full Moon which follows this first progressed new Moon will occur fifteen years later, at around thirty-eight, and the next progressed new Moon fifteen years after that, which means at around fifty-three.

We each experience these progressed new and full Moons at different times in life. Although the cycle itself is thirty years, varying slightly according to how fast the Sun and Moon are moving, progressed lunations can occur at any age, depending on the lunar phase under which one is born. It is not a fixed cycle like transiting Saturn, which makes its return at the same time in everyone's life. It is highly individual. What does this cycle mean? It is not the same as the progressed Moon aspecting its own place, which *is* a fixed cycle, completing its first round when we are twenty-eight years old. The progressed new and full Moons are related to the ongoing and changing expression of the natal Sun-Moon phase through different signs, houses, and aspects to natal planets, and they mark the endings and beginnings of different phases of life. They are extremely important, especially since we experience few of them in a lifetime. Like the Moon's nodes, they reflect an intersection of solar meaning and lunar embodiment, and the houses in which they fall in the natal and progressed charts reflect the spheres of life in which these endings and beginnings are likely to manifest.

The lunar phase at birth

We are all born with a particular relationship between the Sun, the individual self, the core of the personality, and the Moon, the instinctual antennae which allow us to relate to others and to the world. The Sun symbolises meaning and purpose, while the Moon symbolises the function of relationship. At birth, the Sun is like an empty vessel, not yet filled with life experience. The life purpose has not yet manifested in the world of form. It has not been born; it is not yet embodied. The Moon goes out into the world and touches and feels, eats and digests, and once it has gathered a sufficient amount of experience it brings this back to the Sun and pours it into the Sun's waiting vessel. This experience is processed in terms of the inner core of the individual, and shaped and ordered according to the individual's values and aspirations. Thus the sense of individual identity develops, primarily on the basis of what the Moon reflects back by way of physical and emotional experience. This is why we look at the phase of the Moon under which a person is born, because it tells us the very special rhythm underpinning this alternating movement outward toward experience and inward toward the core of meaning.

If one is born under a new Moon, the Moon is right next to the Sun, so the way in which one gathers experience is coloured by an intense sense of "I". One can never forget oneself in the midst of experience. There isn't really much ebb and flow or give and take, because everything is related back immediately to oneself. This gives great intensity and focus, but also a certain obliviousness in terms of other people's "otherness". It is why people born under a new Moon tend to seem very powerful and even overwhelming to other people. Even if it is a new Moon in Pisces, there is something about it that is very solar, because there is no distinction between one's experience of others and one's sense of personal identity. There is only one flavour of ice cream available, and one cannot imagine that any others exist.

If one is born under a full Moon, the Moon is at its furthest possible distance from the Sun – 180° – so there is a dichotomy between who one is and how one experiences others. One is constantly checking what other people feel and need, and the awareness of others' "otherness" is very intense. Thus relationships are very dominant in one's life, and it is often hard to define oneself without feedback. The Moon is "full" of experience, brimming over with it, but it has not yet begun the long return journey back to the Sun. One may put oneself in situations where one is constantly affected by important relationships, and there is a strong feeling of the necessity for compromise in order to live in harmony with others as well as retaining loyalty to oneself.

The new Moon and the full Moon are the two extremes. In between are all the gradations. When the Moon is forming its first square from the Sun, for example, there is a sense of tension, a push-pull feeling of ambivalence like an adolescent leaving home for the first time. "I want to go out and experience things," says the Moon to the Sun, "but no, I don't really want to, but yes, I really need to have some breathing space of my own, but no, I would rather stay home with you." There is sometimes a slightly aggressive edge to this phase of the Moon, with timidity and great sensitivity lurking underneath. There is often great energy in bursts, but also sudden periods of anxiety and loss of direction.

I think you get the general idea. I don't want to spend too much time on the natal lunar phase. Dane Rudhyar's book, *The*

Lunation Cycle[11], is an invaluable exploration of the lunar phases, and you might also try to catch one of Darby's excellent seminars on the Moon.[12]

Audience: What about when it is just behind the Sun?

Liz: Rudhyar called this the Balsamic phase. The Moon is within sight of home, and it is burdened by its fund of experience. It is a little weary. It is carrying everything back to the Sun, and isn't really interested in going out into the world to get yet more experience when it has already had quite enough. Rudhyar describes this phase as portraying a reflective, self-sacrificing quality. One is chewing over all the experiences one has gathered, prior to the imminent new Moon, and there isn't much desire to reach out for new experience. Other people may find the individual withdrawn and often inaccessible, yet at the same time there is little self-interest. This phase of the Moon describes a deeply reflective and indrawn way of being, whereas the Moon just in front of the Sun is like a child shouting, "What's out there? I want to go and explore!"

The lunar phase at birth describes the way in which we gather emotional and physical experience in the world and process it to build the foundations of the identity. It does not describe personality – that is the domain of the signs and aspects. It describes a way of being in life. The progressed new and full Moons indicate critical times when this very individual process of gathering and digesting experience will be most powerfully highlighted, and in what domain of life.

Progressed lunations aspecting natal planets

If each of you will take the time after the seminar to work out when and where these progressed new and full Moons occur in

---

[11]Dane Rudhyar, *The Lunation Cycle,* Servire-Wassenaar, Netherlands, 1967.

[12]Two of these have now been published – see Darby Costello, *The Astrological Moon,* CPA Press, London, 1996 (2003).

your own chart, you will get a sense of a deep, cyclical drumbeat marking the major turning points in life. It is rather like a piece of music – say, a sonata. The progressed new and full Moons are the indicators of when one movement ends and a new one begins, and in what key and at what tempo each of the movements will be played. These progressed lunations are programmed from birth, because they are dependent on the lunar phase under which one is born. The timing, the houses in which they fall, and the aspects they make to natal planets are all highly individual. Whatever phase of the Moon you are born under, your first progressed new Moon will occur dependent on that, and then the next one will always occur around thirty years later, usually in the subsequent zodiac sign.

Sometimes a progressed new or full Moon will form an aspect to a natal placement. This highlights the natal planet or configuration, and involves its meaning with the critical time reflected by the progressed lunation. When a progressed new Moon aspects a natal planet, a new cycle begins which is coloured by that planet. When a progressed full Moon aspects a natal planet, a time of fruition has arrived which is coloured by that planet. The spotlight is suddenly focused on that natal placement, and the stage director says, "It's time, get out on stage."

Earlier, one of you mentioned the last progressed new Moon in Tony Blair's chart, and what decision he might have made at the time. This progressed new Moon, at 20° Gemini, formed a grand trine with the natal Moon and the natal Saturn–Neptune conjunction. That heralded the beginning of a new life cycle, highlighting his idealism, his need to be of service, and his powerful urge to manifest his ideals in the public arena. In fact the progressed Moon will have to reach 5° Capricorn, in opposition to progressed Sun in 5° Cancer, for this new phase of life to come to fruition. It is not yet at that stage. The progressed Moon will form a first quarter square to the progressed Sun when the progressed Moon is at 28° Virgo and the progressed Sun at 28° Gemini, which will be in late summer next year. The progressed full Moon is still around eight or nine years away.

This thirty-year cycle is going to focus on the natal Saturn-Neptune conjunction. That does not mean nothing else in the chart is relevant. Important transits and other progressed aspects will highlight other areas of the chart, as we have seen. But the main way in which Mr. Blair develops his individual goals and aspirations will be coloured by natal Saturn-Neptune trine natal Moon. That is what is fuelling his ambitions from within, and because it is a grand trine it is likely that he has been fired, for the last six years, by a grand trine sense that it is all "right" and "meant" and will inevitably come to pass. However, progressions describe the internal development pattern, not whether an event will occur, and this sense of everything being "meant" may or may not be justified by external circumstances.

Audience: I have noticed, studying the progressed lunation cycle, that there is a similar quality to all the experiences which happen under the progressed lunations. Through every progressed lunation cycle, at the same junctures the same kinds of things happen. I am thinking of Jung, who at his first progressed full Moon experienced his father's death. At the second progressed full Moon his mother died. I have observed that there is some quality in the events which is repetitive.

Liz: There is a repeating quality because the source of the progressed lunation cycle is the natal Sun-Moon relationship, which includes the houses and signs in which the natal Sun and Moon are placed. Ultimately this is where the "results" show themselves, because progressed aspects, like transits, trigger what is potential within the birth chart, and put flesh on the bare archetypal bones. It may be that separation from or conflict with a loved one was a repeating theme in Jung's cycle because he was born under a last quarter Moon (which, according to Rudhyar, involves translating conflict into inner conviction or philosophy), with the natal Sun in the 7th, the house of relationships. But the immediate focus of each successive progressed lunation will depend on the house in which it falls, and what natal planets are aspected.

Audience: By "focus", do you mean the events?

Liz: No, I mean the psychological and teleological focus, although important events often accompany or immediately precede the progressed lunations. The ultimate products of these progressed lunations will always pertain to the development and expression of the natal Sun and Moon, and there will be an inherent thread of meaning running through all the progressed lunations because of this. But the focus of what this period of life is about will involve the configurations aspected by the progressed new or full Moon, and the houses – natal and progressed – in which the lunation falls.

Wherever a progressed new Moon falls, one can catch a glimpse of what area of the natal chart will be in the spotlight for the next thirty-year cycle. This is a big but extremely subtle cycle, and often we do not get a real sense of what it is about until we have been through at least one and perhaps even two rounds. It is hard to get perspective on it if one has not yet experienced a progressed new Moon, or one has not yet got very far into the second cycle. On the theoretical level it is of course possible to make sense of it at any time, but often the penny doesn't drop until one looks back and sees the underlying pattern. It is hard to recognise that everything has come back round again until it comes back round again. But understanding it on the theoretical level may be very helpful, because the decisions we make at the time of progressed lunations may have repercussions for a very long time, and we can make those decisions with a greater awareness of their implications.

Audience: With a progressed New Moon, what house does it activate – the house in the progressed chart or the birth chart?

Liz: Both. But the levels are different. The natal houses describe an innate design. They are a "given", in the sense that the planets in them, and the signs on their cusps, describe the underlying pattern according to which one's life is lived. In those houses emphasised by the presence of natal planets, we are "fated", because we are impelled to encounter or create certain experiences, develop certain qualities and perceptions, and produce certain results in the world.

Let's say that your natal Sun is in the 10th house, and your natal Moon is in the 9th. Putting it very briefly, you would therefore have a deep instinctive need to understand your experiences in the context of a larger, more universal pattern. This would make you feel at peace with life. You would also want to take what you have learned and create something special with it, which you can offer to society and thereby make your mark on the world. This would make you feel you are fulfilling your purpose.

Now, let's say that the first progressed new Moon falls in the 11th. The area of your life which this new cycle highlights is therefore your sense of connection with the larger human family, your involvement with the collective, your ideals, and your sense of vision beyond the purely personal. These are all 11th house issues. Ultimately this progressed new Moon, which might well open up an awareness of your place in the bigger evolutionary pattern, will strengthen those natal placements, Sun in the 10th and Moon in the 9th, so that your concern with religious, spiritual or philosophical matters and your need to make your mark on the world are both activated. A new cycle is beginning in which you are likely to become more truly who you are because of your contact with new people and ideas.

But you also need to look at the house in which this progressed new Moon falls in the progressed chart. Let's say that it is the 10th, because by progressed motion all the house cusps as well as the planets will have moved. This lunation might even be conjunct the progressed MC. This progressed 10th house then becomes the immediate arena of activity, the sphere where things are likely to "happen". You might discover a strong sense of vocation, or experience big changes in your work, or you might have to face issues around the mother. But your perception of belonging to a larger human family – the natal 11th in which the lunation falls – is opened up as a result of these worldly changes. The progressed chart is where we have got to now. So the progressed house in which the lunation falls is the outer form of what we see happening. But the deeper level is the house which is triggered in the natal chart, and ultimately what is really highlighted is the relationship of natal Sun and Moon.

I think we have to get used to looking at everything in doubles and even triples if we are to make sense of progressions and transits in any depth. This can be a bit irritating for anyone who likes to have simple, two-dimensional interpretations. But nothing living is that simple. A doctor can look solely at an immediate physical symptom and orientate his or her treatment according to that alone, but a wiser doctor will want to know the health history of the family, the circumstances in which one is placed, any repetition of the symptom pattern, and something of the patient's emotional state at the time.

Secondaries and solar arcs

It is worth the effort to get past the very natural human need to have only one answer, and to be flexible enough to see different perspectives of any planetary movement. The different systems of progressing a chart also require this flexibility. There is no single "right" method of progressing a chart. Every method has its followers and every method works on one level or another. It is a good idea to use two systems rather than only one, because they tend to back each other up as well as highlighting different levels of the personality which are being activated.

Take, for example, the dilemma of whether to use secondary progressions or solar arc progressions. Secondaries seem to be more "psychological", in the sense that most people understand the term. Often they don't correlate with external events. But they invariably reflect psychological states. Sometimes events are linked up, but usually we will find that triggering transits are involved if that is the case. But solar arc progressions have a very impersonal feeling about them. They are often used in connection with midpoints, and they are better indicators of events than secondaries.

Why should this be? Secondary progressions involve moving the planets each according to its own rate of speed. If we understand this symbolically, we are "tracking" the different drives within the individual according to their different rates of unfoldment, and the internal dynamics of the chart – the aspect patterns and house placements – will be constantly changing. Solar arc progressions involve moving everything in the chart according to the Sun's daily rate of motion. This means that the internal dynamics of the chart will not change, because everything is moving at the same rate of speed. Therefore solar arc progressions are only relevant in relation to the birth placements, while secondaries are relevant in relation to each other, and to the progressed houses through which they are moving. The subtleties of secondaries reflect the subtleties of the individual's inner "weather", while solar arcs are much starker in their inexorable triggering of the birth chart.

The Ebertin school uses solar arc progressions over midpoints. Perhaps this is one of the reasons why some of the interpretations in *The Combinations of Stellar Influences* are often very concrete, and do not allow much room for the transformative effect of individual consciousness. We have much more of a sense of process with secondary progressions. Sometimes the two overlap. The progressed Sun is the same in both systems, so solar progressions are both psychological and concrete. But one might find a secondary progressed aspect to one natal planet, and a solar arc progressed aspect to a different planet, occurring at the same time. They are completely different, yet one can see how the first describes the psychological background to the external experience of the other. It may not be practical to put that much work into a client's chart if the session is only an hour or two. But I would strongly recommend that you do this with your own charts. Take a time in your life when a lot was happening, progress the chart by both systems, and try to put them together. Then add the transits, which are usually reliable triggers for both systems of progression.

It is easier to grasp the difference between the natal and the progressed chart. One is innate and the other is where we have got to. Try to stretch your perspective when you work with transits and progressions, because you will have to look at several different things at once. At a certain point one gets brain fatigue, and the chart begins to look like a cauliflower. Then it is time to stop and mow the lawn, or go back to the essential structure of the birth chart, the ultimate arbiter of how all transits and progressions are expressed. The difficulty of juggling many different perspectives at once is one of the reasons why a lot of astrologers try to come up with a formula for progressions. First they feel impelled to decide that one system alone is correct. Then they say, "Let's work out when an event is likely to take place," and they try to work out a ratio of timing between the exactness of a progressed aspect and the exactness of a triggering transit. There is an enormous pressure on us to try to interpret progressions and transits based on some kind of mathematical formula, because we want to know when to take out life insurance and when to book our airline tickets.

The trouble is that any action or event on the material plane is not isolated from the psyche of the person performing that action or experiencing that event. And the psyche is different in different people. It processes things at different rates of speed. Complexes may take longer in some people than in others to make an impact on consciousness. Events mean different things to different people, as we have seen, and we are working with something living that we cannot reduce to a mathematical formula.

The question of orbs

The same dilemma arises with orbs. There is sometimes great difficulty in grasping the idea that a transit or a progressed aspect has an orb, just as a natal aspect does. Let's say that a person is born with the following configuration: Moon in 11° Gemini conjunct Uranus in 18° Gemini, both opposition Mars in 16° Sagittarius. When we read this natally, we know that these aspects have an orb. In other words, they "work" within a certain degree of exactness. Here there is a 5° orb for the Moon-Mars opposition, a 2° orb for the Mars-Uranus opposition, and a 7° orb for the Moon-Uranus conjunction. Although none of these aspects is exact, we acknowledge them as operative aspects.

If we are working with transits and progressions, the same applies. The aspect is operative even if is not exact. Let's say that transiting Saturn enters Gemini. From the moment that it moves into this sign, it is within 10° of conjuncting the natal Moon, and it will already begin to make itself known. And it will continue to make itself known even when it has moved on to 28° Gemini, because then it will still be within orb of conjunction to Uranus. This transit does not describe something that happens only within the short period when the aspects are exact. It covers a period of roughly two years, and the feelings, responses, events, actions, perceptions, and process which the transit describes will go on for that entire period.

At certain junctures there may be greater intensity – for example, when Saturn stations, or when another transit, such as Mars, lines up with the transit of Saturn. But greater intensity may not mean a greater propensity to manifest. It may mean greater consciousness of what is occurring within. This is why a transiting heavy planet entering a new sign may have great impact, even though it may be a long way away from an exact aspect to a natal planet. We are already starting to feel it, and because we react to these internal changes in highly individual ways, we may precipitate events long before or after the time of the exact aspect.

Audience: But with the progressed Sun, that means an aspect has a ten-year buildup! And another ten years to wind down!

Liz: Yes, it does. Is this so strange? The Sun is the most important single factor in the chart, because it symbolises our essence, our life purpose, and our sense of connection with the divine. The progressed Sun doesn't lurch from aspect to aspect with nothing in between. It connects one planet with another, slowly and deeply, moving into a new aspect while still within orb of an earlier one, gradually shedding light on the different natal planets and their relationship with each other, and revealing an inherent design. We will get no predictive precision from the progressed Sun, unless we work with midpoints. And midpoints also have an orb of one or two degrees, and are often part of a chain with natal planets and other midpoints, so that the progressed Sun moves from one to the next while still activating the last one. Why should we imagine that the psyche grows and develops in little fragmented spurts? Nothing in nature grows like this.

Dreams can reveal the gradual unfoldment of transits and progressed aspects long before the exact aspect and before the full import of it reaches consciousness. Something has already begun in the unconscious. One can see the approaching shape of the transit or progression, sometimes – in the case of Pluto or the progressed Sun – several years before it is expressed in outer life. The dream content gradually takes on images and feelings which we associate with the planet. For example, we associate Saturn with climbing mountains, or struggling across arid desserts where there is no water, or having to break up rocks or carry huge burdens, or constructing buildings. Figures we associate with Saturn – old men and women, authority figures, police in uniform, and so on – also begin to appear. The isolation and withdrawal of Saturn are also evident in the emotional tone of the dreams. This juxtaposition of analytic work with astrological symbolism has taught me a great deal about the psychological nature of planetary movements.

We don't know when things may manifest during the course of the process. The exact aspect may pass with a disappointing lack of important events. Perhaps it depends on whether it is necessary for something to manifest. Also, manifestation itself has many levels. An event can break something open, or it can bring something to fruition. If it breaks something open, it will come in the early stages of a transit or progressed aspect. If it is a way of resolving something, it will come in the later stages. An event may reflect completion as well as precipitation. Or we may experience several different events. Some may have to do with bringing unconscious issues into consciousness, and others may have to do with resolving them and making necessary changes in outer life. Events can occur at any point during the process. All we can be reasonably sure of is the meaning of the transit and how it is likely to feel to the person. And if we have some knowledge of his or her setup in life, we can make educated guesses about how things are likely to unfold, based not only on the planets and houses involved, but also on the immediate circumstances, character, and level of awareness.

Applying and separating aspects in childhood

I would like to look for a moment at progressions in childhood, especially in relation to what applying and separating aspects reveal. Let's go back to our example natal configuration – Moon in 11° Gemini conjunct Uranus in 18° Gemini, with both opposition Mars in 16° Sagittarius. Because we know that the progressed Moon has to travel 7° to reach its exact conjunction with Uranus, we can work out that this conjunction will be exact at around seven months of age. This is an applying aspect, because the Moon is the faster-moving of the two, and it is moving toward, not away from the conjunction. We can also work out that, at around five months old, the progressed Moon will be exactly opposition Mars. This opposition is also an applying aspect. Finally, the Mars-Uranus opposition is an applying aspect, because Mars is moving more quickly than Uranus by progressed motion. Mars usually travels at around 40' per day, but unlike the Sun and Moon, it may be retrograde, and this must be taken into account. If it is moving at its normal rate of motion, progressed Mars would arrive at the exact opposition with Uranus at approximately three years old.

Thus we have got three specific times in the early part of life when these applying natal aspects are exact by progressed motion. What are they describing? The two lunar progressions are exact during the first year of life. All applying lunar aspects are exact during the first year, because even allowing for a wide orb of 10°, the progressed Moon's motion of roughly 1° a month means that all its applying natal aspects will reach exactness within ten months after birth. Because the Moon is related to the experience of mother, these special times when applying lunar aspects are exact will probably describe experiences and feelings relating to the mother and the family environment.

Audience: What about separating lunar aspects? What would it mean if Uranus were in 11° Gemini, and the Moon in 18° Gemini? That aspect would be exact before birth.

Liz: If you think about it, you will realise that most separating lunar aspects, except those with a 10° orb, will be exact during the mother's pregnancy. I believe these aspects relate to experiences and feelings which mother and unborn child share during the gestation period.

Audience: Could progressed Moon opposition Mars have to do with breast feeding?

Liz: Possibly. Or it may have to do with disruption in the home, or with the mother experiencing tension, illness, or problems with the father. There might be anger or even violence in the domestic environment. It could coincide with a change of residence. A child's experience in such a case may reflect tension and anger. Young children are not always as amenable to moving as their parents are, even if the new home is bigger and better – it is a forcible disruption of their security. This aspect suggests conflict with the mother, although a child of five months is not yet in a position to articulate this in any coherent way. The feeling that one must battle to assert one's needs is an innate property of any hard Moon-Mars aspect, which is why the aspect has a reputation for being aggressive. But the exact timing of the aspect by progressed motion tells us what kind of external situation has helped to crystallise this attitude in early life. This aspect can sometimes coincide with childhood illness, but once again, there is usually an important psychological background to such illnesses, reflected by the tension of the opposition.

If this were a separating aspect, with Mars in 11° Sagittarius and the Moon in 16° Gemini, the opposition would be exact five months before birth. At this time the child is still in the womb. What then might the aspect describe?

Audience: Something disruptive or violent during the mother's pregnancy.

Liz: Yes, it is giving us a picture of difficult prenatal events, experiences, and feelings. Once again, the mother's situation and emotional state are relevant. Illness, excitement, upset or upheaval during pregnancy may not be part of adult consciousness, but such things may be part of one's bodily memories, and if they are triggered one may respond instinctively and compulsively without understanding why. It is generally accepted that the mother's condition and feelings during pregnancy are an important psychological factor in our development.

When the progressed Moon moves away from the opposition to Mars and conjuncts Uranus at seven months old, these two experiences will be connected. They are part of the same configuration, and the progressed Moon will be within orb of the opposition to Mars while it is conjuncting Uranus. So we may assume that something is going on in this family which crystallises the child's natal aspects during the first year of life. Great tension and instability are suggested. We don't know precisely what form this might take. But we know that the progressed Moon is involved in some very turbulent aspects at a very young age. The aspect "holds" the memory of these experiences, and they give a concrete "reason" for the tension, hair-trigger responses, and energetic "thank you very much but I'll do it myself" stance of the configuration in adulthood. The mother did not mysteriously "implant" the configuration in the child's chart. The relationship with the mother is a conduit through which the configuration takes on flesh and the complex develops personal associations.

When an important transiting planet comes into Gemini later in the person's life, and moves over this configuration, this transit does not pertain only to where the person is now. It is going to invoke that earlier time when the progressed Moon opposed Mars and conjuncted Uranus. All the anxiety, tension, anger, and instability from this early period will be constellated. This in turn will affect how the person responds to the transit, and these childhood feelings, rising to the surface and invading the present, may tip the balance if there is a choice of responding to the transit positively or negatively.

It may be important to recognise the invasion of the present by the past, because we can then respond to the present with greater consciousness. The meaning of a Saturn transit over the Moon is archetypal, but we cannot apply the same personal interpretation to everyone because not everyone has the same childhood memories. Each person has to contend with highly individual responses to a transit or progressed aspect to the natal Moon.

Audience: You could also be looking at the family's emotional memories. I always find that certain degrees repeat in families. If they are hit by a transit the whole family may be affected.

Liz: I have found this as well. If particular degrees are echoed in other family charts, or in the composite charts between family members, then a powerful transit will trigger the whole family, because a family complex has been activated. The particular degree may not always be in the same sign, but it is often in the same quadruplicity, and frequently in opposite signs. Observing the way in which family complexes are triggered by transits underlines the need for us to be as flexible as possible in understanding what transits and progressions describe. We see only a little bit of the picture if we look at them as indicators of isolated events.

Transit cycles

The progressed lunation cycle has its own individual timing. Transit cycles like those of Saturn and Uranus are different, because we all experience them at around the same age. They reflect archetypal human experiences linked to particular stages of life. Their emotional and material manifestations vary enormously, but their basic meaning is the same for all of us. A Saturn return is all about the process of growing up psychologically. Whatever house and sign natal Saturn is in, whatever aspects it makes, and whatever other factors appear in the chart, we are challenged to mature during the course of this cycle, willingly or kicking and screaming every inch of the way. Consciously or unconsciously, we crystallise as individuals, and are impelled to separate from the family matrix.

Major transit cycles such as Saturn, Chiron, Uranus, and also Neptune – which will not complete its entire round in one lifetime, but which will generally manage at least a square and maybe an opposition – reflect an inner process. The critical stages of these cycles often coincide with important external events, but such events need to be seen as adjuncts of the inner process, rather than as things separate unto themselves. The external events are rarely predictable unless we know something about the person's background and situation, and can then add reasoned assumptions to the astrological picture.

It is what events precipitate or reflect inside us that seems to be the relevant thing in interpreting these cycles. In one sense it doesn't really matter what happens, because whatever happens, it focuses us on the quality or complex that is seeking consciousness and expression in life. In the case of Saturn, for example, we are focused on our sense of separateness and our need to find an inner self-sufficiency which can help us to survive in life. Each segment of the Saturn cycle is in some way part of the same theme.

Example chart 2

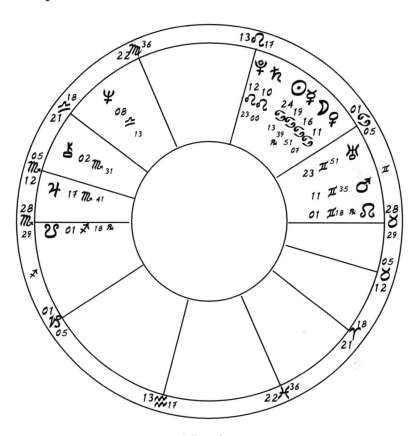

Miranda
[Birth data withheld for reasons of confidentiality]

Here is a chart given to me by someone in the group. We can look at the progressed chart in a moment. What did you want to explore?

Miranda: It's Neptune transiting opposition my Sun that I am most concerned about. It's already been across it once and now it's going to make a station right in that degree. I've also just finished with Pluto on my Ascendant, and now it's opposition the Moon's node.

Liz: To make any sense of the transits and progressions, we have to look first at the natal chart. The Sun is in the 8th house, along with five other planets. Venus is at 11° Cancer, then the Moon at 16° Cancer, then Mercury at 19° Cancer, and then the Sun at 24° Cancer. Then there is a Saturn-Pluto conjunction, at 10° and 12° Leo respectively. All the Cancer planets are trine natal Jupiter in 17° Scorpio. The Sun is also square natal Chiron at 2° Scorpio. So transiting Neptune isn't only opposing the Sun. It has been moving across this group of planets for a very long time, opposing first Venus, then the Moon, then Mercury, and finally the Sun. When it enters Aquarius it will square natal Chiron and eventually oppose the natal Saturn-Pluto conjunction. Neptune is transiting through the 2nd house, and natal Neptune, which we also have to consider, is in the 10th, conjunct the MC. We have to take all these things into account to make sense of the Neptune-Sun transit.

This is a watery chart, by sign and by house, and with such a powerful emphasis in the 8th and 12th in water signs, your receptivity to the inner world is likely to be very great. There may be difficulty in establishing boundaries, especially as there are no planets in earth signs – although what you may lack in definition you undoubtedly make up for in a deep faith in life and a sense of connection with other people. However, I have found that people with a great emphasis in the 8th often discover their relationship with the inner world through loss and emotional upheaval – it demands an inner journey of a committed kind. Otherwise there may be a sense of victimisation, and a feeling that one is at the mercy of forces one cannot understand or do anything about.

Miranda: I do have a problem with boundaries. It is especially bad right now. That is why I am a little afraid of this transit. I don't need yet more dissolving!

Transiting Neptune opposition the Sun and Moon

Liz: Let's try to make some sense of transiting Neptune opposition the Sun. What does it mean and what is it likely to feel like?

Audience: Confusion. Loss of identity.

Liz: Those are classic Neptunian emotional experiences. Moreover, this is an unearthed chart, presenting us with a nature which is imaginative, idealistic, romantic, and inclined to live in a world of potentials. The limitations of hard reality are not usually the flavour of the month for someone lacking earth, even without a Neptune transit. The natural response to stress, for all of us, is to fall back on our strengths and avoid our weaknesses. Any hard aspect from a transiting planet, especially an outer planet, reflects a time of stress. Miranda's strengths lie in her fine imagination and her ability to empathise with others' feelings. Her weaknesses lie in her reluctance to accept the limits of the earthy plane, the chief one of which is separateness.

The Moon in the 8th emphasises this – there is a powerful need to experience safety through losing oneself in one's emotions. When there is pressure, this is a natural line of escape – to seek intense emotional involvement in the hope of getting away from painful feelings of isolation and limitation. A hard transit of Neptune is likely to aggravate this inclination because one feels so lost and confused. This transit would probably increase the need to escape into alternative realities or intense relationships that initially seem to get Miranda's mind off her loneliness, but which are not likely to turn out very satisfactory in the end.

Miranda: That's me!

Liz: These are some of the emotional ramifications of the transit. What is its teleology, and what is its potential?

Audience: It's been opposing all the 8th house planets. They would all be connected.

Liz: Yes, it has been picking them off, one by one. Let's start with the Moon, to get some background. What is the meaning of Neptune opposition the Moon?

Audience: That would really make her want to escape.

Liz: On the level of meaning, transiting Neptune opposition the Moon might reflect a process of breaking down habitual family patterns of relating. New feelings and new relationship patterns would begin to emerge, which reflect more of Miranda's individual needs, and less of her mother's. With all those planets in the 8th, there is a lot of inherited family patterning on the emotional level. Neptune will start breaking down all the old emotional responses through its characteristic activation of the longing to go home. It is a regressive pull. This is likely to generate a great deal of anxiety, and in turn a powerful desire to escape the inevitable change which is required. Most importantly, it may break down any idealisation of and identification with the mother, and bring to the surface many difficult emotional issues from early childhood. It is a process of separation from the mother, and this separation is likely to begin with a powerful need to be close to mother, or even to become her in order to be close. How is mother described in the birth chart?

Miranda: Neptune in the 10th!

Liz: Yes, and it is square the Moon in the natal chart, so it is a mother-significator to begin with. The Neptune-Moon transit would inevitably bring up themes of sacrifice, suffering and victimisation. It seems you need to learn not to be your mother, by becoming her for a while and finding out that you have other options.

Miranda: My mother recently died.

Liz: I am not surprised. There is often a strange synchronicity between the inner separation from a parent and the parent's actual death. And you got involved in a relationship that proved painfully disappointing?

Miranda: Yes, as a matter of fact I did. He wasn't what I thought. I began to realise I was becoming my mother, with all the resentment and disappointment and feeling cheated.

Liz: That is what I think this Neptune-Moon transit means. An old pattern of relationship is breaking down – an old model of what it is to be a woman, which is rooted in the family background and in the mother, who appears as the archetypal victim. Your sense of yourself as a woman has been submerged in this identification.

Miranda: I saw my mother die. It was really horrible. Not just physically – she was also in a lot of confusion. When she died the real truth of her relationship with my father began to come out.

Liz: This has obviously been proving a very painful transit. But what it seems to be doing on the level of meaning is giving you back your Sun and Moon. The Sun and Moon are in the 8th house, and this suggests that you have been unconsciously carrying a psychological inheritance which, in effect, keeps you underwater and unformed. I think it is ultimately necessary for anyone with an 8th house emphasis to understand the family emotional history, because there is always excess psychic baggage which makes itself known through compulsive relationship patterns and emotional states. With a strong 8th house, it is essential to recognise the reality of the unconscious.

Neptune is now opposition the Sun and is activating your sense of yourself – but in a Neptunian way. If this had been another transiting planet, the same meaning would have underpinned this period of your life, but the feelings and events would have probably been quite different. The means by which you are reclaiming your emotional identity from the matrix of the family psyche is through becoming Neptune for a while, which in your chart means becoming your mother – since Neptune in the 10th is her significator. Evidently you have to live this through in a way which makes you conscious of it, so that you can disengage from it.

Very often, powerful hard transits to the Sun precipitate a recognition of who we are through discovering who we are not. We become conscious by recognising our unconsciousness. We are denied something, and we only realise what we value and want by recognising that what we have is what we *don't* want. Through loss or suffering or sacrifice, a realisation dawns of what we are actually made of. It is often how Neptune works. We only discover what we care about most deeply through losing it, or through having to live without it for a while, or through discovering that we never had it. Ultimately, the meaning of this transit is enormously creative. But the experience of it has clearly been pretty awful.

Miranda: Yes.

Liz: Transiting Neptune is often no fun by opposition or square to the Sun. It can constellate very powerful and very unpleasant experiences and feelings. It also seems that the stronger the sense of will and identity, however nascent, the more difficult it is. But what it reveals about the Sun is extremely important.

Audience: So the transit is the means, not the end.

Liz: Yes. Any progressed or transiting aspect to the Sun ultimately activates the Sun. The transit will pass, but the Sun remains. If the Sun is in natal aspect to Neptune, then the "means", as you put it, may not feel so alien. One has been living with it all one's life. But it is the Sun which is constellated by this transit.

Audience: You would say this regardless of which planet was transiting.

Liz: Yes, I believe the natal planet is the key to the meaning of the progression or the transit. Now let's have a look at Miranda's progressed chart, to see whether any progressed aspects add to our understanding of what is happening at the moment.

Progressed planets over natal Saturn and Pluto

Audience: I am looking at the Saturn-Pluto conjunction at the very end of the 8th house. This is the end of tempestuous, intense relationships, before the step of emerging and understanding. It seems that all endings are extremely painful and they involve great breakdowns of some kind. Now, in terms of secondary progressions, what I see is that all the inner planets are behind that conjunction. So it seems to me that there is a threshold through which all the inner planets have to pass as they progress. They have to get swallowed up and expelled out into the 9th house. The destiny of this life means going through a particular threshold, which marks the end of 8th house stuff and an emerging into some kind of new vision of things. But it is very painful, with great loss every time. Also, her resistance is very strong. It is as if she pushes things to the limit, maybe unconsciously. There is great resistance to change.

Liz: Yes, you are describing the characteristic strength and resistance of Saturn-Pluto in the 8th. This conjunction says, "I will not give up and I will not let go, and you can't make me." There is enormous tenacity. It is anything but Neptunian – the defences and boundaries are obsessively strong. You are making a very important point. Let's look at the timing of the inner planets progressing over Saturn-Pluto. Can you give us a quick biography, Miranda? The progressed Sun arrived on Saturn when you were around sixteen, and on Pluto at around eighteen. What happened at that age?

Miranda: I can't remember anything specific. I remember feeling terribly depressed and suicidal. But I can't remember an event.

Liz: This is a solar progression. The events in themselves were evidently not important enough for you to have remembered them, but the inner experience was of extreme depression, verging on the point of suicide. Do you remember why? Was it loneliness?

Miranda: Yes. I always used to think that as I got older, everything would change, and I would be happy. As I was growing up I could always make myself feel better by imagining that just around the corner was some kind of wonderful life. Then I began to think, "Things are not going to change, they are still the same." I don't remember any big relationship bust-up. I had difficulties, but no worse than anyone else's. But I can remember that feeling, at around sixteen, that I had been deluding myself, and that nothing would change.

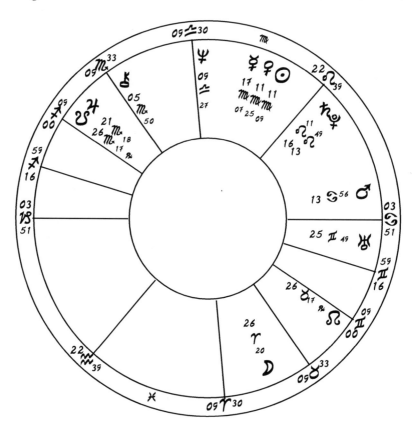

Miranda
Progressed chart set for 8 June 1996

Liz: I can't think of a better way of expressing both the feeling and the meaning of progressed Sun on Saturn. One has to acknowledge life's limits, and it can be deeply depressing and lonely for a person with such a romantic and idealistic nature. Secondary progressions in themselves are not that concerned with events, and you are illustrating that. You realised that you are alone and separate, an individual in incarnation, which is extremely painful for a

Cancerian temperament, and particularly painful for a sixteen-year-old.

The progressed Moon would have reached the Saturn-Pluto conjunction when you were under two years old. You probably don't have a memory of what happened at that age, but there must have been some experience of deep isolation, and perhaps physical rejection as well. Your mother may have gone through something painful at that time which underlined your feeling of being separate and having to fight for your own survival. Something secret or painful might have been going on in the family, and the atmosphere may have been very difficult for you.

Progressed Mercury would have arrived at Saturn-Pluto at about the same time as the progressed Sun, which suggests that your mental attitudes were particularly negative and dark, and you might have found it hard to communicate your feelings to anyone. Progressed Mars hasn't got there yet – it is still in Cancer, and it will be a very long time before it reaches Saturn-Pluto. But after the progressed Sun and Mercury, progressed Venus arrived there, at about the time of your Saturn return or just before – around twenty-nine. What was happening then?

Miranda: I made a suicide attempt.

Liz: So the isolation of Saturn-Pluto becomes virtually unbearable when it is triggered. Have you felt suicidal under this Neptune-Sun transit?

Miranda: Yes. But it isn't as bad as it was when I was twenty-nine. I wouldn't do anything about it now. I just think about it.

Liz: Neptune is rarely actively self-destructive. It just wants to go home, if the opportunity arises –"If a bus rolls over me, I don't really mind." The threshold that everything has to get past seems to be the intense experience of aloneness.

Audience: Isn't the progressed Ascendant opposite the Sun? I thought it moved at the same speed as the progressed Sun.

Liz: The Ascendant progresses at variable speed, depending on the sign and the latitude of birth. Scorpio, Sagittarius and Capricorn are signs of slow ascension in northern latitudes and progress at less than 1° per year. Aries and Taurus are signs of rapid ascension, and progress at more than 1° per year. The progressed Ascendant is at 8° Capricorn, and is in fact square natal Neptune. There is no escaping Neptune at the moment, is there? Or perhaps it would be more accurate to say there is no escaping mother. This progressed square from the Ascendant activates natal Neptune, so the individual you are becoming – the particular way in which you are learning to express yourself in life – is in conflict with the longing for fusion and return to the source reflected by Neptune. The struggle between transiting Neptune and natal Sun is echoed by this progressed aspect. Transiting Neptune activates the Sun in the 8th, which says, "Good God, I have been asleep all my life. I have been at the mercy of the family psyche. Now I want to be an individual. I have to find my own way. But it's cold out there, and it's hard to leave the birth canal." This conflict necessitates looking beneath the surface of life, because that is the path of the Sun in the 8th. In the midst of all this, you can't make everything nice by trying to create a state of fusion with a lover, although it is likely that you would try.

Miranda: I did try. But I suppose it was doomed from the start.

Liz: Meanwhile the progressed Ascendant has moved into Capricorn, an earth sign. There is no earth in the birth chart. This suggests that during the last ten years or so, since the Ascendant progressed out of Sagittarius, you have begun to learn containment, structure, and acceptance of limits. Now this increasing ability to live within the confines of reality has reached a crisis point, and is in direct collision with the Neptunian longing to retreat from life through emotional fusion, which is bound up with your relationship with your mother.

Looking at these two planetary movements – transiting Neptune opposition Sun and progressed Ascendant square Neptune – there is a certain inevitability about trying to escape the conflict in the arms of a lover-redeemer. But it would probably prove impossible to make such a relationship work, not because the planets are "fating" you to have a bad relationship, but because your emotional state at the moment is, in large part, that of a very young child. Any feelings and fantasies you might have about a partner are likely to be heavily coloured by that, which makes it pretty hard to maintain a relationship of equals. Also, the kind of person who is attracted to a woman in such a state of childlike need and confusion is likely to be the kind of person who feeds off being in control. That is not a good recipe for mutual respect.

Miranda: I feel I desperately need some structure in my life. I know I need to do this myself, and not through somebody else. It has a lot to do with material independence.

Liz: Yes, that is the voice of the Ascendant progressed in Capricorn. But seeking anything "desperately" is not a good place to begin. If you flail about wildly trying to create structures that are secure just because you want to alleviate your anxiety, you may find that these too prove disappointing, because you are being driven by the same compulsion to find a safe womb. If you build something because you really value it, then you are starting on firm ground. But if your structures are meant to replace a relationship that hasn't worked out, then I think it is wise to be especially attentive, especially when dealing with material matters.

The Greeks were very intelligent when dealing with divine interference. They understood deity as having many facets, each reflected by a particular god or goddess, and any of these facets could prove difficult and demanding at particular junctures in life. If one wanted to make friends with a god, one made an offering which that particular god liked. One didn't give the gods something alien to their individual natures. One didn't go to Mars and offer him flowers, because Mars loves the clash of arms and the glory of victory, so how can he be expected to appreciate tulips? One didn't go to Apollo and offer him one's enemy's bloody head, because Apollo is a scholar and a gentleman and dislikes chaos and mess. The Greeks always tried to give the god what the god wanted, not what the individual found it easy to give. There is great wisdom in working with transits and progressions from this perspective.

The natal planet which is triggered by a transit is the operative god. What does the Sun want? It certainly doesn't want self-abnegation and a lot of weeping and self-pity, because, as I said, Apollo is a gentleman and dislikes chaos. This god appreciates efforts at consciousness, because this is what he symbolises, as god of wisdom and foresight. If you try to make an offering that is not part of Apollo's nature, then the god will reject it. Because the Sun is your essential individuality, a relationship in which you are seeking redemption by losing yourself in another person is not likely to be pleasing to the god. But consciousness and creative work are the right sort of offering.

If you are trying to build secure financial structures in order to feel safe, that is not likely to please Apollo either. If you are finding a way of being creative which also earns you money, the god might approve of that, because Apollo and his Muses favour all efforts at self-expression from the heart. But he becomes bored and irritated by blind panic. As long as the Sun is being activated by Neptune, there is pressure on you to develop yourself as an individual, independent of your emotional background. As long as you are aligned with that need, regardless of the chaos around you, you will be in harmony with the meaning of the time.

Audience: As Neptune goes into Aquarius, it will be in her 2nd house, and it will trine the Moon's north node. That is a revolutionary thing – she will find destiny and direction.

Liz: Transits aspecting the nodal axis are very interesting. I think they are important, although I am not sure I would use the word "destiny" as being especially applicable to the nodes. But the nodes seem concerned with manifestation, because they symbolise the intersection of the Sun and Moon. They are a kind of gateway through which both the solar sense of purpose and the lunar experience of the material world are expressed. But I have found that they are more connected with relationship than with anything else, and here the nodal axis straddles the Ascendant/Descendant axis. This transit is already within orb, and I suspect it pertains not only to anchoring the creative imagination in form – that is Neptune transiting through the 2nd – but also to the possibility of a different and more fulfilling kind of relationship.

Miranda: So there is light at the end of the tunnel.

Liz: Yes, but there is also light in the middle of the tunnel. You have been in that tunnel for a long time, and you have begun to see what the walls are made of. That means there is already light – even if it doesn't feel that way at the moment.

Miranda: I have had both Uranus and Neptune making oppositions in my chart for such a long time – nearly ten years. Neptune opposing my Sun has probably been the hardest of all the outer planet transits that I have been through. It's much worse than Pluto over my Ascendant.

Liz: I believe you. I cannot imagine why people glamorise Neptune. It can be positively awful in hard aspect transits, because everything feels as though it is coming unglued. Pluto might be rough, but it mobilises the survival instincts. And with all your planets in the 8th, and Scorpio on the Ascendant, Pluto is actually an old friend.

Accidents and progressions and transits to Mars

Audience: I have a question about a friend's chart. She has a Mars-Saturn square, and her Moon is opposition Uranus, right on the MC/IC axis. Now she is in the middle of a Saturn return, and the progressed Moon is in Aries, and she has the progressed Sun square Mars, and she was told by an astrologer to be very careful because she has a propensity for accidents. She got very upset and frightened, as you can imagine.

Liz: This sort of interpretation is quite unhelpful. Progressed Sun square Mars may activate a lot of aggression and anger, but it is important that the person understands what this is all about, rather than simply being told that something awful might happen.

A "propensity" for accidents is something which is as psychological as anything else. What does this picture tell you on an emotional level? And on the level of meaning?

Audience: Well, it could be that what these aspects make her feel right now is self-assertion, a kind of initiative, impetus, a need to start new things, searching for some kind of personal independence. If there is frustration, then she may get angry, and drive faster, and have a crash.

Liz: Yes, that is getting closer to why difficult aspects involving Mars sometimes manifest in unpleasant events. But progressed Sun square Mars can be very positive too, if the person is in touch with Martial drives and can find a constructive outlet. We need to know where the Mars-Saturn square is placed by house.

Audience: Mars is in the 7th, square Saturn in the 10th.

Liz: If Mars is going to erupt in an unconscious way, it will probably do so in the sphere of relationships. It is not in the 3rd, which might pertain to mental and physical coordination, and it is not in the 8th, which might pertain to sudden emotional eruptions of a destructive or self-destructive kind. It is more likely that your friend will pick fights with people, or get them to pick fights with her. Natal Mars in the 7th tends to give personal power away to other people, and then anger builds up because there is a feeling that one is not in control of one's life. This might be particularly strong in your friend's case because of the involvement of Saturn with Mars, which could reflect a lot of inhibition and a fear of expressing aggression because of early issues with the mother. Saturn is, after all, in the 10th. Your friend may have a propensity to give away personal authority to the people with whom she is involved. She needs to find the courage to make her own decisions.

Audience: So you would see accident-proneness as an expression of unconscious aggression turned against oneself.

Liz: Often. If there is a repeating pattern of accidents, it may be an expression of something which is running loose and manifesting externally because it has not been integrated internally. Certainly this can be said of repetitive accidents which one causes oneself through carelessness. But because the unconscious is psychoid, it may also be said of accidents in which we are apparently not to blame. I don't doubt that some accidents, especially those which are fatal, are somehow part of the underlying destiny, and one cannot find any personal liability, conscious or unconscious. But "proneness" suggests a pattern, and where there are patterns there are usually complexes at work. Sometimes a run of small accidents can be interpreted as a kind of inner red warning light – something is on the move in the psyche, and the individual is not paying sufficient attention to its meaning.

This is a fraught issue which gets some people very worked up, but I think it needs to be explored. Many of these "accident-prone" patterns I have heard about seem to be linked with Mars in great trouble in the birth chart. There is a pocket of aggressive, fiery energy which is split off from consciousness. It is a complex which is autonomous and manifests in physical reality when the appropriate transit or progressed aspect acts as a trigger.

One of the most "accident-prone" people I have encountered has an 8th house Mars in Pisces. It is a singleton in the western half of the chart, with no aspects except squares to a group of planets in Gemini. This man is a very kind, civilised, nonaggressive individual. But he is constantly having accidents, or finding himself in the middle of other people's accidents. Every time something transits Mars, he encounters an accident. Some of these accidents are clearly self-generated, but others are quite bizarre – restaurants catch on fire while he is eating in them, or ferocious animals break out of the zoo just when he happens to be in town.

I believe there is a big, pulsating, fiery, red, autonomous complex at work here, not unlike the kind of things we see with poltergeist activity – but to the ordinary observer they are accidents, and the poor man is accident-prone. Such a pattern can be worked with. It is not a fate in the literal sense. But working with a difficult, split-off Mars means that one must face one's primitive rage and potential for violence, and for some people – especially civilised airy types – this is exceedingly painful.

Audience: I am glad to see that everybody else is nodding agreement, and I agree with you. The other interpretation did worry me.

Liz: Instead of having an accident, perhaps your friend should have punched the astrologer.

Audience: Well, I would have liked to do that myself.

Liz: Obviously, if one is a reckless driver with a history of traffic violations, and one has difficult transits to Mars, then one needs to be sensible and exercise restraint. But it might be wiser to ask oneself first *why* one is a reckless driver, before looking in the ephemeris every day to see when there is a bad aspect coming up.

Transiting Saturn opposition Neptune

Now let's look at the transit of Saturn through the 4th house, opposition natal Neptune in the 10th in Miranda's chart. They are sextile in the birth chart, and natal Saturn is in the 8th. Transiting Chiron is in the 10th, and it is stationing now, opposing transiting Saturn and conjunct natal Neptune. What does this configuration suggest?

Audience: Illness.

Liz: What is a Saturn-Neptune illness as distinct from other kinds of illness? Both Ebertin and Robert Pelletier mention illness in relation to Saturn-Neptune. What does this mean?

Audience: Depression. The poisoning of ideals.

Liz: Yes, one's ideals may undergo serious tarnishing. Usually what is left is indestructible, and what is tarnished belongs to the world of the infant. The child's Neptunian dream-world of perfect oneness is recognised as no longer viable. Reality comes along and cracks the egg. Transiting Saturn is in the 4th – you may feel homeless, parentless, alone in the world, without roots. Often people get very depressed during the course of this aspect, and if they get depressed enough without understanding why, they may also express their feelings through the body, because they are grieving on a very profound level. This aspect describes grieving for a lost womb-world, and it may also reflect grief for your mother. You said she died recently. When?

Miranda: In the spring of 1995.

Liz: That is just over a year ago. Do you feel you have been able to grieve for her?

Miranda: I don't know how far I've gone into it. I suppose the honest answer is no.

Liz: You may be in the middle of grieving now, because I think that is, in part, what the aspect reflects on the emotional level. You have described a painful, unpleasant and undignified death, to which you were witness. The sadness and world-weariness which you feel now may be linked with your mother's death, even if you have not been conscious of the link. When the mother is symbolised by Neptune, she is more than one's personal mother. She is the archetypal source of life, the divine womb from which one comes and to which one will eventually return. A close identification with this archetypal mother means one may unconsciously carry the illusion of being immortal, and always in relationship with her. Separation means not only the loss of a person, but also the loss of Eden. It is like being thrown out of Paradise. One experiences one's aloneness and vulnerability in a very intense and acute way.

Audience: Transiting Saturn will trigger the natal Saturn-Neptune sextile. So Saturn can bring Neptune's ideals down into reality. It has to do with making something concrete out of her most cherished dreams, and accepting the limitations of those dreams.

Liz: Yes, the process of anchoring one's dreams inevitably involves accommodating the human experiences of loss, limitation, and disappointment – all the Saturnian hard realities. The potential is there, and the opposition is going to trigger that potential. Psychologically, you are parting ways with both parents, and with the whole family past.

Miranda: My father is very old and in hospital. I have been thinking I may lose him as well.

Liz: There is a possibility you may lose him. But it is the inner separation which is most relevant, and the realisation of what your parents have meant to you. On an inner level, transiting Saturn and Chiron ploughing into natal Neptune suggests letting go of a long-standing fantasy of a perfect family, perfect love, and perfect relationship. This is a deep and lifelong dream. Natal Venus is square Neptune, so you are tremendously romantic, and do not cope easily with other people's failings. You want all your relationships to be beautiful, wonderful, perfect, kind, and seamlessly loving. That is not the reality that you have encountered. This dream is now going through the fire. One parent has died and the other is old and ill, and you have just experienced a relationship failure as well. Love has proven to be imperfect, and immortality has proven to be an illusion. If you became ill during this transit, it might be because you were not facing these feelings of disillusionment and world-weariness, and so they might somatise. Saturn-Neptune illnesses are linked with the process of grieving for a lost Paradise. It is not enough to say "illness". It is a kind of soul-sickness, which may be expressed as physical illness if it has no other outlet.

Miranda: I suppose I'm pretty infantile about all this.

Liz: Grieving for a lost Paradise doesn't necessarily make you infantile – it means there is a childlike side of you which always has one eye on the eternal. A lot depends on whether you can contain that child and honour its vision while living effectively in this world. I think you are waking up to your Sun as a result of this Neptune transit. You can only live the Sun if you are not paralysed by the fear of loneliness. The real imaginative and emotional gifts of Cancer can only open up if you take Saturn-Pluto on board and accept the limitations of love.

Audience: I can confirm what you were saying about feeling homeless with transiting Saturn in the 4th. Wherever you live, there is some kind of loneliness and isolation, and at a very deep level you have to stand alone in the place you are living.

The response of the client to prognosticative advice

Audience: I have found that when I give advice to clients about transits and progressions, they usually do exactly the opposite. I wonder why I bother. Do you think there is something in people that has to reject what the astrologer tells them?

Liz: Not as a general rule, no. When somebody goes to the trouble of coming along and spending money for a chart reading, generally he or she makes the effort to listen. But a lot depends on what you mean by "advice", and how you are offering it. Telling people what they should or shouldn't do under a particular transit or progression may provoke some deep need in the client to exercise free will, because the archetypal background of an astrological reading unconsciously invokes a sense of fate and a cosmos which could grind one's will down if it so pleased. If the astrologer then adds to the client's sense of impotence by saying, "If you don't do what I say, such-and-such will happen," the client may understandably feel impelled to prove the astrologer wrong. I do not believe our job is to give advice of a kind which takes away the client's decision-making capacities. It is more relevant to help the client understand the options reflected by a particular transit or progression, and the deeper issues underlying the situation.

If you try to tell someone something when he or she is not interested in hearing it, then it may prove a waste of time. Lack of interest usually occurs when the client is bullied into consulting the astrologer by an insistent spouse, lover, friend or parent, or when the astrologer, filled with good intentions, offers unsolicited advice.

But usually people come for a chart interpretation because they are in crisis of some kind. Either it is an obvious crisis, or they are feeling lost and confused. Most of the time an important transit or progression is hovering about, and this provides the underlying "reason" for the consultation, whether the client is fully conscious of it or not. Clients generally come along because they are changing, and therefore they tend to be open to new perspectives.

Audience: What about when you predict events?

Liz: I don't predict events; that is not my area of focus. Sometimes I may see something screamingly obvious, such as transiting Saturn conjunct the IC and square the Sun in the chart of a client who has a ninety-eight-year-old father in hospital with a fatal illness. It does not take a mind of great genius to work out that the father will probably die. In that sort of instance I might tell the client the father's death is probable, because the client already knows it is probable; the doctor has said so. But unless a situation is so clear that there isn't really any other option for the transit, then I don't think we can know how that transit is going to come out. We can talk about what it means, and how it might feel, and we can discuss options and possibilities. But usually my only advice is to suggest that the person needs to become more conscious of what is going on inside. Then he or she can make more intelligent choices.

When we are unconscious, we are predictable, but that is not because of transits. It is because of character. Earlier, I asked Miranda if she had been through a disappointing relationship. This is not because the Neptune transit "made" it happen. It is because the individual psyche responds consistently to pressure and change, according to its nature. Miranda is a romantic and has difficulty in creating firm boundaries and coping with loneliness. If she feels unhappy, lonely, or depressed, another person is likely to seem like the path to redemption, and she might expect too much. Miranda recently lost her mother, and all the feelings associated with that loss would inevitably creep into her relationship. The model of the feminine provided by Miranda's mother in early life is also a difficult model, because it portrays woman as sacrificial victim. With that background, Miranda would be likely to slip into this role, until she became aware that it was her mother's role, which does not suit her as a whole individual.

If Miranda had come to see me in the midst of all this, and had said, "I have just fallen in love!", I could have replied, "Be very careful, because Neptune transits are very tricky." But what does "careful" mean? Ring the chap up and tell him to sod off? Get involved sexually but remain emotionally detached? How could a Cancer-Scorpio nature manage that? I would more likely have talked about why Miranda's emotional state made her especially vulnerable, rather than advising her to avoid the relationship. She would have hurled herself into the relationship anyway. That is not willful refusal to accept the astrologer's advice. It is inner necessity.

When complexes are thumping about, one does not listen to other people's advice. It would spoil all the fun. But consciousness can make painful experiences worthwhile, and may alter their ultimate outcome. Our business is not to tell people to avoid experiences. It is to help people understand why they have been drawn into certain experiences, so that they can get something positive out of the experience if they choose to go through it. If it is possible to act on sound advice, people generally do, from enlightened self-interest. But transits and progressions reflect the triggering of complexes, and activated complexes and sound advice repel each other like oil and water. If someone is inwardly compelled to go through something, that may be the only way he or she is going to learn.

It is possible to work with a complex so that its expression is more creative. But we cannot do this on paper. On paper, during the course of these powerful Neptune transits, Miranda could theoretically have avoided picking the wrong love object. That would have spared her a good deal of pain and disappointment. But if she had not picked the wrong love object, she would not have discovered herself behaving like her mother, and she would not be able to affirm her right to be happy as herself. She could only achieve that awareness in the midst of the experience. Pain and disappointment have helped her to understand why she has chosen people who don't treat her well, and who make her feel like her mother felt. Consciousness can help her to avoid such destructive relationships. She will always be a romantic who needs to be needed, and no one will ever provide the perfect union she dreams about. But next time, she may be less likely to pick a lemon.

More on applying and separating aspects

Audience: Can I ask a technical question? Earlier on, you were talking about applying aspects. I'm a little confused about this. If I have Uranus in 11° Gemini, and Saturn in 16° Gemini, then Uranus will progress toward Saturn, and one day, if I'm still alive, the conjunction will be exact. Is that an applying aspect?

Liz: Technically, no. One day progressed Uranus may indeed reach natal Saturn. But in an applying aspect, the faster-moving planet is moving into exact aspect with the slower one. Uranus moves much more slowly than Saturn. This is technically a separating aspect – unless Saturn is retrograde, in which case it is applying backward into the conjunction. If you have the Sun at 3° Taurus square Saturn in 9° Leo, that is an applying aspect; the Sun progresses more quickly than Saturn. It would make the exact square at six years of age. If Saturn were at 3° Taurus and the Sun at 9° Leo, Saturn might eventually reach the exact square with the Sun, and that time would certainly be critical, but it is not an applying aspect. The Sun is moving away from Saturn, and that gives the natal aspect a different tone.

Audience: And you don't count progressed aspects which aren't already in the birth chart?

Liz: Of course they are important. But they are not referred to as "applying". The progression of any planet from birth forms a continuous story, and all the aspects it makes by progression, whether they are applying or come about later in life, are part of the story. But the applying and separating aspects of the Moon are especially relevant in childhood, because they are exact during pregnancy and the early months of life and can tell us a great deal about early family patterns.

Audience: And you look at the progressed Moon applying to the natal planet, not the progressed planet? Like, in your example, progressed Mars?

Liz: At five months of age, Mars won't have moved much. Progressed Moon completing an opposition to progressed Mars will occur at virtually the same time as progressed Moon opposing natal Mars. With aspects occurring later in life, such as Miranda's progressed Ascendant square natal Neptune, it is well worth looking at both the natal and progressed recipient of the aspect. I mentioned this when we were looking at Tony Blair's chart. His progressed Ascendant has already finished conjuncting natal Uranus, but it has not yet made the exact conjunction to progressed Uranus.

Audience: But that is not an applying aspect.

Liz: No, not in the technical sense. There is no Ascendant-Uranus conjunction in the birth chart.

Audience: Thank you. Now I have one final question, which is about orbs. I can understand that orbs are important with the transits. But would you use the same orb for progressions?

Liz: Yes, they are within orb when they get within 10°. Because of this, the heavy planets can take a lifetime to close a birth aspect by progressed motion.

Audience: Then what is the point of looking at the progression? If it is always within orb, then it is in the natal chart, and that's that.

Liz: The closer the two planets get by progressed motion, the hotter the issue becomes. One lives with such aspects all one's life, but they gradually become stronger, and when they are exact there is usually a critical phase when the meaning of the aspect is expressed in outer life. Such movements reflect lifelong developments. We should never get impatient with slow-moving planets. They take a long time to do their job. If you're in a hurry, concentrate on the progressed Moon.

Progressed stations of planets

Audience: What about progressed planets making stations?

Liz: When a planet stations by progression, the station lasts for several years in the case of the fast-moving planets, and longer in the case of the slower planets. It will probably happen only once in a lifetime, although sometimes progressed Mercury or Venus may go stationary direct or retrograde in childhood and then make another station retrograde or direct in adulthood. When a planet stations, it begins to slow down many days before the station, which in progressed motion means many years.

As a planet slows up for a station retrograde, it begins to introvert. It turns around and heads back to where it came from. It looks back over its shoulder, if planets have shoulders, and reflects on the past and on the inner world. The person no longer feels impelled to express that planet's energy in external life. If the planet is moving quickly enough, it may repeat aspects to other planets which it already made when it was moving direct. It's like a traveler who has turned around and is now revisiting places he stopped at on the outward journey. One notices different things the second time around. This recapitulation of aspects gives the person the opportunity to discover deeper dimensions of these already visited planets.

A planet that is retrograde at birth may station and go direct. Then it may go over its natal place on its journey forward. For example, Mercury may be retrograde at birth. It moves back to an earlier point in the zodiac, and then it stations, goes forward, and moves over its natal place. That may reflect a time when the person feels he or she is really learning to communicate. Mercury has completed its introvert period, and is now ready to move out into life and make spontaneous contact with others, which may have been difficult while it was retrograde. There may be a feeling of reclaiming something. I remember one client describing this as "getting something back that I lost long ago." Very often interests, hobbies, or talents that one thought one had lost in childhood are resuscitated and enrich the person's adult life.

A progressed outer planet may make a station. It slows up a long time before the actual station, and remains within the same two or three degrees for a couple of months, which in progressed motion means sixty years. So it is, in effect, stationary for most of one's life. It is not going to move very far, nor make any aspects other than the ones it made in the birth chart. In its particular sphere of life it dominates, but it has a limited range of movement and is not amenable to much development. These stationary slow-moving planets may reflect generational patterns and complexes. We can live them in creative ways, and our attitude toward what they represent may alter, but we may not have the option of shifting them to any significant degree.

Example chart 3

Liz: Here is another chart from the group. What do you want us to focus on, Paul?

Paul: I would like to look at what is going on in my 12th house, because it is something I am a little bit confused about.

Liz: All right, we can begin with the confusing 12th house, although I think we will have to consider sooner or later the fact that you are also in the middle of your Saturn return. Let's have a look at the progressed chart together with the natal.

Progressed Moon over a natal T–cross

The progressed Moon has been moving through the natal 12th house for around twelve months. It has just entered Virgo, and is coming up to natal Jupiter in 1° Virgo in the 12th. About a year ago it made its first lunar return at 18° Leo. In the last few months, as it moved through the last decanate of Leo, it opposed natal Sun at 24° Aquarius and natal Mercury in 28° Aquarius, and squared natal Neptune in 26° Scorpio. It also formed quincunxes to natal Mars and

Chiron in 27° Pisces, and conjuncted progressed Jupiter in 28° Leo. So it has been very busy for quite some time, and now it is about to complete its passage across a natal T-cross, which involves natal Moon, Jupiter, Sun, Mercury, and Neptune. At the same time that the progressed Moon has been making these aspects, transiting Pluto has also been busy on this natal T-cross, although for a much longer time. Having finally moved into Sagittarius, at present it is squaring Jupiter, and also squaring the progressed Moon.

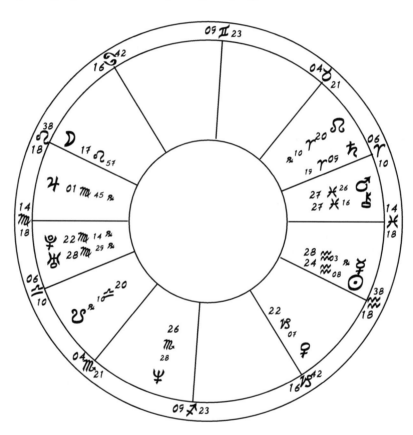

Paul
[Birth data withheld for reasons of confidentiality]

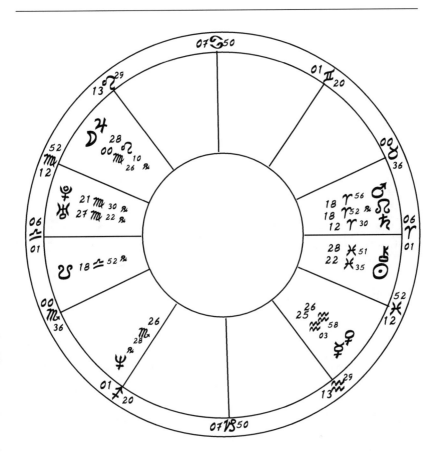

Paul
Progressed chart set for 8 June 1996

There are many other powerful movements going on, not least the progressed Sun in 22° Pisces opposition natal Pluto, and progressed Venus in 26° Aquarius square natal Neptune. Transiting Pluto was squaring progressed Venus at the same time it transited over Neptune, and transiting Saturn, while it was in the last decanate of Pisces, triggered the progressed Sun applying to the opposition to natal Pluto. Last year must have been one hell of a year. But for the moment let's focus on the progressed Moon and transiting Pluto completing their passage over the T-cross. We need to make some sense of this T-cross to understand what the transiting and progressed aspects are about. Any ideas?

Audience: The oppositions run from the 12th to the 6th. So the collective psyche needs to be expressed in practical ways. Things which have existed in the spiritual realm have to manifest.

Liz: Yes, this T-cross has something to do with learning to manifest, in a practical and useful form, ideals and dreams of a spiritual and imaginal kind. It may also involve learning to work with the stuff of the collective psyche, the "ancestors", and transforming this inheritance into skills which can be applied to bring order into material reality. Jupiter in the 12th square Neptune in the 3rd suggests a deep intuitive connection with the religious and spiritual past, but Sun in Aquarius in the 6th needs to work this into a rational system of thought applicable in everyday life.

Paul: That rings a few bells.

Liz: You need to make your psychological and spiritual inheritance manifest in a highly individual way, which both honours your vision and is useful to others. The transit of Pluto over natal Neptune and square progressed Venus may have brought some pain and disillusionment with it – perhaps a feeling that all the grand dreams you once had for helping humanity, not to mention achieving perfect relationships, have to be compromised and tailored to suit the world you live in. That kind of compromise might not be very welcome to an Aquarian. Transiting Pluto square the Sun and Mercury might make you feel, on the one hand, deeply committed to what you believe is your "destiny", and, on the other hand, profoundly uneasy about the power issues which that destiny involves.

Pluto has been transiting across the T-cross for several years. The progressed Moon there may ground these issues through direct emotional experience. The vague but insistent sense of destiny which Pluto has brought up might be more accessible to you, because the progressed Moon allows you to make it personal. You might be able to clarify your diffuse, boundless quality of vision and idealism, and put it into some kind of tangible, useful form which makes rational sense and is relevant to other people. However, the progressed Moon moving through the 12th is a period of gestation. One is not clear about anything, and the process may be going on without your being able to feel secure or confident that you are moving in the right direction. And I cannot help looking at the progressed Sun opposing Pluto, and feeling that your whole sense of identity is undergoing demolition and rebuilding.

Paul: Yes. The sense of ideals, combined with the sense of wanting to do something practical, is something that in previous years I have experienced in different ways. I used to live in the mountains, in the countryside. I was part of an association for rebuilding ancient buildings, and did a lot of landscape gardening. Then life turned around, and I find myself here in London studying astrology. I have had a proposition of work right now, a very serious proposition which involves great effort, great commitment. Although I feel all this great idealism and enthusiasm, I very often feel very sad, and have lost contact with any real motivation. It is as though there is great energy and then there is a form of passivity, and I think that one of my deepest fears about life is going through life not achieving anything tangible. All this is linked with my father, because he was an astrologer himself. He died not long ago.

Liz: So you are very literally trying to anchor your spiritual inheritance through pursuing the same profession as your father. I would like to look at transiting Saturn as well as the progressed Moon in the 12th, because the Saturn return, which is now occurring in the 8th house, also has bearing on the family inheritance. So does Pluto transiting square the progressed Moon, which seems to mark the end of a chapter of life and the beginning of a new one, with an attendant sense of loss and grief.

Sadness and passivity are characteristic of the progressed Moon in the 12th, especially with transiting Pluto squaring it, but that is not the whole story. The Saturn return is a crucial transit, and it is linked to the solar and lunar progressions because they are occurring at the same moment. A lot of the sad feelings you are experiencing could also be connected with progressed Venus square natal Neptune, which can describe a sense of grief, loss and sadness. It is the loss of a dream of love, of something beautiful that seems to be fading away in the distance; and there is a lot of pain and yearning. And the Saturn return is also concerned with the loss of childhood.

Paul: I have a very mixed feeling of pain, grief and relief, with some happiness as well, because I know it is something I have to go through. But at the same time, with great horror I am facing a period where I see that it is necessary for me to be alone – not in the sense of not seeing anybody, but in the sense of no longer demanding things from other people that I have to do myself.

Liz: You are, of course, giving voice to the meaning of your Saturn return. You have articulated it beautifully without any need for embellishment by me. You are also articulating the emotional tone of progressed Sun in the 7th opposite a 1st house Pluto. Isolation is often very much part of Pluto's transits and progressions, and you may also be discovering that, despite the gregariousness of an Aquarian Sun, you need and want to be alone in order to pursue your own path.

I wonder whether you may be putting more emphasis on the role your father plays in this than he actually merits. His death has clearly been a powerful and transformative event, since it occurred during the course of these transits and progressions. He also looms very large for you because he was an astrologer, and you are one yourself. From the aspects to your Sun – square Neptune, opposition Jupiter, quincunx Pluto – it seems he was a very magnetic and powerful man, whom I believe you deeply loved and idealised. But you may have felt let down by him, and are very confused by the ambivalence of your feelings. The Saturn return is not really about your father. It is about the father principle. In some ways your image of your father, the powerful astrologer, allows you to stay a boy.

As long as he is up there on the mountaintop, big and important and complex, you can remain a *puer*. If you let him go and allow him to rest in peace, it means that you are a man and must then live your Saturn. Your skills and abilities have to be put to the test in the world, and you need to do it in your own way, not your father's. There may be some guilt in discovering that perhaps he was not all that good an astrologer. In some ways you may want your father to go on being a big issue, because it keeps you on the threshold of maturity.

Paul: Last night I had some very strong inner experiences which were reflective, not verbally reasoned, and I could see that in many things I am similar to my father. We were born on the same day. I can see that many of my own aspirations and fears are very similar to his. Last night I was feeling particularly uneasy, because I felt it was important that I could manage to differentiate between myself, my own fears and aspirations, and his, in order to really be able to live my life. I am a bit worried. I worry why I am really doing astrology. Why I am working at this? Who am I doing it for? And although I like it a lot, I am worried that maybe I should be doing something else.

Audience: You have to discard your family in order to become a real person.

Liz: I am not sure "discard" is the appropriate word. The people we love cannot be "discarded". It is a much slower, subtler process, and the transit of Pluto moving over Paul's T-cross reflects just how slow and subtle it is. But I think this differentiation you hope for has already happened. If you had not already begun to make the separation, you would not be asking these questions. The separation has already taken place inwardly, and now you are experiencing the loss. If you were still identified with your father you wouldn't be capable of saying, "What are my aspirations, and how are they different from his?"

This inner separation has left you in what sounds to me like a sane and healthy place, although it isn't a very happy one at the moment. You are questioning who you are and what you are doing, which is absolutely appropriate for the Saturn return, as well as for progressed Sun opposition Pluto. You are no longer your father's mirror and protegé – you are yourself, for better or worse. The semi-divine father of your fantasies is disappearing, and the one who remains was a mortal man. I think you have already performed the task that you are convinced you must do in the future.

Paul: There is a point around the 12th house which confuses me. In order to get in touch with planets in the 12th, we may have a lot of hard work, because we may have lacked actual models out there in the world. So we say, "What is this about? I have never seen this before. No one in my family ever showed it." I was telling you about my difficulty at doing certain things or saying, "This is what I want to do, so I am going to do it!" with a sense of joy and faith. It touches on religious feelings and religious issues. I feel that, if I am to go back to some kind of inner reality which is the source of my own being, it will involve a cutting off from the past. I feel that I will never be able to communicate with anybody in the family.

Liz: You may have to part from them on a psychological level, and accept that you will not experience the kind of emotional support you have hoped for. This is often the case with an 8th house Saturn, which can bring hard lessons about emotional self-sufficiency. There is usually a lack of emotional sharing in the family background. One simply has to grow up without it. This doesn't mean you have to cut yourself off from your family. But your expectations may be too high. You could maintain reasonable relations with them, if you can accept the situation as it is. Virgo rising may be adaptable enough to get on with them on an everyday level and not begrudge them their inability to understand you. Inwardly, you may have to let them go. The religious source you speak about may lie further in the past than your father, and with the natal Moon in the 12th, that is where you are most naturally inclined to turn for inner peace and safety.

Audience: Natal Saturn is trine the Moon, so transiting Saturn will also trine it during the Saturn return.

Liz: Yes, it is trine the Moon, so the Saturn return is, among other things, concerned with developing emotional self-sufficiency and separateness – something which was always innately there, but which perhaps the Moon square Neptune obscured in the past.

Audience: Saturn is also conjunct the Moon's north Node. I think that means his path lies in learning to stand alone. I don't mean he can't have a relationship. But Chiron is also in the 7th house. There is a whole issue around dependency and independence, and mistrust of other people at the same time as being very needy and idealistic.

Liz: I wish we had time to look at this chart in greater depth. But it seems that the thing you are so worried about on the conscious level is already in place on the unconscious one. The separation has occurred and the new life has begun, but the ego hasn't caught up yet. Your sadness and apathy may be the inevitable consequences of leaving a chapter of life behind. Something is paid up and finished, but it is all you have ever known, and you don't know what to do without it. You feel lonely and alone, but you have already moved on, and it is a question of letting the past go. Your sadness and confusion are natural and healthy. When the progressed Moon crosses the natal Ascendant in a little over a year, I think you will be ready to show to the outer world what has been gestating in the inner one.

Paul: The Moon will cross the Ascendant just after Saturn finishes its return. That is nice timing. It is a new beginning.

Liz: Yes, it is a new beginning. We have come full circle, and are back to the nature of events. When does an event really happen? Your father's death has already occurred, but inwardly it is occurring only now. You fear a separation from the family, but it has already happened on the psychological level. Now you are facing the repercussions in terms of your sense of identity and your relationship with the family. It sounds to me as if you are exactly where you need to be, even though at the moment it may not feel like a pleasant place.

Thank you for letting us discuss the chart. I am sorry we don't have more time, but I am afraid we have come to the end of the seminar. Thank you all for participating.

Bibliography

Costello, Darby, *The Astrological Moon,* Vol. 6, CPA Press, London, 1996.

Greene, Liz, *The Outer Planets and Their Cycles,* CRCS, Reno, Nevada, 1983.

Hillman, James, "Betrayal", in *Loose Ends,* Spring Publications, Zürich, 1975.

Rudhyar, Dane, *The Lunation Cycle,* Servire-Wassenaar, Netherlands, 1967.

About the Centre for Psychological Astrology

The Centre for Psychological Astrology was founded in 1983 by Dr Liz Greene and Howard Sasportas. Since its inception, the CPA has become world renowned for its unique and inspiring application of a variety of psychological approaches to astrology. The Centre continues to foster the cross-fertilisation of the fields of astrology and depth, humanistic and transpersonal psychology. Together with MISPA it hosts a unique webinar programme providing an original, informal and inspiring framework for both beginners and experienced astrologers.

Past CPA seminars are available as books and e-books through the CPA Press.

For further information about the current programme of seminars and webinars, to receive mailings and browse the CPA Press astrology books, visit: www.cpalondon.com or contact the Administrator, Juliet Sharman-Burke at: juliet@cpalondon.com

The **Online Introductory Certificate Course** with John Green provides a foundation in the basics of psychological astrology. Run as real time online tutorials, students can interact with the tutor and other students, ask questions and watch recorded sessions.

For further information, contact John at: webmaster@cpalondon.com

About the Mercury Internet School of Psychological Astrology

The Mercury Internet School of Psychological Astrology (MISPA) offers a 2 year Diploma Course, and students who have completed the CPA's Foundation Course, or similar, are eligible to enrol.

For further information visit: www.mercuryinternetschool.com or write to info@mercuryinternetschool.com

Made in the USA
Columbia, SC
08 September 2023

22628234R00143